Afro-American Reference

Recent Titles in
Bibliographies and Indexes in Afro-American and African Studies

Black-Jewish Relations in the United States: A Selected Bibliography
Compiled by Lenwood G. Davis

Black Immigration and Ethnicity in the United States: An Annotated Bibliography
Center for Afroamerican and African Studies, The University of Michigan

Blacks in the American Armed Forces, 1776-1983: A Bibliography
Compiled by Lenwood G. Davis and George Hill

Education of the Black Adult in the United States: An Annotated Bibliography
Compiled by Leo McGee and Harvey G. Neufeldt

A Guide to the Archives of Hampton Institute
Compiled by Fritz J. Malval

A Bibliographical Guide to Black Studies Programs in the United States: An Annotated Bibliography
Compiled by Lenwood G. Davis and George Hill

Wole Soyinka: A Bibliography of Primary and Secondary Sources
Compiled by James Gibbs, Ketu H. Katrak, and Henry Louis Gates, Jr.

Afro-American Demography and Urban Issues: A Bibliography
Compiled by R. A. Obudho and Jeannine B. Scott

Afro-American Reference

AN ANNOTATED BIBLIOGRAPHY OF SELECTED RESOURCES

Compiled and edited by
Nathaniel Davis

Bibliographies and Indexes in Afro-American and African Studies, Number 9

Greenwood Press
Westport, Connecticut • London, England

Library of Congress Cataloging-in-Publication Data

Davis, Nathaniel.
Afro-American reference.

(Bibliographies and indexes in Afro-American and African studies, ISSN 0742-6925 ; no. 9)
Bibliography: p.
Includes indexes.
1. Bibliography—Bibliography—Afro-Americans.
2. Afro-Americans—Bibliography. I. Title. II. Series.
Z1361.N39D37 1985 [E185] 016.973'0496 85-21942
ISBN 0-313-24930-X (lib. bdg. : alk. paper)

Library of Congress Catalog Card Number: 85-21942
ISBN: 0-313-24930-X
ISSN: 0742-6925

First published in 1985

Greenwood Press
A division of Congressional Information Service, Inc.
88 Post Road West, Westport, Connecticut 06881

Printed in the United States of America

The paper used in this book complies with the Permanent Paper Standard issued by the National Information Standards Organization (Z39.48-1984).

10 9 8 7 6 5 4 3 2 1

CONTENTS

PREFACE

Many individuals contributed to and influenced this bibliography. Without their support this compilation would not have been possible. Those individuals whose contributions were indispensible and to whom I am most grateful include: Jean Leonard, Lawrence Gutierrez, and Erwin Sanvictores, who assisted in the gathering and computer input of the bibliographical data; Dr. Beverly Robinson, Dr. Richard Yarborough, Richard Chabran, John Overholt, and Moshe Kaufman, who provided invaluable suggestions and support; Kathy Harris, Joan Slottow, and Shirley Nordhaus of the UCLA Office of Academic Computing who provided guidance and consultation in the design of the text editing computer file; and Betsy Coles and the UCLA University Research Library ORION User Services staff, who provided guidance and consultation involving the specialized use of ORION, the UCLA Library online catalog. Warm and sincere thanks also go to Assistant Librarian Eunice Posnansky, and Library Assistants Natalie Glover and Fumio Omari who contibuted to the gathering of the bibliographical data. Suggestions and support from Dr. Joseph Holloway, Dr. Vicki Mays, Dr. Halford Fairchild, Dr. M. Belinda Tucker, Dr. Waddell Herron and Dr. Claudia Mitchell-Kernan are also greatly appreciated. Support from the UCLA Institute of American Cultures and the UCLA Center for Afro-American Studies was substantial and is most appreciated. Support from the UCLA Graduate School of Library and Information Science and the UCLA Mini-Grant Program is also gratefully acknowledged. Finally, a very special thanks goes to Ruth Elizabeth Burks, who served as copy editor for earlier drafts, and also provided moral support and encouragement when obstacles, problems, and setbacks ocurred. I acknowledge my debt to the above persons and institutions for any positive and helpful features which this bibliography contains. It is my pleasure to share with them the credit for whatever value this bibliography will have for library users. I, however, am fully responsible for the content and format of this present work and for any errors of omission or commission.

INTRODUCTION

This general annotated bibliography of Afro-American studies reference sources attempts to fill a long-standing gap in the bibliographical literature. The last two general compilations of Afro-American reference sources were: Guy T. Westmoreland's *An Annotated Guide to Basic Reference Books on the Black Experience*, 1974; and Edith Fisher's *Focusing on Afro/Black American Research: A Guide and Annotated Bibliography to Selected Resources in the University of California, San Diego, Libraries*, 1975. Both were well-designed and highly useful, but are now somewhat dated.

More recent Afro-American reference publications have been devoted to specialized topics dealing with women, religion, literature, children, the family, and so on, most of which are cited in this compilation. These specialized publications, although invaluable and needed additions to the bibliographical literature, are useful primarily to the specialist, or to a limited number of persons engaged in research on a specific topic. Moreover, these specialized bibliographical compilations have not included many topics in Afro-American studies, such as anthropology, the black male, psychology, sociology, and blacks in the armed forces. This may have been due to a lack of interest on the part of bibliographers or to an apparent dearth of available resources in these areas.

This bibliography was designed to allow both academic and public library users to identify and locate those resources pertinent to their needs for Afro-American studies public awareness and academic information. Included are the major Afro-American library reference resources which are or should be available in large public and academic libraries. While not exhaustive, this bibliography may serve as a point of departure for research on most aspects of Afro-American history and culture, and should be adequate to satisfy the reference needs of most non-specialists.

The main focus of this bibliography is on the Afro-American experience in the United States, and an attempt was made to cover the full interdisciplinary subject range of Afro-American studies. A section devoted to the black experience in the Caribbean, and Central and South America is also included.

Most of the works cited are devoted exclusively to Afro-American studies. Some cover several minority groups. Others are not specific to Afro-American or minority groups, but provide some significant coverage of Afro-Americans in areas not well-covered by specifically Afro-American bibliographical tools.

The majority of the items listed are specifically reference materials, i.e., bibliographies, bibliographical guides, indexes, dictionaries, almanacs, or directories, and almost all of these are in book form. Selected anthologies are also included. Periodical articles or articles in books, with few exceptions, are not included.

Some materials which do not fit within the strict definition of a library reference source have also been included because they contain useful bibliographies, indexes, important data, or state of the art information on topics inadequately covered by more standard reference tools. Indeed, some of these sources are of equal or greater value as references than some of the standard reference sources.

This work is arranged into major subject categories and cites 642 selected resources which are numbered consecutively throughout. Most of these items were selected on the basis of their demonstrated usefulness in providing library reference assistance to students, faculty, and the general public at a large academic institution (UCLA).

The basic bibliographical citation for each entry includes the author, title, place of publication, publisher, date of publication, number of pages, and series title. In addition, most works include a descriptive annotation, which emphasises the reference qualities of the work and usually consists of brief statements on the content, scope, arrangement, and usage, as well as mention of the presence of bibliographies and indexes. Other features such as tables, charts, graphs, photographs, and illustrations, are also mentioned where significant and applicable. With few exeptions, the annotations are based on the editor's personal examination of the works.

When possible, Library of Congress subject headings which apply to the work are included with the entries following the notation SUBJECT(S). These headings provide additional information on the contents of the work and may serve as a guide to the user when conducting subject searches in local libraries for additional works of interest. It should be noted that certain limitations apply to the use of these headings. These subject headings have been assigned by either the UCLA Afro-American Studies Library, the Library of Congress, the UCLA Library Technical Services Department, and/or other libraries across the nation which subscribe to OCLC. It is possible that local public or academic libraries may assign other subject headings to the same work and other works falling within the the same subject category. It should also be noted that the subject headings that appear with the entries were used by the Library of Congress at the time of publication and these same headings may not be currently in use. More recent publications falling within the same subject categories may have different headings. Further, Library of Congress subject headings assigned to Afro-American related materials often lack some degree of specificity or relevance to the works to which they have been assigned. This remains a central problem in the area of bibliographical control of Afro-American related resources. However, if one tries to imagine or arrive at more suitable possibilities for standardized Afro-American subject headings, one can appreciate the enormous effort which the Library of Congress has devoted to this problem, and the tendency to criticize their inadequacies is tempered by a realization of the severity and magnitude of the problems involved. Despite such occasional limitations, which must be discovered on a case-by-case basis, the subject headings for the entries can, in most cases, serve as a valuable, supplementary guide when evaluating book contents, and when searching for additional library materials.

Separate author, title, and subject indexes conclude this volume. The number appearing after each entry refers to the citation number rather than a page number. The subject index terms are based on those used by the Library of Congress. In those instances where the headings were not sufficiently specific or relevant, or were too unwieldy for a book publication subject index, it was necessary to modify and supplement the terms. At the same time, efforts were made to maintain standardization in the use of the subject index terms.

In some instances, the placement of works within the subject categories also presented problems. Some of the works included have contents which fall within several subject categories, or are so unique that they would require a separate category of their own. Since it was not practical to create numerous categories containing only one or two works, a number of the entries appear in categories with which they are not entirely compatible. However, a review of the entries within the categories, combined with the use of the indexes, should allow the user to identify all works which are relevant, in part or as a whole, to any particular topic.

In light of the vast number of works of relevance to Afro-Americans, no claim is made that this work is a definitive listing of the important reference works and texts which may serve as reference sources. There are omissions, and it is acknowledged that some important works may have been overlooked. In addition to any omissions, this bibliography will inevitably contain its share of errors. I welcome comments, criticism, or suggestions which might be incorporated in future editions of this work.

Afro-American Reference

GENERAL REFERENCE SOURCES

Almanacs and Encyclopedias

1. Hornsby, Alton. *The Black Almanac*. 4th rev. ed. Woodbury, NY: Barron's Educational Series, Inc., 1977. 358 p.

This almanac covers the years 1619 to 1976. Chapters are divided into historical periods, with year and major events listed and described. Tables are included which give data such as the percentage of blacks in school, the number of elected officials, and income levels. A selected, discursive bibliography arranged by chronological period is included, and an author-title-subject index are also included.

SUBJECT(S): Afro-Americans--History--Chronology.

2. Low, W. Augustus, ed., and Cleft, Virgil A., assoc. ed. *Encyclopedia of Black America*. NY: McGraw-Hill, 1981. 921 p.

This first, complete encyclopedic volume on black America contains an exceptionally comprehensive survey of of virtually every topic in Afro-American history, life, and culture, and may serve as a point of departure for more in depth research. Arranged in an easy-access, A to Z format. Each major entry includes a selected bibliography. Cross references interrelate all information on a given topic. Illustrations and a name and subject index are included.

SUBJECT(S): Afro-Americans--Dictionaries and encyclopedias. Encyclopedias.

3. National Urban League. *The State of Black America*, 1976-.

This annual publication is considered an authoritative statement on the current state of black America, and is widely quoted. It includes informative essays by a number of distinguished scholars addressing current critical issues. Recommendations for corrective action, and a chronology of the events of the preceding year are included.

SUBJECT(S): Afro-Americans--Periodicals.
Social and Economic Conditions.

4. Ploski, Harry A., and James Williams, eds. and comps. *The Negro Almanac: A Reference Work on the Afro-American.* 4th ed. New York: Wiley, 1983. 1550 p.

This exceptionally useful work brings together information on virtually every aspect of the history, culture, as well as the current status of blacks in the United States, and can serve as a point of departure for more in depth research. A section on blacks living elsewhere in the Western hemisphere is included. An extensive selected bibliography, and a general index are also included.

SUBJECT(S): Afro-Americans--Dictionaries and encyclopedias.
Almanacs.

5. Smyth, Mabel M. *The Black American Reference Book.* Englewood Cliffs, NJ: Printice-Hall, 1976. 1026 p.

A comprehensive almanac covering many aspects of Afro-American history and culture. An extensive bibliography and an author-subject index is included.

SUBJECT(S): Afro-Americans--Dictionaries and encyclopedias.

Dictionaries

6. Baskin, Wade, and Richard Runes. *Dictionary of Black Culture.* New York: Philosophical Library, 1973. 493 p.

This dictionary lists people, places, and subjects in Afro-American culture and history.

SUBJECT(S): Afro-Americans--Bibliography.
Afro-Americans--Dictionaries and encyclopedias.

7. Dalgish, Gerard M. *A Dictionary of Africanisms: Contributions of Sub-Saharan Africa to the English Language.* Westport CT: Greenwood Press, 1982. xviii, 203 p.

This unique dictionary lists African or African derived words and phrases, and provides correct pronunciation, the definition as used in English, the African derivation, and references to usage in Western and African publications.

SUBJECT(S): English language--Provincialisms--Africa, Sub-Saharan--Dictionaries.
English language--Foreign elements--African--Dictionaries.
African languages--Glossaries, vocabularies, etc.
Africa, Sub-Saharan--Languages--Glossaries, vocabularies, etc.

8. Kellner, Bruce, ed. *The Harlem Renaissance: A Historical Dictionary for the Era*. Westport, CT: Greenwood Press, 1984. 576 p.

This work of nearly 800 entries, contains a wide range of information about the personalities, places, and events that relate to black arts and letters, politics, and theater during the Harlem Renaissance, through the 1920s. Appendices provide a listing of plays, musical entertainments, lists of publications by and about black Americans, and a comprehensive glossary of Harlem slang of the period.

9. Major, Clarence. *Dictionary of Afro-American Slang*. New York: International Publishers 1975. 127 p. SERIES: New World Paperbacks.

A list of slang words, used or created by Afro-Americans. For each word, the definition, date of usage, and geographical region of usage, are provided. An introductory essay, and a bibliography on Afro-American slang are also included.

SUBJECT(S): Afro-Americans--Language (New words, slang, etc.)
English language--Slang--Dictionaries.
English language in the United States.

10. Nunez, Benjamin. *Dictionary of Afro-Latin American Civilization*. Westport, CT: Greenwood Press, 1980. xxxv, 525 p.

A highly useful historical and descriptive dictionary of terms, phrases, and biographies of selected Afro-Latin political leaders, writers, and other important personalities. Over 4,500 entries, taken from English, French, Portuguese, and Spanish sources, are listed in alphabetical order, and defined in their geographical and historical context. A brief bibliography of dictionaries, glossaries, books, monographs, articles, and periodicals is included. Subject and name indexes are also included.

SUBJECT(S): Latin America--Civilization--African influences--Dictionaries.
Caribbean area--Civilization--African influences--Dictionaries.

11. Puckett, Newbell Niles. *Black Names in America: Origins and Usage*. Edited by Murray Heller. Boston: G. K. Hall, 1975. xix, 561 p.

This work lists and discusses Afro-American names, as found in slavery lists, population reports, and college records produced between 1700 and the 1930s. A dictionary of names providing information on African origins, meaning, and ethnic group and gender identification, is included. A bibliography of important sources is also included.

SUBJECT(S): Blacks--Names.
Names, Personal--United States.

General Bibliographies

General bibliographies which cover several areas of Afro-American studies are cited below. Specialized subject bibliographies are cited within the appropriate subject sections.

12. Blazek, Ron, Janice Fennell, and Frances Masterson McKinney eds. and comps. *The Black Experience*: *A Bibliography of Bibliographies*, *1970-1975*. Chicago: The Adult Library Materials Committee, Reference and Adult Services Division, American Library Association. 1978. 67 p.

A bibliography of bibliographies citing materials "readily available and easily acquired by public and academic libraries." Bibliographies published in book form, Council of Planning Libraries bibliographies, bibliographical articles in journals, and a list of bibliographies not examined by the compiler are cited. Includes an index of individual compilers and editors, and an index of subject headings.

SUBJECT(S): Bibliography--Bibliography--Afro-Americans.
Bibliography--Bibliography--Blacks.
Afro-Americans--Bibliography.
Blacks--Bibliography.

13. Davis, Lenwood G. *Index to CPL Bibliographies on Blacks*, *Related to Blacks*, *on Africa*, *and Related to Africa*, *numbers 869-1310*. Monticello, IL: Council of Planning Librarians, 1977. 5 p. SERIES: Council of Planning Librarians. Exchange Bibliography, no. 1374.

This index offers guidance to black-related bibliographies scattered throughout several volumes of Council of Planning Libraries bibliographies published between 1875 and 1977.

SUBJECT(S): Council of Planning Librarians.
Bibliography--Bibliography--Blacks.

14. Fisher, Edith Maureen *Focusing on Afro-Black American Research: A Guide and Annotated Bibliography to Selected Resources in the University of California, San Diego Libraries.* San Diego: Instructional Services Department, University Library, University of California, San Diego 1975. xii, 80 p. SERIES: Ethnic Studies Publication, no. 1.

A useful, classified, annotated list of almanacs, encyclopedias, handbooks, manuals, and bibliographies on literature, music, politics, history, religion, and black women. An author-title index is included. Instructions on how to use the library are also included.

SUBJECT(S): Afro-Americans--Bibliography--Catalogs.

15. Gubert, Betty Kaplan, comp. *Early Black Bibliographies, 1863-1919.* New York: Garland Publishing, Inc., 1982. xiii, 380 p. SERIES: Critical Studies on Black Life and Culture, vol. 25. SERIES: Garland Reference Library of Social Science, vol. 103.

This work contains reprints of nineteen old, rare, and out-of-print bibliograhies on Afro-Americana. The criteria for inclusion were rarity, originality, uniqueness, and scholarly siginificance. The purpose of this collection is to make available to researchers, scholars, librarians, teachers, and students sources of early information by and about black people. An index is included.

SUBJECT(S): Bibliography--Bibliography--Afro-Americans.
Afro-Americans--Bibliography.

16. Jackson, Clara O. *A Bibliography of Afro-American and other American Minorites Represented in Library and Library-Related Listing.* New York: American Institute of Marxist Studies, 1970; Supplement, 1972.

17. Matthews, Geraldine O., comp. *Black American Writers, 1773-1949: A Bibliography and Union List.* Boston: G. K. Hall, 1975. xv, 221 p.

A bibliography identifying over 1600 authors of monographs. Entries are arranged by subject, and cover the social sciences, religion, history, philosophy, language, science, art, and literature. Library location information is provided. An author index and a bibliography are included.

SUBJECT(S): Afro-Americans--Bibliography--Union lists.
Catalogs, Union--Southern States.

18. Miller, Elizabeth W., comp. *The Negro in America: A Bibliography*. Foreward by Thomas F. Pettigrew. 2nd ed., rev. and enl. by Mary L. Fisher. Cambridge: Harvard University Press, 1970. xx, 350 p.

A selectively annotated bibliography of works on Afro-American history, culture, and politics. Books, periodicals, and government reports are included. A guide to sources and an author index are also included.

SUBJECT(S): Afro-Americans--Bibliography.

19. Newman, Richard, comp. *Black Access: A Bibliography of Afro-American Bibliographies*. Westport, CT: Greenwood Press, 1984. xxviii, 249 p.

A comprehensive and highly useful bibliography of over 3,000 bibliographies. Entries are arranged in a single alphabet by author. Book-length bibliographies, and bibliographies in books, pamphlets, articles, essays, chapters in books, indexes, exhibition catalogs, calendars, checklists, and guides to manuscript and archival collections are cited. All subject areas are covered, with special strengths in history, literature, discographies of blues and jazz, race relations, and the social sciences. The relatively neglected areas of folklore, children's literature, and religion are also covered. It also identifies retrospective, obscure, and specialized bibliographies. Bibliographies are included only if they are "separately published" or have independent existence as a book, pamphlet, article, or chapter in a book. Bibliographies that are appendices to monographs are excluded. A subject index provides detailed access to names, academic institutions, sponsoring organizations, and libraries. A Chronological index indicates the inclusive dates covered by the bibliographies and facilitates comparative studies and the study of particular periods.

SUBJECT(S): Bibliography--Bibliography--Afro-Americans.
Afro-Americans--Bibliography.

20. New York (City). Public Library. *No Crystal Stair: A Bibliography of Black Literature*. New York: New York Public Library 1971. 63 p.

Arranged by subject, this selected bibliography of basic works includes reference materials and works on history, politics, sociology, psychology, religion, economics, education, and sports. Author and title indexes are included.

SUBJECT(S): American literature--Afro-American authors.

21. Peavy, Charles D. *Afro-American Literature and Culture Since World War II: A Guide to Information Sources*. Detroit: Gale Research Co., 1979. xiv, 302 p. SERIES: American Studies Information Guide Series, vol. 6. SERIES: Gale Information Guide Library.

A bibliography of books, articles, essays, and dissertations. Divided into two parts: the first cites works according to subject categories, including politics, culture, psychology, women, sociology, and television; the second part lists resources on individual authors of fiction and non-fiction. Author, title, and subject indexes are included.

SUBJECT(S): American literature--Afro-American authors--Bibliography.
American literature--20th century-- Bibliography.
Afro-Americans--Bibliography.
Reference books--Afro-Americans-- Bibliography.
United States--Civilization--1945-- Bibliography.

22. Porter, Dorothy Burnett, comp. *The Negro in the United States: A Selected Bibliography*. Washington: Library of Congress; 1970. x, 313 p.

This bibliography of 1,781 entries is arranged by subject and covers all areas of Afro-American studies. The items were selected on the basis of the frequency of requests at large college libraries, and their availability at the Library of Congress. Most items cited were written between 1940 and 1969. Annotations are included only when needed to clarify contents. An author-subject index is included.

SUBJECT(S): Afro-Americans--Bibliography.

23. Porter, Dorothy Burnett, comp. *A Working Bibliography on the Negro in the United States*. Ann Arbor, MI: Xerox, University Microfilms, 1969. 202 p.

This bibliography of 1,996 entries is arranged by subject and covers all areas of Afro-American studies. Most items cited were written after the turn of the century. There are no annotations. A name index is included.

SUBJECT(S): Afro-Americans--Bibliography.

24. Rowell, Charles Henry. *Afro-American Literary Bibliographies: An Annotated List of Bibliographic Guides for the Study of Afro-American Literature, Folklore, and Related Areas*. Ph.D. diss., Ohio State University, 1972. 220 p.

This unpublished doctoral dissertation is an annotated bibliographical guide to published and unpublished bibliographies of primary and secondary materials that are useful in the study of Afro-American literature and folklore and allied fields. The compilation is divided into four major sections: 1) Literature, 2) Folklore and Music (including discographies), 3) Journalism, and 4) Selected Background Sources containing cross-references to various entries. The entries are numbered consecutively throughout. Included among the published bibliographies are those devoted to particular literary genres, individuals authors, specific subjects, instructional materials, and general bibliographies which contain primary and secondary materials covering the entire area of Afro-American studies. Some of the bibliographies are parts of other works, such as studies, anthologies, and collections. Some are bio-bibliographical sketches of writers, bibliographical essays, and essays which mention or discuss numerous works not listed in other bibliographies. Also included are serial bibliographies, periodicals which publish reviews and notes on new books, guides to master's theses and doctoral dissertations, and catalogs and guides to special library collections and archives. The unpublished bibliographies include master's theses and doctoral dissertations which are themselves bibliographies or contain extensive bibliographies of significant materials.

SUBJECT(S): Afro-Americans--Bibliography.

25. Thompson, Edgar Tristram, and Alma Macy Thompson, comps. *Race and Region: A Descriptive Bibliography.* Chapel Hill: University of North Carolina Press, 1949. xii, 149 p.

Originally published in 1949, and reprinted in 1971, this bibliography provides references to material about Afro-Americans published before the modern civil rights movement. Books, periodicals, and pamphlets on slavery, Afro-American culture, and race relations are included. Entries are arranged by subject, and then alphabetically by author. An author index is included.

SUBJECT(S): Afro-Americans--Bibliography.
Race relations--Bibliography.
Afro-American race--Bibliography.

26. Welsch, Erwin K. *The Negro in the United States: A Research Guide.* Bloomington: Indiana University Press, 1965. xiii, 142 p.

A discursive, bibliographic guide to resources on Afro-Americans. Material is arranged in seven sections and sub-arranged by historical period. The subjects covered are science, philosophy, race, historical and sociological background, major issues through 1968, and the arts. Appendices list bibliographies, periodicals, and national and state organizations. Author and subject indexes are included.

SUBJECT(S): Afro-Americans--Bibliography.

27. Westmoreland, Guy T. *An Annotated Guide to Basic Reference Books on the Black American Experience*. Wilmington, DE: Scholarly Resources, Inc., 1974. x, 98 p.

This is one of the first annotated bibliographies of general reference works on Afro-Americans. Part I includes general reference works such as guides, biographical sources, encyclopedias, indexes, and general bibliographies. Part II lists reference works on historical, political, social, economic, and cultural topics. Annotations provide content abstracts and assess usefulness. There is a addendum consisting of works not personally examined by the compiler. Author, title, and subject indexes are included.

SUBJECT(S): Afro-Americans--Bibliography--Bibliography.

28. Work, Monroe Nathan, comp. *A Bibliography of the Negro in Africa and America*. 1928. Reprint. New York: Octagon Books, 1965. xxi, 698 p.

This classic compilation lists over 17,000 books, pamphlets, and periodical articles, "covering the most worth while publications in different languages issued before 1928." Most works cited are in English. Divided into two parts: part I pertains to Africa and part II to America. Each part is further divided into chapters dealing with a wide variety of topics. One section of Part II covers the West Indies and Latin America. An index is included.

SUBJECT(S): Afro-Americans--Bibliography.
Afro-Americans in Africa--Bibliography.
Afro-Americans in America--Bibliography.

Catalogs and Guides to Major Collections

This section includes catalogs to some of the nation's largest and most outstanding library collections on Afro-Americans. These catalogs tend to be retrospective in scope and do not cite the most recent publications. Also, some of the works cited may be rare and difficult to locate in local libraries. Dispite these limitations, These massive works often represent near-exhaustive compilations for the chronological periods and topics covered.

29. Chicago Public Library. Vivian G. Harsh Collection. *The Chicago Afro-American Union Analytic Catalog: An Index to Materials of the Afro-American in the Principal Libraries of Chicago*. Boston: G. K. Hall, 1972. 5 vols.

An annotated, author-title-subject catalog of books, periodicals, reports, proceedings, yearbooks, art catalogs, and domestic and foreign periodicals on "every phase of Afro-Americana" produced between the 1500s and 1940.

SUBJECT(S): Afro-Americans--Bibliography--Union lists.
Catalogs, Union--Illinois--Chicago.

30. Chicago Public Library. Vivian G. Harsh Collection. *The Dictionary Catalog of the Vivian G. Harsh Collection of Afro-American History and Literature*. Boston: G. K. Hall, 1978. 4 vols.

An author-title-subject catalog of over 20,000 books, periodicals, pamphlets, manuscripts, microfilm, records, tapes, posters, and artifacts. All areas of Afro-American studies, from the 1500s to the late 1970s are covered. It is particularly strong in religion, sociology, politics, art, music, literature, and Afro-American, Caribbean, and Chicago history. It also includes 1,000 titles of children's literature related to Afro-American studies.

SUBJECT(S): Afro-Americans--Bibliography--Catalogs.
American Literature--Afro-American authors--Bibliography--Catalogs.

31. Race Relations Information Center. *Directory of Afro-American Resources*. New York: R.R. Bowker Co., 1970. xv, 485 p.

Although somewhat dated and incomplete, this remains a valuable source of information on Afro-American library resources and special collections. It covers 2,108 federal, state, and local government agencies, private offices, and organizations, which together house 5,365 collections. The size and content of each collection is described. An index of organizational names and an index of personal names is included. A bibliography of works consulted is also included.

SUBJECT(S): Afro-Americans--Library resources.

32. Fisk University Library. *Dictionary Catalog of the Negro Collection of the Fisk University Library*. Nashville, Tennessee. Boston: G. K. Hall, 1974. 6 vols.

A catalog of the black studies collection of the Fisk University Library in six volumes, with author, title, and subject entries arranged in a single alphabet. It lists 35,000 books and pamphlets produced between the late-eighteenth century and 1974. All areas of Afro-American life are included. Abolitionist literature is well represented.

SUBJECT(S): Fisk University, Nashville. Library.
Afro-Americans--Bibliography--Catalogs.
Africa--Bibliography--Catalogs.

33. Hampton Institute, Hampton, VA. Collis P. Huntington Library. *A Classified Catalogue of the Negro Collection in the Collis P. Huntington Library, Hampton Institute*. Compiled by Mentor A. Howe and Roscoe E. Lewis. St.Clair Shores, MI: Scholarly Press, Inc. 1971. x, 341 p.

Originally published in 1940, this catalog contains approximately 14,800 books and 1,300 manuscripts, clippings, periodicals, and pamphlets. Slavery and its economic and religious aspects, the Abolitionist movement, black art, music, and religion are well covered. It is especially strong on materials relating to the Civil War and Reconstruction. The main focus is on Afro-Americans in the United States. Some items relating to Africa are also included. An author index is included.

SUBJECT(S): Black race--Bibliography--Catalogs.

34. Howard University, Washington, D.C. Library. *Dictionary Catalog of the Arthur B. Spingarn Collection of Negro Authors*. Boston: G. K. Hall, 1970. 2 vols.

A catalog of books, pamphlets, and ephemera produced by black literary authors, from the late-eighteenth century through 1970. Authors, titles, and subjects are interfiled in a single alphabet. Most material is by blacks in the United States, but there are also many entries by Afro-Cuban and Afro-Brazilian authors. An appendix indexes black composers and their music.

SUBJECT(S): Spingarn, Arthur Barnett, 1878-.
American literature--Afro-American authors--
Bibliography--Catalogs.
Music--Bibliography--Catalogs.

35. Howard University, Washington, D.C. Library. Moorland Foundation. *Dictionary Catalog of the Jesse E. Moorland Collection of Negro Life and History*. Boston: G.K. Hall, 1970. 9 vols.

Anti-slavery books and pamphlets comprise a major part of the collection. In addition, there is material on Afro-American religion, masonry, the YMCA movement, and the history and administration of Howard University.

SUBJECT(S): Afro-Americans--Bibliography--Catalogs.

36. Library Company of Philadelphia and the Historical Society of Pennsylvania. *Afro-Americana, 1553-1906: Author Catalog of the Library Company of Philadelphia and the Historical Society of Pennsylvania*. Boston: G.K. Hall, 1973. xiii, 714 p.

An author catalog of books, pamphlets, manuscripts, and broadsides by or about Afro-Americans. These items are part of the collection of the Library Company and Historical Society of

Pennsylvania. A subject index is included.

SUBJECT(S): Library Company of Philadelphia.
Historical Society of Pennsylvania.
Afro-Americans--Bibliography--Catalogs.
Slavery in the United States--Bibliography--Catalogs.
Africa--Discovery and exploration--Bibliography--Catalogs.

37. New York City. Public Library. Schomburg Collection of Negro Literature and History. *Dictionary Catalog of the Schomburg Collection of Negro Literature and History*. Boston: G.K. Hall, 1962. 9 vols.

A catalog of over 36,000 books by or about Afro-Americans with author, title, and subject entries arranged in a single alphabet. Roughly half of the citations are on Africa. Most works cited are in English. A few are in French, German, and Spanish. Books, phonograph records, sheet music, manuscripts, newspapers, and periodicals are listed.

SUBJECT(S): American literature--Afro-American authors--Bibliography--Catalogs.
Literature--Black authors-- Bibliography--Catalogs.
Blacks--Bibliography--Catalogs.
Afro-Americans--Bibliography--Catalogs.

38. New York City. Public Library. Schomburg Center for Research and Black Culture. *Bibliographic Guide to Black Studies*. Boston: G.K. Hall, 1975-.

This work updates and supplements the *Dictionary Catalog of the Schomburg Collection of Negro Literature and History*. Issued annually, it lists publications cataloged during the past year by the New York Public Library. It provides a comprehensive survey of nonserial literature by and about people of African descent, wherever they live, and regardless of subject matter, language, or national origin.

SUBJECT(S): Schomburg Center for Research and Black Culture.
Afro-Americans--Bibliography--Catalogs.
Blacks--Bibliography--Catalogs.
Literature--Black authors--Bibliography.
Afro-Americans--Bibliography--Catalogs--Periodicals.
Black race--Bibliography--Catalogs--Periodicals.
Blacks--History--Bibliography.
Afro-Americans--Study and teaching--Bibliography--Catalogs.
Black race--Bibliography--Catalogs.

39. Smith, Jessie Carney. *Black Academic Libraries and Research Collections: An Historical Survey*. Westport, CT: Greenwood Press, 1977. xvii, 303 p. SERIES: Contributions in Afro-American and African Studies, no. 34.

An important study on the history of black colleges and the development and status of their libraries. Eighty-nine, four year or graduate level institutions are covered. The emphasis is on the library collections, and information on their history, scope, content, strengths, and effectiveness in curricular and research activities provided. A bibliography and an index are included.

SUBJECT(S): Afro-American university and college libraries. Afro-Americans--Library resources-- United States.

BIOGRAPHICAL SOURCES

General Biographical Sources

This section cites collected biographical sources which cover individuals working in many fields and living in the United States. A few works also include blacks living elsewhere in the world. Biographical sources on scientists and inventors are covered in that section. Biographical sources devoted to blacks woring in specific fields or disciplines are cited within the appropriate subject section.

Biographical sources devoted to a single individual are not included in this bibliography. Available book bibliographies or biographies on particular individuals may be easily identified by searching a library catalog under the name of the individual. (The Malcolm X *bibliography by Lenwood Davis was included* because it contains citations to works which also provide information on Black Muslims and on Malcolm X's followers.)

40. Abajian, James de T. *Blacks in Selected Newspapers, Censuses and other Sources: An Index to Names and Subjects.* Boston: G.K. Hall, 1977. 3 vols.

This three-volume index cites information on known and obscure black personalities, organizations, and subjects. It indexes newspapers, periodicals, census records, and other sources of the nineteenth and twentieth and centuries. It is especially good for retrieving information pertaining to the first half of the of the twentieth century. All information sources are listed in bibliographies at the beginning of volume I. Each entry includes names, dates (when known), occupation, and information source.

SUBJECT(S): Afro-Americans--Genealogy--Indexes. Afro-Americans--Biography--Indexes.

41. Adams, Russell L. *Great Negroes, Past and Present*. Illustrated by Eugene Winslow. Edited by Davis P. Ross, Jr. 3d ed. Chicago: Afro-Am. Pub. Co., 1969. Reprint 1972. ix, 212 p.

This work contains brief biographies of men and women in politics, science, business, religion, education, art, music, literature, and the theater. Entries are arranged by subject and time period. Accompanying each biography are source notes and illustrations. A name index is included.

SUBJECT(S): Afro-Americans--Biography--Juvenile literature. Afro-Americans--Africa--Biography--Juvenile literature.

42. Alford, Sterling G. *Famous First Blacks*. New York: Vantage Press, 1974. 105 p.

This work lists and provides brief information on black firsts in Afro-American history. Entries are arranged alphabetically under subject categories. Areas covered include awards, honors, business, the church, and the military.

SUBJECT(S): Afro-Americans--Biography--Dictionaries.

43. Brignano, Russell Carl. *Black Americans in Autobiography: An Annotated Bibliography of Autobiographies and Autobiographical Books Written Since the Civil War*. Durham, NC: Duke University Press, 1974. ix, 118 p.

A a bibliography of 147 black autobiographies written between 1865 and 1973. Annotations provide basic information on each autobiographer's life. Slave narratives are also cited. Reprints of autobiography published before 1865 are cited in a separate checklist. Indexes by experience, occupation or profession, geographical location, educational institution, and title are included.

SUBJECT(S): Afro-Americans--Biography--Bibliography. Slaves--United States--Biography--Bibliography.

44. Campbell, Dorothy W. *Index to Black American Writers in Collective Biographies*. Littleton, CO: Libraries Unlimited, 1983. 162 p.

This exceptionally useful index provides bibliographical references to biographical information on over 1,800 black American writers appearing in collective biographies. Included are creative writers, biographers, autobiographers, historians, pioneer journalists, literary critics, illustrators of books, and scholar/bibliographers. Over 267 reference sources, published between 1837 to 1982, are indexed in this work, and each source contains biographical information on at least two black authors. Many of the writers included are not well known and are not found in standard biographical sources. Entries are arranged alphabetically by authors' name.

SUBJECT(S): Afro-American authors--Biography-- Bibliography.
Afro-American authors--Biography--Indexes.

45. Contee, Clarence G., and Sharon Harley. *A Pan-African Index to Current Biography, 1940-1970*. Monticello, IL: Council of Planning Librarians, 1976. 20 p. SERIES: Council of Planning Librarians. Exchange Bibliography, no. 951.

This index provides cites short, concise biographies of Afro-Americans and Africans published between 1940 and 1970 in *Current Biography*. The 259 entries, cover 188 black Americans, 65 Africans, and 15 West Indians. Listed alphabetically, each entry includes name, date, type of work, and reference to the issue of *Current Biography*.

SUBJECT(S): Current biography yearbook--Indexes.
Biography--20th century--Indexes.
Afro-Americans--Biography--Indexes.
Blacks--Biography--Indexes.

46. Logan, Rayford Whittingham. *Dictionary of American Negro Biography*. 1st ed. New York: Norton, 1982.

This outstanding work contains biographical essays on more than 700 significant individuals in Afro-American history who were deceased prior to January 1, 1970. In addition to famous explorers, inventors, politicians, physicians, scientists, artists, cowboys, etc., this book also includes other important lesser-known figures. Each entry provides substantial information on the subject and concludes with a list of sources for further information. Unfortunately, an index of names by occupation or activity is not included.

SUBJECT(S): Afro-Americans--Biography.

47. Page, James Allen. *Selected Black American Authors: An Illustrated Bio-Bibliography*. Boston: G. K. Hall, 1977. xv, 398 p. SERIES: A Reference Publication in Black Studies.

This collection of biographies includes 453 Afro-American authors, poets, playwrights, and essayists from the eighteenth century to the present. Each entry provides date and place of birth, career experience, and citations to the author's works. Title and subject indexes and a bibliography are included.

SUBJECT(S): American literature--Afro-American authors--Bio-Bibliography.
Afro-American authors--Biography.

48. Page, James A. and Jae Min Roh, comps. *Selected Black American, African, and Caribbean Authors: A Bio-Bibliography.* Littleton, CO: Libraries Unlimited, 1985. 408 p.

This work provides biographical and bibliographical information on 632 Afro-American, Caribbean, and African authors published in the United States from the eighteenth century to 1985. Literary and non-literary writers are covered, including novelists, poets, playwrights, literary critics, and essayists concerned with civil rights, social and political issues, and theology. Publishers and editors who have had a significant impact on Afro-American writing are also included. Caribbean and African writers are included only if they have lived, studied, or published in the continental United States. The entries are arranged alphabetically by author's name. Each entry includes biographical information, a bibliography of the author's works, and sidelights on the writer's canon or status. The bibliography under each author is divided into the categories of fiction and nonfiction, then arranged chronologically. When possible, the genre and subject matter of each title is indicated. A general bibliography of sources is also included. Nationality rosters for Caribbean and African writers, and occupational and title indexes are included.

SUBJECT(S): American literature--Afro-American authors--Bio-bibliography.
Afro-American authors--Biography.
Blacks--Biography--Indexes.

49. Robinson, Wilhelmena S. *Historical Afro-American Biographies.* Cornwells Heights, PA: Publishers Agency, 1978. xii, 291 p. Series: International Library of Afro-American Life and History.

This collected work contains brief biographies on over 500 historical personalities considered to be representative of the socioeconomic aspects of Afro-American life. The individuals lived from the fourteenth through the twentieth century. Photographs, an index of last names, and an index by major activities are included.

SUBJECT(S): Afro-Americans--Biography.

50. Rogers, Joel Augustus. *World's Great Men of Color.* Edited with an introcommentary and new bibliographical notes by John Henrik Clarke. rev. ed. New York: Macmillan; London: Collier-Macmillan, 1972-73. 2 vols.

This two-volume work contains 200 biographies of important men and women of black African descent, from ancient Egypt through the 1940s. Biographies are arranged by geographic region. Volume I includes Egypt, Asia, and Africa. Volume II covers Europe, South and Central America, the West Indies, and the United States. It also contains a chapter on "Europeans who had some African blood, which was not generally known to their contemporaries," and others who have been "arbitrarily classified as whites." Illustrations and portraits are included. References are cited at the end of each biography.

SUBJECT(S): Afro-American race--Biography.
Biography--Blacks.

51. Rush, Theressa G., Carol F. Myers, and Esther S. Arata, eds. *Black American Writers Past and Present: A Biographical and Bibliographical Dictionary*. Metuchen, NJ: Scarecrow Press, 1975. 2 vols.

This comprehensive bio-bibliography covers over 2,000 black American writers from the early 18th century to the early 1970s. West Indian and African writers who lived or are published in the United States are also included. Authors are arranged alphabetically. Each entry includes brief biographical sketches, a list of works written by the author, a list of critical works on the author, and a portrait photo or illustration. Appendices list the names of noted critics, historians, and editors. An extensive bibliography is also included.

SUBJECT(S): American literature--Afro-American authos--Bio-bibliography.

52. Shockley, Ann Allen and Sue P. Chandler. *Living Black American Authors: A Biographical Directory*. New York: R.R. Bowker, 1973. 220 p.

An alphabetical listing of authors of books, periodical aricles, plays, television scripts, filmstrips, and editors. For each entry, occupation, dates, education, family, professional experience, memberships, awards, publications, and mailing address are included. A list of black publishers and a title index are included.

SUBJECT(S): American literature--Afro-American authors--Bio-bibliography.
American literature--20th century--Bio-bibliography.

53. Spradling, Mary Mace. *In Black and White: A Guide to Magazine Articles, Newspaper Articles, and Books Concerning More than 15,000 Black Individuals and Groups*. 3d ed. Detroit, MI: Gale Research Co., 1980-.

Updated periodically, this two-volume reference book provides biographical and bibliographical information on over 15,000 black individuals and groups, arranged alphabetically by name. The citations are drawn from periodicals, newspapers, and books. An occupation index is included.

SUBJECT(S): Afro-Americans--Biography--Indexes.

54. Toppin, Edgar Allan. *A Biographical History of Blacks in America Since 1528*. New York: McKay, 1971. X, 499 p.

This work presents Afro-American history as seen from the point of view of its famous personalities. It includes an alphabetically arranged collection of biographies of famous Afro-Americans, and a collection of fifteen essays on Afro-American history, from African origins through 1970. An extensive bibliography, and an author-title-subject index are included.

SUBJECT(S): Afro-Americans--Biography.
Afro-Americans--History.

55. *Who's Who Among Black Americans*. Northbrook, IL: Who's Who Among Black Americans, Inc., Pub. Co., 1977-.

This biographical dictionary contains brief biographies on thousands of noted contemporary blacks in the United States. The individuals are included on the basis of leadership and career achievement. Data for each person includes date of birth, family, education, publications, memberships, awards, military service, present position, and address. Geographical location and occupation indexes are included.

SUBJECT(S): Afro-Americans--Biography.

Scientists and Inventors

56. Carwell, Hattie. *Blacks in Science: Astrophysicist to Zoologist*. Hicksville, NY: Exposition Press, 1977. 95 p.

Includes biographical sketches of twenty-six outstanding, but relatively unknown black scientists. The appendix contains an extensive list of black inventors and their inventions. A brief bibliography, illustrations, and a name index are included.

SUBJECT(S): Afro-American scientists--Biography.

57. Driver, Paul J. *Black Giants in Science*. New York: Vantage Press, 1978. 83 p.

Written for young adults, this work provides brief biographies of twenty-four famous and little-known black men and women in the field of science. Entries are arranged alphabetically. Portraits and a brief bibliography are included.

SUBJECT(S): Afro-American scientists--Biography.
Black scientists--Biography.

58. Haber, Louis. *Black Pioneers of Science and Invention*. New York: Harcourt, Brace & World, 1970. vii, 181 p.

This work discusses the significant contributions made by fourteen black scientists and inventors and the roles they played in the development of scientific progress in the United States. These individuals are rarely cited in science text books. Portraits, bibliographical references, and a general index are included.

SUBJECT(S): Afro-American scientists.
Afro-American inventors.

59. Ho, James K. *Black Engineers in the United States: A Directory*. Washington, D.C.: Howard University Press, 1974. xix, 281 p.

This directory lists the names of 1,511 black engineers out of an estimated total of 7,000, as of 1974. It provides brief biographical data, including date of birth, current employment, history, education, marital status and name of spouse, memberships, and current address. Indexes are included.

SUBJECT(S): Afro-American engineers--United States--Directories.

60. Newell, Virginia K. *Black Mathematicians and Their Works*. Ardmore, PA: Dorrance, 1980. xvi, 327 p.

This volume contains biographical sketches and research articles by selected black Ph.D mathematicians and mathematics educators. An appendix provides lists of universities where blacks received doctorates in mathematics, and where black mathematicians are employed.

SUBJECT(S): Afro-American mathematicians.
Mathematics--Addresses, essays, lectures.

61. Van Sertima, Ivan, ed. *Blacks in Science: Ancient and Modern*. New Brunswick, NJ: Transaction Books, 1983. 202 p.

This collection of essays is the first book in English to give serious treatment to the technologies of early Africa. Chapters are devoted to ancient African technological advances and scientific discoveries in the fields of astronomy, agriculture, architecture, engineering, aeronautics, mathematics, medicine, metallurgy, navigation, physics, and writing systems. It also includes essays on the paradigms of African science. Of special interest are the chapters on Afro-American scientific and technological achievements. A useful bibliographical guide to the literature and biographical sketches of contributors are also included.

SUBJECT(S): African scientists.
Afro-American scientists.
African inventors.
Afro-American inventors.
Scientists--United States.

Doctoral Dissertations

62. *Dissertation Abstracts International. A: The Humanities and Social Sciences.* Ann Arbor, MI: University Microfilms International, 1930-. Also available in microfiche. Ann Arbor, University Microfilms. Continues: *Dissertation Abstracts. A: The Humanities and Social Sciences.*

A monthly publication containing author-prepared abstracts and indexes to doctoral dissertations in the humanities and the social sciences accepted at over 400 universities in North America. Dissertations relating to Afro-Americans can be identified through use of the title-keyword index. To identify dissertations by Afro-Americans, the name of the author must be known. An author index is included.

SUBJECT(S): Social sciences--Abstracts--Periodicals.
Humanities--Abstracts--Periodicals.
Dissertations, Academic-- Abstracts--Periodicals.
Dissertations, Academic--Abstracts.
Dissertations, Academic--United States--Abstracts.

63. *Dissertation Abstracts International. A, The Humanities and Social Sciences. B, The Sciences and Engineering. Cumulated Author Index.* Ann Arbor, MI: Xerox University Microfilms, 1974-.

This quarterly publication provides a cumulative author index for: *Dissertation Abstracts International. A, The Humanities and Social Sciences*,as well as*Dissertation Abstracts Abstracts International B, The Sciences and Engineering.*

SUBJECT(S): Dissertations, Academic--indexes.

64. Peebles, Joan. *Black Studies: A Dissertation Bibliography.* Ann Arbor, MI: University Microfilms International, 1978-1980. 2 vols.

This two-volume work cites dissertations on every aspect of the study of black Americans. It supplements Earle West's *A Bibliography of Doctoral Research on the Negro, 1933-1966.* Volume I is entitled *A Bibliography of Doctoral Research on the Negro,*

1967-1977. Volume II is entitled *Black Studies II*, and lists titles published by University Microfilms International from 1977 through 1980, plus 877 additional dissertations from the period 1940-1976 not covered by West or Volume I. Also listed are 175 masters theses completed 1948 to 1979. Both volumes group citations into broad subject categories, and each includes an author index. Citations include order information.

SUBJECT(S): Afro-Americans--Bibliography.
Afro-Americans--Study and teaching--Bibliography.
Dissertations, Academic--United States--Bibliography.

65. West, Earle Huddleston. *A Bibliography of Doctoral Research on the Negro, 1933-1966 and Supplement*. Washington, D.C.: Xerox, 1969. vii, 134 p.

A list of 1,452 doctoral dissertations, arranged in broad subject categories, covering every aspect of black life in the U.S. An author index is included.

SUBJECT(S): Afro-Americans--Bibliography.
Dissertations, Academic--United States--Bibliography.

ORGANIZATIONS

66. Black Resource Guide Incorporated. *The Black Resource Guide*. Washington D.C.: Ben Johnson, 1983, 109 p.

This national directory is designed to inform the public of available sources of assistance and information in the United States. It lincludes businesses and major corporations; colleges and universities; libraries, museums, and book stores; news and media organizations and associations; church, fraternal, civil rights, and national organizations; bar associations; and adoption agencies.

SUBJECT(S): Afro-Americans--associations, institutions, etc.
Afro-Americans--directories.
Afro-Americans--societies.

67. *Encyclopedia of Associations*. Detroit: Gale Research Co., 1956-. 5 vols.

This comprehensive guide to national and international organizations includes selected black organizations in the United States. Although its coverage of black organizations is not complete, it can be a valuable information source. It is updated around every two years. Use of the organization title and keyword index allows quick access to the black organizations listed. A geographic index arranged by state and city, and an index of the chief executives of the organizations are also included.

SUBJECT(S): Associations, institutions, etc.--Directories.
Associations, institutions, etc.--United States--Directories.

68. Cole, Katherine W., ed. *Minority Organizations: A National Directory*. Garrett Park, MD: Garrett Park Press, 1978-.

A directory of Alaskan Indian, Native American, Asian-American, Hispanic, and Afro-American organizations arranged by title in a single alphabet. Each entry provides address, telephone number, and activities. Title, geographical area, and function indexes are included. Also includes a glossary. Sources of information are also listed. Although it is a cumbersome task to identify the various of black-oriented organizations, it is nonetheless a valuable resource. Updated periodically.

SUBJECT(S): Minorities--United States--Directories.

69. Sanders, Charles, and Linda McLean, eds. *Directory: National Black Organizations*, New York: Afram Associates, 1972.

A list of business, professional, charitable and religious organizations. Each entry includes organization name, address, activities, membership rules, publications, date organized, officers, contact person, and statement of purpose. A list of other directories, and a title index are included.

SUBJECT(S): Afro-Americans.
Afro-Americans--Societies, etc.

70. Yearwood, Lennox S., ed. *Black Organizations: Issues on Survival Techniques*. Washington, D.C.: University Press of America, Inc., 1980. xxi, 260 p.

A collection of essays by black scholars addressing issues relating to survival techniques for black organizations. The types of organizations discussed include: colleges and universities, the church, civic and community groups, social clubs, professional organizations, athletic conferences, and social welfare. A selected list of organizations and a bibliography are included.

SUBJECT(S): Afro-American organizations.
Afro-Americans--Societies, etc.--Congresses.
Afro-Americans--Social conditions--1975- --Congresses.
Organizations.

AFRO-AMERICAN LIBRARIANSHIP

71. Clack, Doris H. *Black Literature Resources: Analysis and Organization.* New York: M. Dekker, 1975. viii, 207 p. SERIES: Books in Library and Information Science, vol. 16.

A study and analysis of the problems of bibliographical organization of black resources. It contains a guide to all classification numbers and subject headings reserved for black resources in the Library of Congress system which were in use through 1975. Non-relevant classification notations and subject headings (those which do not clearly indicate that the a work relates to Afro-Americans) used by the Library of Congress has used to identify black resources are also listed. Some of the classifications and subject headings listed in this work are now dated and no longer in use by the Library of Congress. The most important change by the Library of Congress since the publication of this work has been the abandonement of the term "Negro(es)" and the adoption of the term "Afro-American" to refer to works relating to blacks living in the United States; and the use of the term "Black(s)" to refer to blacks living elsewhere in the world outside the United States. Most of the classifications and headings are still in use and the study as a whole is valuable for those interested in the problems of bibliographical control of Afro-American library materials. A source bibliography, a general bibliography, and an index are included.

SUBJECT(S): Subject headings--Afro-Americans.
Classification--Books--Afro-Americans.
Classification, Library of Congress.

72. Josey, E. J., and Shockley, Ann Allen, eds. and comps. *Handbook of Black Librarianship.* Littleton, CO: Libraries Unlimited, Inc., 1977. 392 p.

This important source provides information on the relationship of Afro-Americans to libraries and librarianship. The history of and issues in black librarianship are explored. Library resources in Afro-American and African Studies, black-owned bookstores, and black publishers are listed. There are chapters on: library education in black colleges; public libraries in black communities; and black academic libraries. An author-title-subject index is included. See also Mass Media - General Sources section for additional book publisher sources.

SUBJECT(S): Afro-Americans and libraries.
Afro-American librarians.
Afro-Americans--Library resources.
Libraries--Special collections--Afro-Americans.
American literature--Afro-American authors.

JOURNAL ABSTRACTS AND INDEXES, BIBLIOGRAPHIES AND GUIDES

Current Journal Abstracting and Indexing Services

Journal, or periodical, abstracting and indexing (A & I) services are generally the only library resources which make possible a systematic and efficient identification and retrieval of the current periodical literature. The utilization of A & I services is therefore indispensible to library users attempting to identify the most recent periodical articles or information on a particular topic. This section cites selected current A & I services which, collectively, provide a comprehensive coverage of the current periodical literature relating to Afro-American studies.

Only one of these A & I services, *Index to Periodical Articles by and about Blacks*, indexes exclusively black periodicals. The other A & I services index both black and non-black periodicals devoted to particular disciplines or subject areas. In so doing, these other A & I services provide some coverage, more or less complete, of the periodical articles in those respective disciplines or subject areas which relate to Afro-Americans.

A list of periodicals scanned or indexed is usually included with these publications; and it is often indicated whether the indexing of the contents of a particular periodical or category of periodicals is partial or complete.

The complexities of arrangement and ease of use will vary, and this is noted in the annotations when these factors are significant. In each instance, the instructions on use accompanying these publications should be consulted to maximize positive search results.

The indexing terms used by the A & I services to identify articles relevant to blacks also varies from service to service, and it is important that the reader apply several possible subject terms in the course of a subject search effort. Relevant subject index terms commonly used include: AFRO-AMERICAN(S), BLACK(S), and NEGRO(ES). Other commonly used terms, which are generally relevant include: DISCRIMINATION, ETHNIC--, INTEGRATION, MINORITIES, RACE--, RACISM, and SEGREGATION. Frequently, a relevant work will not be entered under one of the above obviously relevant terms, but will begin with a specific subject term, i.e., Education, Family, History, or Politics, and then be subdivided by the term Afro-Americans, or Blacks, etc. These idiosyncracies regarding the indexing of Afro-American related articles are usually not indicated in the instructions on use. The user is therefore advised to search under both those terms which are obviously relevant to Afro-Americans as well as under specific subject or discipline terms and phrases.

Items which cover periodicals and magazines as a form of the mass media and relating to the field of journalism are cited in Mass Media - Journalism.

73. *ABC POL SCI. A Bibliography of Contents: Political Science & Government*. Santa Barbara, CA: ABC Clio Press, 1969-.

An index to current periodical literature in international affairs, law, government, political science, sociology, and economics. *ABC POL SCI* lists and indexes the tables of contents of over 300 journals, 33 of which are published in foreign countries. It is cumulated annually, and every five years.

SUBJECT(S): Political science--Bibliography--Periodicals.
Political science--Bibliography.

74. *America: History and Life*, Santa Barbara, CA: Clio Press, 1964-.

One of the most comprehensive abstracting and indexing services covering current literature on North American history (United States and Canada) from pre-historic times to the present. Approximately 2,000 scholarly journals published in English and in many foreign languages are covered. It is exeptionally useful due to its extensive and reliable coverage of Afro-American related articles which are widely scattered in the general periodical literature. Several exclusively Afro-American journals and a large number of high Afro-American content journals are included. In addition to periodical articles, articles in books, book reviews, and dissertations are also cited. It currently appears in four parts: Part A. "Article abstracts and citations," 1964-, issued three times a year; Part B. "Index to Book Reviews," 1974-, issued two times a year; Part C. "American History Bibliography, Books, Articles and Dissertations," 1974-, issued annually; and Part D. "Annual index," 1974-. Author and subject access to items indexed is provided. It's complex arrangement requires a careful study of the instructions on use. Information contained in *America: History and Life* since 1964 is available online for computer searches though DIALOG Information Services, Inc.

SUBJECT(S): United States--History--Periodicals-- Indexes.
Canada--History--Periodicals--Indexes.

75. *Art Index*. New York: H. W. Wilson, 1929-.

A quarterly author and subject index to periodical publications in the fields of fine arts, graphic arts, crafts, art history, architecture, archeology, city planning, industrial design, interior design, landscape architecture, museology, photography and films, and related topics. Approximately 250 periodicals are indexed, including English and foreign publications. Yearbooks and museum bulletins are also covered. Each issue contains a book review index section arranged alphabetically by author of book. *Art Index* is cumulated annually.

SUBJECT(S): Art--Periodicals--Indexes.
Art--Bibliography.

76. *Arts & Humanities Citation Index* (*A&HCI*). Philadelphia: Institute for Scientific Information, 1977-.

A comprehensive index to the world's current periodical literature in the fields of the arts and humanities. Over 5,500 journals are covered, as well as selected books. It is highly useful in that it permits the quick identification of related works by citing sources (usually endnotes or footnotes) which are included in a particular work. It's complex arrangement requires a careful study of the instructions on use. Issued three times a year, with annual cumulations.

SUBJECT(S): Periodical--Indexes.
Humanities--Periodicals--Indexes.
Arts--Periodicals--Indexes.

77. *Bibliographic Index*: *A Cumulative bibliography of Bibliographies*. New York: H.W. Wilson Company, 1937-.

A comprehensive subject index to bibliographies published separately or appearing as parts of books, pamphlets, or periodical articles. It is limited to bibliographies which have fifty or more citations. The emphasis is on Germanic and Romance language publications. In addition to books and pamphlets, the sources include 2,600 periodical titles which are regularly examined. Entries are arranged alphabetically by author under specific subject headings based on the Library of Congress Subject Headings. Issued three times a year and cumulated annually.

SUBJECT(S): Bibliography--Bibliography--Periodicals.

78. *Criminal Justice Abstracts* (*CJA*). Monsey, NY: Willow Tree Press, Inc., 1968-. Continues: *Abstracts On Crime and Juvenile Delinquency*.

A quarterly abstracting and indexing service covering international periodical and other literature relating to criminal justice policies, theories, and programs. Approximately 200 periodicals, as well as selected reports, books, dissertations, and proceedings are covered. The index is cumulated annually. Also available on microfilm.

SUBJECT(S): Crime and criminals--United States--Abstracts.
Juvenile delinquency--United States--Abstracts.

79. *Current Index to Journals in Education* (*CIJE*). Phoenix, AZ: Oryx Press, 1969-.

A monthly annotated index to current periodical literature on education and related topics. Issued as a companion piece to *Research in Education*. Topics covered include: higher education; junior colleges; elementary and early childhood education; adult, career, and vocational education; counseling and personnel services; reading and communication skills; educational management; handicapped and gifted children; languages and linguistics; information resources; rural education and small schools; science, mathematics, and environmental education; social studies/social science education; teacher education; tests, measurement, and evaluation; and urban education. Approximately 750 English-language journals are covered, and approximately 20,000 items are indexed each year. Several exclusively Afro-American journals are covered. Access is provided by author, subject, and by journal title. *CIJE* is cumulated semiannually. Information in *CIJE* is available online for computer searches.

SUBJECT(S): Education--Periodicals--Bibliography.
Education--Periodicals--Indexes.
Education--Information services.
Educational research--Periodicals--Indexes.

80. *Education Index*. New York: H. W. Wilson Co., 1929-.

A monthly author and subject index to over 300 current periodicals in education and related fields. Yearbooks and monographs are also indexed. Topics covered include: education, including administration and supervision; preschool, elementary, secondary, higher and adult education; teacher education; vocational education; counseling and personnel service; teaching methods and curriculum; audiovisual education; comparative and international education; special education and rehabilitation; and education in specific subject fields. Each issue contains a book review section arranged alphabetically by author of book. Cumulated annually.

SUBJECT(S): Education--Bibliography--Periodicals.
Education--Periodicals--Indexes.

81. *Humanities Index*. New York: H. W. Wilson Co., 1974-. Continues in part: *Social Sciences and Humanities Index*.

A quarterly author and subject index to over 250 current periodicals in the humanities. The fields of archaeology and classical studies, area studies, folklore, history, language and literature, literary and political criticism, performing arts, philosophy, religion and theology, and related subjects are covered. Each issue contains a book review index arranged alphabetically by author and title of book. Cumulated annually.

SUBJECT(S): Periodicals--Indexes.
Humanities--Periodicals--Indexes.

82. *Index Medicus*. National Library of Medicine. Bethesda, MD: U.S. Dept. of Health, Education, and Welfare, Public Health Service, National Institutes of Health, National Library of Medicine, Washington, D.C.: Supt. of Docs., U.S. G.P.O., 1879-. SERIES: DHHS Publication, no. (NIH).

A comprehensive monthly author and subject index to the world's current biomedical literature. Over 2,600 English and foreign-language periodicals are covered. In addition to journals in the medical and health sciences, there are representative journals in the fields of biometry, botany, chemistry, entomology, physics, psychology, sociology, veterinary medicine, and zoology. Articles pertinent to Afro-Americans which are scattered throughout the general medical literature are well represented. The medical literature pertaining to blacks throughout the world, especially South Africa, is also well represented. However, the one exclusively black medical journal, *National Medical Association Journal*, is not covered. Each issue also contains the *Bibliography of Medical Reviews* which includes those articles which are well documented surveys of the recent biomedical literature. The annual cumulation, *Cumulated Index Medicus*, and an abridged version, *Abridged Index Medicus*, are issued separately. MEDLINE, the online version of the index, is available for computer searches through DIALOG Information Services, Inc. and Bibliographic Retrieval Services, Inc. (BRS).

SUBJECT(S): Medicine--Periodicals.
Bibliography of Medicine--Periodicals.

83. *Index to Periodical Articles by and About Blacks*. Boston: G. K. Hall, 1950-.

An annual author-title-subject index to articles and book reviews by and about Afro-Americans which appear in approximately 23 Afro-American journals. It is the only current periodical indexing service devoted exclusively to Afro-American content periodicals. All aspects of Afro-American history and culture are covered, with extensive coverage given to the period from the early days of the Civil Rights movement to the present. A book review section arranged alphabetically by author of book appears with each annual volume. Poems and short stories, drama reviews, motion picture reviews, music reviews, and record reviews are also indexed. Subject index terms are based on the Library of Congress Subject Headings. Continues: *Index to Periodical Articles By and About Negroes*. It should be noted that only a fraction of periodical literature relating to Afro-Americans is indexed in this work. The numerous Afro-American related articles which appear in journals having contents not exclusively black, are not covered by this publication. The user must consult the other abstracting and indexing services to identify those relevant articles appearing in the non-exclusively Afro-American content journals.

SUBJECT(S): Afro-American periodicals--Indexes.

84. *International Political Science Abstracts*. Documentation Politique Internationale. Paris, International Political Science Association, 1951-.

A bimonthly indexing and abstracting service covering international periodical literature relating to political science, including international relations. Topics covered include methods and theory, political thinkers and ideas, governmental and administrative institutions, political process, public opinion, attitudes, parties, forces, groups, elections, and national and area studies. Approximately 800 periodical are indexed, and a list of the titles is included with each issue. Articles written in English are abstracted in English. Articles in other languages are abstracted in French. Article titles are translated into English and French as appropriate. Author and subject indexes are cumulated annually and appear in the final issue of each volume.

SUBJECT(S): Political science--Abstracts.
World politics--1945- --Abstracts.
International law--Abstracts.

85. *LLBA, Language and Language Behavior Abstracts*. La Jolla, CA: Sociological Abstracts, Inc., 1967-.

Comprehensive, quarterly abstracts to the world's current periodical literature on linguistics, language behavior, and related topics. Approximately 1,500 journals are indexed. The literature relating to Afro-Americans is well represented. Conference proceedings and occasional papers are also indexed. Abstracts accompany each entry. Access is provided by author and subject indexes, which are cumulated annually in separate volumes. Titles and abstracts for articles in foreign language journals are translated into English. Information contained in *LLBA* since 1973 is available online for computer searches through DIALOG Information Services, Inc.

SUBJECT(S): Linguistics--Abstracts--Periodicals.
Language and languages--Abstracts--Periodicals.
Language--Periodicals.

86. *MLA International Bibliography of Books and Articles on the Modern Languages and Literatures*. Modern Language Association of America, 1921-.

An annual comprehensive international bibliography of books and periodical articles falling into the categories of modern languages, literatures, folklore, and linguistics. It is issued in four volumes: Volume 1, British, American, Australian, Canadian, New Zealand, and West Indian literatures; Volume 2, European, Soviet, Asian, and African literatures; Volume 3, Linguistics; Volume 4, General literature and related topics; and Volume 5, Folklore. Entries are arranged alphabetically by author under literary, chronological period, or geographical categories.

Over 3,000 periodical titles are covered. In addition to periodical articles and books, dissertations, proceedings, and festschriften are included. Author and subject indexes, and a source list are included with each volume. Black related literature, linguistics, and folklore are fairly well represented, making this an important source for students and researchers in those fields. Information contained in this work since 1970 is available online for computer searches through DIALOG Information Services, Inc., and Bibliographic Retrieval Services, Inc. (BRS).

SUBJECT(S): Languages, Modern--Bibliography.
Literature--History and criticism--Bibliography.

87. *The Music Index.* Detroit: Information Coordinators, 1949-.

A monthly author and subject index to current music periodical literature. Indexes over 400 journals. Book reviews, reviews of music performances and recordings, and obituaries are also indexed. Cumulated annually.

SUBJECT(S): Music--Indexes.
Subject headings--Music.
Music--Periodicals--Indexes.

88. *Psychological Abstracts.* Washington, D.C.: American Psychological Association, 1927-.

Comprehensive monthly abstracts of the world's current literature in psychology and related fields. Over 1,000 journals, as well as selected books and technical reports are indexed. An abstract accompanies each entry. Author and subject indexes are included with each issue. The indexes are cumulated every six months, and every three years. The online PsychINFO Database contains all records published in *Psychological Abstracts* since 1969 and is available for computer searches through several commercial vendors including, DIALOG Information Services, Inc. and Bibliographic Retrieval Services, Inc. (BRS).

SUBJECT(S): Psychology--Periodicals.

89. *Readers' Guide to Periodical Literature.* New York: H. W. Wilson Co., 1900-.

An author and subject index to current popular and general interest periodicals published in the United States. Over 180 periodicals are covered. A book review section is included. Issued twice each month except in February, July, and August, when it appears monthly.

SUBJECT(S): Periodicals--Indexes.

90. *Sage Race Relations Abstracts* (*SRRA*). London,Beverly Hills, CA: Sage Publications Ltd., 1976-. Continues: *Race Relations Abstracts*.

Quarterly abstracts covering the world's current literature in English on race relations. Topics covered include community relations; attitudes; adjustment and integration; associations, organizations, and pressure groups; culture and identity; crime and delinquency; demographic studies; discrimination; economic studies; education; employment; family and adoption; health; housing; immigration and emigration; language; police; religion and race; women; and young people. Approximately 300 journals are indexed. Selected books and government documents are also covered. Although the emphasis is on Great Britain, materials pertaining to Afro-Americans in the United States are also cited. Author and subject indexes are cumulated annually.

SUBJECT(S): Ethnopsychology--abstracts.
Psychology, Social--abstracts.
Race Relations--abstracts.
Sociology--abstracts.
Ethnopsychology--Abstracts--Periodicals.
Race problems--Abstracts--Periodicals.
Sociology--Abstracts--Periodicals.

91. *Social Sciences Index*. New York: H. W. Wilson Co., 1974-. Continues in part: *Social Sciences & Humanities Index*.

A quarterly author and subject index to periodicals in the social sciences, including: anthropology, economics, environmental sciences, geography, law and criminology, planning and public administration, political science, psychology, sociology, the social aspects of medicine, and related subjects. A book review section is included with each issue. It is cumulated annually.

SUBJECT(S): Periodicals--Indexes.
Social sciences--Periodicals--Indexes.
Periodicals--indexes.
Social Sciences--indexes.

92. *Social Sciences Citation Index* (*SSCI*). Philadelphia: Institute for Scientific Information, 1973-.

A comprehensive index to the world's current periodical literature in the fields of the social sciences. Over 4,500 journals are covered, as well as selected books. It is highly useful in that it permits the quick identification of related works by citing sources (usually endnotes or footnotes) which are containged in a particular work. It's complex arrangement requires a careful study of the instructions on use. Issued three times a year, with annual and five-year cumulations.

SUBJECT(S): Social Sciences--Indexes.

93. *Sociological Abstracts*. San Diego: Sociological Abstracts, Inc. 1953-.

An abstracting service covering the world's literature in sociology and related fields. Over 1,500 journals, as well as selected books and conference proceedings are indexed. The literature pertaining to Afro-Americans is well covered. Issued five times annually. Each issue includes author, subject, and source indexes. The indexes are cumulated annually. Included in each issue, is the supplement, "International Review of Publications in Sociology," which provides a bibliography of the books reviews which appear in the journals abstracted. *Sociological Abstracts* is available online for computerized searches through DIALOG Information Services, Inc. and Bibliographic Retrieval Services, Inc.

SUBJECT(S): Sociology--Abstracts.

Journal Bibliographies and Guides

94. Birkos, Alexander S., and Lewis S. Tambs. *African and Black American Studies*. Littleton, CO: Libraries Unlimited, 1975. 205 p. SERIES: Academic Writer's Guide to Periodicals, vol. 3.

A directory of periodicals in African and Afro-American studies, listed alphabetically by title. For each publication, title, frequency, subscription price, subject areas covered, editorial policy, titles of indexing and abstracting services which cover journal contents, and special features are listed. Four indexes listing the journals are also included: unrestricted by subject coverage; chronologically by historical periods; geographically by region; and by topics covered.

SUBJECT(S): Afro-Americans--Periodicals --Directories.
Afro-American race--Periodicals --Directories.
Africa--Periodicals--Directories.

95. Daniel, Walter C. *Black Journals of the United States*. Westport, CO: Greenwood Press, 1982. x, 432 p. SERIES: Historical Guides to the World's Periodicals and Newspapers.

This guide contains historical and descriptive profiles of over one-hundred Afro-American periodicals published between 1827 and the 1980s. Newspapers are excluded. Each entry includes a historical essay providing information on editorial policies, the periodical's development, and the people who played a role in that development. Each entry also includes bibliographical notes of information sources, additional bibliography, a brief list of indexing services which cover the journal, and locations; and a section on publication history which lists title changes, volume and issue data, publisher and place of publication, editors, and circulation statistics. Journal selection was made on the basis of availability of the journals and the strength of the journal's coverage of the black experience. Two appendices are included which provide: a chronology of the journals' founding dates and significant events in black history; and and a listing of journals by geographical location.

SUBJECT(S): Afro-American periodicals--History.
Afro-American periodicals--Bibliography.

96. *Guide to Scholarly Journals in Black Studies*. Chicago, IL: Chicago Center for Afro American Studies and Research, 1981.

This work lists and describes twenty-six currently published black scholarly journals. The information presented for each journal includes: background information, such as publisher, editors, and date founded; journal contents, such as types of material accepted and the range of subjects covered; guidelines for article submission; and subscription information. A topical index to journals and a name index are included.

SUBJECT(S): Afro-American periodicals--Bibliography.
Afro-American periodicals--Directories.
Afro-American periodicals--Guides.

97. Newman, Richard. *Black Index: Afro-Americana in Selected Periodicals, 1907-1949*. Richard Newman. New York: Garland Pub., 1981. xxxi, 266 p. SERIES: Critical Studies on Black Life and Culture, vol. 4. SERIES: Garland Reference Library of Social Science, vol. 65.

An author and subject index to over 1,000 articles on Afro-Americana in over 350 periodicals published in the United States and Great Britain during the first half of the twentieth century. Entries are arranged in a single alphabet. A list of the periodicals with indication of the dates covered is included. Little-known magazines and journals, particularly state historical publications to which systematic access is often difficult are included. Book reviews are listed under author of book and name of reviewer. The *Journal of Negro History*, which publishes its own index, is not included.

SUBJECT(S): Afro-Americans--Periodicals--Indexes.

98. North Carolina Central University. School of Library Science. AfricanAmerican Materials Project. *Newspapers and Periodicals By and About Black People: Southeastern Library Holdings*. Compiled by the African-American Materials Project staff, School of Library Science, North Carolina Central University, and assisted by Lillie Dailey Caster. Boston: G. K. Hall, 1978. xxxvii, 153 p. SERIES: A Reference Publication in Black

Studies.

An alphabetical list of approximately 1000 periodical titles from Africa, the Caribbean, and the United States. Religious, political, fraternal, business, educational, and government publications are listed. For each publication the title, date of first issue (and last where applicable) and location in a Southeastern public or private library is given.

SUBJECT(S): Afro-Americans--Periodicals--Bibliography--Union lists.
Afro-American periodicals--Bibliography--Union lists.
Afro-American newspapers--Bibliography--Union lists.
Blacks--Periodicals--Bibliography--Union lists.
Catalogs, Union--Southern States.

NEWSPAPER INDEXES, BIBLIOGRAPHIES AND GUIDES

Newspaper Indexes

99. *Index to Black Newspapers.* Wooster, OH: Newspaper Indexing Center, Micro Photo Division of Bell Co., 1977-.

Published four times a year, this index covers ten major black newspapers from around the country. Currently, it is the only newspaper index devoted to Afro-American newspapers. Local, state, regional, national, and international items are indexed, as well as editorials, letters to the editor, syndicated columns, and reviews of art exhibits, concerts, motion pictures, plays, phonograph records, etc. Advertising is indexed only where it is "unique," or contains a company's history or position on a major issue. There are two sections: the first lists articles by subject, the second by author. For each article indexed, the title, name of the paper, date, and page number are given. The titles of the newspapers covered are as follows: *Afro-American* (New York Edition), *Amsterdam News* (New York), *Argus* (St. Louis), *Call & Post* (Cleveland), *Chicago Defender* (Chicago), *Daily World*, (Atlanta), *Journal & Guide* (Norfolk), *Michigan Chronicle* (Detroit), *Sentinel* (Los Angeles), and the *American Muslim Journal* (Chicago).

SUBJECT(S): Afro-American newspapers--Indexes--Periodicals.

Newspaper Bibliographies and Guides

100. Campbell, Georgetta Merritt. *Extant Collections of Early Black Newspapers: A Research Guide to the Black Press, 1880-1915, with an Index to the Boston Guardian, 1902-1904.* Troy, NY: Whitston Publishing Co., 1981. 401 p.

This guide lists 333 extant black newspapers arranged geographically by state and city. Each citation contains an abbreviated list of institutions or libraries in the United States owning each title. A directory to the abbreviated list is included. A "prototype" index to *Boston Guardian* is included, and was selected because only a few issues of this newspaper are extant. Notes and a bibliography are included.

SUBJECT(S): The Guardian (Boston, Mass.)--Indexes
Afro-American newspapers--Bibliography.
Afro-American newspapers--Indexes.

101. LaBrie, Henry G., III. *A Survey of Black Newspapers in America* Kennebunkport, Main: Mercer House Press, 1979. 72 p.

This work reports the findings of a 1979 survey which identified 165 current black newspapers published in 34 states and the District of Columbia, 151 of which reported circulations which together totaled 2,901,162 weekly. This reflects a 33.6% circulation decrease and a 22.5% loss in newspaper titles from the findings of a 1974 survey. Contains a directory of current newspapers (daily, weekly, and biweekly), arranged by state, providing address, telephone number, circulation, editor, issue days, the year publication began, number of staff, advertisement rates, and published format. A brief bibliography is included. Although some of the information is dated, this remains a valuable resource.

SUBJECT(S): Afro-American newspapers (American)--Directories.
Afro-American newspapers--Bibliography.
Afro-American newspapers--Surveys.

102. Pride, Armistead Scott. *A Register and History of Negro Newspapers in the United States, 1827- 1950*. Ann Arbor, MI: University Microfilms International, 1981. 426 p.

This register provides a history of black newspapers and a comprehensive listing of 2,700 Afro-American newspapers covering the years 1827 to 1950. The newspapers are arranged geographically by state and city. Forty-one states are represented. It also contains a four-part bibliography which cites works on the history of the Negro newspaper and the Negro press; checklists; directories; and articles from periodicals.

SUBJECT(S): Afro-American press--Bibliography.
Afro-American newspapers--History--Bibliography.

GENEALOGY

103. Blockson, Charles, L. *Black Genealogy*. Englewood Cliffs, NJ: Prentice-Hall, 1977. 232 p.

A bibliography and index are included.

SUBJECT(S): Afro-Americans--Genealogy--Handbooks, manuals, etc.

104. Rose, James and Alice Eichholz. *Black Genesis*. Detroit: Gale Research Co., 1978. xiv, 326 p. SERIES: Gale Genealogy and Local History Series, v. 1.

This handbook provides instructions and sources for genealogical research on blacks in the United States, West Indies, and Canada. Most of the book consists of extensive, annotated lists of primary and secondary resources. Government documents are well-represented. Archives, libraries, and historical societies with significant genealogical collections are also listed. Author, title, and subject indexes are included.

SUBJECT(S): Afro-Americans--Genealogy--Handbooks, manuals, etc.
United States--Genealogy--Handbooks, manuals, etc.

105. Smith, Jessie Carney, ed. *Ethnic Genealogy: A Research Guide*. Forward by Alex Haley. Westport, CT: Greenwood Press, 1983. xxxix, 440 p.

This series of articles, prepared by librarians, historians, archivists, and genealogists, provides instructions and sources for genealogical research on black Americans, American Indians, Asian Americans, and Hispanic Americans. The steps one takes in pursuing ethnic genealogical research are carefully delineated. Techniques, tools, types of records and sources, and needed genealogical supplies are listed. Libraries and historical societies with significant genealogical collections are also listed. Figures, tables, bibliography, and an index are included.

SUBJECT(S): Afro-Americans--Genealogy--Handbooks, manuals, etc.
Asian Americans--Genealogy--Handbooks, manuals, etc.
Hispanic Americans--Genealogy--Handbooks, manuals, etc.
Indians of North America--Genealogy--Handbooks, manuals, etc.
United States--Genealogy--Handbooks, manuals, etc.
United States--Genealogy--Library resources.

HISTORY

History - Chronologies, Fact Books, and Guides

106. Bergman, Peter M. *The Chronological History of the Negro in America*. New York: Harper and Row, 1969. 698 p.

A chronology of events in Afro-American history from the time of Columbus to 1968. Portraits, a bibliography of bibliographies, and an alphabetical index of people, places, and events are included.

SUBJECT(S): Afro-Americans--History--Chronology.

107. Clarke, Robert L., ed. *Afro-American History: Sources for Research*. Washington, D.C.: Howard University Press, 1973. xviii, 236 p.

This collection of essays serves as a guide to materials in the United States National Archives which relate to the government's role in shaping the black experience. Military, diplomatic, presidential, and domestic records are covered. Among the contributors are Alex Haley, John Blassingame, Mary Frances Berry, Andrew Billingsley, and Harold T. Pinkett.

SUBJECT(S): Afro-Americans--History--Sources--Congresses.
Afro-Americans--History--Archival resources--Congresses.

108. Diggs, Ellen Irene. *Black Chronology from 4000 B.C. to the Abolition of the Slave Trade*. Boston, MA: G.K. Hall, 1983. 295 p.

This chronology attempts to place Afro-Americans within the context of world history by annotating events dating back to Egyptian civilization, 4777 B.C. References to major books, tracts, and narratives written by blacks since the sixteenth century are included with the entries. A list of patents issued to blacks with year of issue is also included. This work is most useful for chronicling major themes in pre-colonial African history, events during the Atlantic slave trade, and black protest against the institution of slavery in the Americas prior to its abolition. It may also be useful for students of the African diaspora. A bibliography and index are included.

SUBJECT(S): Blacks--History--Chronology.
Slavery--History--Chronology.
Slave-trade--History--Chronology.
Africa--History--Chronology.

109. Drotning, Phillip T. *A Guide to Negro History in America*. Garden City, NY: Doubleday, 1968. xiv, 247 p.

Provides descriptions of important sites in Afro-American history by state and city. Memorials, churches, schools, libraries, homes, battlefields, forts, and graveyards are included. An index of places and people is included.

SUBJECT(S): Afro-Americans--History.
United States--Description and travel--Guide-books.
United States--Civilization--Afro-American influences.

110. Hudson, Gossie Harold. *Directory of Black Historians, Ph.D.'s and Others, 1975-1976: Essays, Commentaries, and Publications*. Monticello, IL: Council of Planning Librarians, 1975. 196 p. SERIES: Council of Planning Librarians. Exchange Bibliography nos. 870-872.

This guide to black history studies and directory of black historians contains essays on the role of the black historian, black historiography, and the Civil War. The directory contains the names and addresses of black historians, and the names, addresses, and interests of black and white, American and foreign, teachers of black history. A list of black colleges with Ph.D. programs in history is included. Though some of the information may be dated, it can be a valuable source for students of history.

SUBJECT(S): Historians--United States--Directories.
Afro-American historians--Directories.
Afro-Americans--Historiography--Address, essays, lectures.

111. Katz, William Loren. *Teachers' Guide to American Negro History*. Chicago: Quadrangle Books, 1968, 192 p.

This work provides suggestions for integrating Afro-American history into history classes for school children, a description of basic reference sources, and suggested classroom activities. It also contains a chapter on major units in Afro-American history, with each unit accompanied by a bibliography. A chapter on sources of free or inexpensive material is also included. Appendices contain lists of relevant books, American libraries with large black collections, and museums of black history. Illustrations, portraits, and a name-title index are included.

SUBJECT(S): Afro-Americans--History--Study and teaching.
Afro-Americans--History--Bibliography.

112. Salk, Erwin A., ed. and comp. *A Layman's Guide to Negro History*. new, enl. ed. New York: McGraw-Hill, 1967. xviii, 196 p.

A fact book intended to show the "depth of the Negro's contribution to American history." It is for popular rather than scholarly use. It is in two parts: part I, "Fact book," lists important dates and personalities in Afro-American history; part II is a group of thirty-one bibliographies on various subjects, which include print and non-print materials, such as phonograph records. Portraits and illustrations are also included.

SUBJECT(S): Afro-Americans--History--Bibliography.

113. Sloan, Irving J., ed. and comp. *The Blacks in America, 1492-1977: A Chronology & Fact Book.* 4th rev. ed. Dobbs Ferry, NY: Oceana Publications, 1977. x, 169 p. SERIES: Ethnic Chronology Series, no. 2.

A chronology of major events in Afro-American history and culture. There are also chapters which contain lists of Afro-American colleges, organizations, and publications; statistics on the social and educational status of Afro-Americans; and selected quotes by prominent Afro-Americans. A name index is included.

SUBJECT(S): Afro-Americans--History--Chronology.
Afro-Americans.

114. Thorpe, Earl E. *Black Historians: A Critique.* New York: Morrow, 1971, xi, 260 p. 260 p.

An analysis of Afro-American historians and their works. It is arranged in six sections that cover the years 1800 to 1971. A short biography of each writer is followed by an analysis of his or her work. Group portraits, illustrations, a selected bibliography, and an author-title-subject index are included.

SUBJECT(S): Afro-Americans--Historiography.
Afro-American Historians.

115. Wiggins, William H., Jr. "Lift Every Voice: A Study of Afro-American Emancipation Celebrations." *Discovering Afro-America*, ed. by John F. Szwed and Roger D. Abrahams. Leiden: Brill, 1975. pp. 46-57.

This unusual historical essay provides information on the origin and observance of a series of thirteen, little-studied emancipation celebrations. It begins with the first on January 1, 1808, commemorating the termination of America's foreign slave trade, and ends with June 19, 1865 (Juneteeth), celebrating the date of emancipation in east Texas. These celebrations were fashioned by differing historical circumstances and held in various states and locations in the country. Some celebrations, such as Juneteeth, continue to be observed today, while others are no longer recognized. A brief bibliography is included.

SUBJECT(S): Afro-Americans--history.

History - General Bibliographies

There are very few book bibliographies devoted to general Afro-American history. The James McPherson work which covers both history and culture is listed here because of its strong focus on history. The General Bibiographies and the Catalogs and Guides to Major Collections sections, while covering the full range of Afro-American studies, are also generally strong in history. Also, major history texts and periodical articles often include important bibliographies. Several history texts which include bibliographies are listed in the General History Texts and Slavery Texts sections. Among the best retrospective sources for periodical articles is the book by Dwight Smith listed below. *Bibliographic Index* can be useful for identifying bibliographies which appear as a part of current or retrospective books and periodical articles. Additional current and retrospective periodical articles may be identified by consulting sources listed in the Current Journal Abstracting and Indexing Services section.

116. McPherson, James M. *Blacks in America: Bibliographical Essays*. Garden City, NY: Doubleday, 1971. xxii, 430 p.

A comprehensive, bibliographic essay on Afro-American history and culture. It cites works published through 1970, including books and periodical articles. Over 4,000 titles cited are grouped into chronological periods, covering pre-slavery to 1970. An author-title-subject index is included.

SUBJECT(S): Afro-Americans--History--Bibliography.

117. Smith, Dwight La Vern, ed. *Afro-American History: A Bibliography*. Introduction by Benjamin Quarles. Santa Barbara, CA: ABC-Clio, 1974-1981. 2 vols. SERIES: Clio Bibliography Series, nos. 2, 8.

This two-volume annotated bibliography of periodical articles is one of the few devoted to Afro-American history. Together, the two volumes contain over 7,000 articles which appeared in *America: History and Life*, from 1954 to 1978. Volume I covers 1954 to 1972, and Volume II covers through 1978. Entries are arranged by chronological periods, then by subjects covering several areas: traditions in Afro-American culture, blacks in colonial America, slavery and freedom, Reconstruction, blacks in twentieth century America, and the contemporary scene since 1945. Some foreign language materials are cited. Author and subject indexes and a list of periodicals are included. For articles published since 1978, see current issues of *American: History and Life*.

SUBJECT(S): Afro-Americans--Bibliography.

History - Documents

This section cites selected document collections which cover the full range of Afro-American history, as opposed to a limited chronological period or topic. Documents relating to slavery are cited under History - Slavery. Document collections relating to other topics are cited in the appropriate subject section.

118. Aptheker, Herbert, ed. *A Documentary History of the Negro People in the United States*. New York: Citadel Press, 1969, 1974. 3 vols.

This is a collection of historical documents arranged chronologically by period, covering the years 1661 to 1910. Each section is prefaced by an introduction, which places the material in its historical context. Speeches, addresses, testimonies, reports, and newspaper articles are included. Bibliography and indexes are included.

SUBJECT(S): Afro-Americans--History--Sources.

119. Bergman, Peter M., and Jean McCarroll. *The Negro in the Congressional Record*. New York: Bergman Publishers, 1969.

This multi-volume work contains portions of the Congressional Record concerning Afro-Americans, dating from 1774 to 1863. Each volume provides a table of contents. There are no indexes or bibliography.

SUBJECT(S): Afro-Americans--History--To 1863--Sources.
Slavery--United States--History--Sources.

120. Ducas, George, and Charles Van Doren, eds. *Great Documents in Black American History*. Introduction by C. Eric Lincoln. New York: Praeger Publishers, 1972.

This document collection contains essays, letters, and speeches on Afro-Americans from colonial times through 1970. Most items were written by black authors. Each has a short introduction placing the work in the context of Afro-American history. Drawings and photographs of the authors and illustrations of important events are included. A list of document sources and an author-title-subject index are also included.

SUBJECT(S): Afro-American--History--Sources.

121. Frazier, Thomas R., ed. *Afro-American History: Primary Sources*. New York: Harcourt, Brace & World, Inc., 1970. xiv, 514 p.

A collection of documents by blacks intended to serve as an introduction to Afro-American history. They are reproduced in their entirety or in abridged form. Documents are arranged chronologically in fourteen sections covering the colonial period to 1970. Each section has a brief introduction, contains three to five documents, and is concluded with a bibliography for further reading. Each document is introduced with a short note placing the item in its historical context. Included are descriptions of black life, statements of black leaders, and position papers of black organizations. The works concludes with a general bibliography.

SUBJECT(S): Afro-Americans--History.

122. Romero, Patricia H., ed. and comp. *I Too Am America: Documents from 1619 to the Present*. Cornwells Heights, PA: Publishers Agency, 1978. iv, 304 p. SERIES: International Library of Afro-American Life and History.

A collection of documents written from 1619 through the 1960s, arranged chronologically. Most were written by Afro-Americans, and were selected because they reveal the dramatic aspect of the struggle for equality. Slavery, abolition, Reconstruction, the late-nineteenth and early-twentieth centuries, and the civil rights movement are covered. Annotations provide information on the historical context in which the documents were produced. Many of the items have been edited. A few illustrations, facsimiles, maps, and an index are included.

SUBJECT(S): Afro-Americans--History--Sources.

History - General Texts

It was not possible to cite all or most of the many general texts on Afro-American history. The few general texts cited below were selected for their scholarly and reference value and to provide those not familiar with Afro-American history with a point of departure. It is not suggested that the many outstanding general histories not included are of less value than those which are. A few history texts relating specifically to slaverly are also included in this bibliography and are cited in the Slavery Texts section.

123. Adler, Mortimer J., Charles Van Doren, and George Ducas., eds. *The Negro in American History*. rev. ed. Chicago: Encyclopedia Britannica Corp., 1972, 3 vols.

This three volume collection of essays is intended to present the "role of the Black man in the life of this continent." It contains a total of 186 selections, by 134 different authors, drawn from *Annals of America*, a twenty-volume work on American history. The essays cover historical, political, social, and economic topics in Afro-American studies from 1567 to 1968. Drawings, photographs, and biographies of the authors are included. Each volume includes an author index.

SUBJECT(S): Afro-Americans--History--Sources.

124. Berry, Mary Frances and John W. Blassingame. *Long Memory: The Black Experience in America*. New York: Oxford University Press, 1982. xxi, 486 p.

This general history text covers Afro-American history from Africa to through the 1970s. It is more thematic in approach than narrative, and focuses on those subjects most revealing of the complexities of the black experience in America. The title chosen for this book symbolized the authors' rejection of the view of Afro-Americans as an atomized, rootless people and their emphasis on cultural continuities and on succeding generations building on the lessons learned and passed on through oral tradition. Illustrations, an extensive bibliography, a chronology, and an index are included.

SUBJECT(S): Afro-Americans--History.
Afro-Americans--Civil rights.
United States--Race relations.

125. Franklin, John Hope. *From Slavery to Freedom: A History of Negro Americans*. 5th ed. New York: Knopf, 1980. xxvii, 554 p.

This classic work provides a comprehensive general history of blacks in the United States. Bibliographical notes and an index are included.

SUBJECT(S): Afro-Americans--History.
Slavery--United States--History.

126. Katz, William Loren, comp. *Eyewitness: The Negro in American History*. New York: Pitman Pub. Corp., 1967. xix, 554 p.

This four-volume work covers the history of blacks in America from their origins in Africa through 1973. Over 1000 photographs, facsimiles, and drawings are included. Volume 1 covers Africa to the Civil War; volume 2, Reconstruction to 1945; and volume 3, the civil rights movement to the black revolution. Volume 4 is a yearbook of major events and personalities of 1972, and contains special reports on Africa, blacks in films, obituaries, and a calendar of events, 1971-1972. Volume 3 contains indexes for volumes 1-3; volume 4 has its own index.

SUBJECT(S): Afro-Americans--History--Sources.

127. Meier, August and Elliott Rudwick. *From Plantation to Ghetto*. 3rd ed. New York: Hill and Wang, 1976. vi, 280 p. SERIES: American Century Series.

A brief, analytical, interpretive, interdisciplinary survey of Afro-American history from the West African heritage to the early 1970s. The focus is on what was happening with Afro-Americans, and it is assumed that the reader is familiar with general United States history. An extensive bibliography and an index are included.

SUBJECT(S): Afro-Americans--History.

SLAVERY

Slavery - Bibliographies

128. Dumond, Dwight Lowell. *A Bibliography of Antislavery in America*. Ann Arbor: University of Michigan Press, 1961. 119 p.

According to the author, "no item of major importance" is left out of this bibliography of American and British anti-slavery literature. The British material is included only because of its use in the United States. Items are arranged alphabetically by main entry. Books, articles, sermons, reports, and correspondence are included. There are no annotations.

SUBJECT(S): Slavery--United States-- Antislavery movements--Bibliography.

129. Fowler, Julian S., ed., and Geraldine Hopkins Hubbard, comp. *A Classified Catalogue of the Collection of Anti-Slavery Propaganda: In the Oberlin College Library*. Oberlin, OH: Oberlin College Library, 1932. 84 p.

A catalog of 1,590 entries, all by Americans, citing anti-slavery society publications, religious and moral literature, legal and economic works, personal slave narratives, biographies, children's literature and poetry, songs, anthologies, newspapers, and periodicals. The appendix describes British anti-slavery material and American pro-slavery works. Includes author-subject index.

SUBJECT(S): Slavery--United States--Bibliography.

130. Jacobs, Donald Martin, ed. *Antebellum Black Newspapers: Indices to New York Freedom's Journal (1827-1829), The Rights of All (1829), The Weekly Advocate (1837), and The Colored American (1837-1841)*. Westport, CT: Greenwood Press, 1976. xii, 587 p.

This work contains indexes for four abolitionist newspapers, published between 1827 and 1841, in New York City. Each index includes author and subject entries arranged alphabetically. Each entry gives date, page, and column in which the article appeared.

SUBJECT(S): Afro-American newspapers--New York (City)--Indexes.

131. Smith, John David, comp. *Black Slavery in the Americas: An Interdisciplinary Bibliography, 1865-1980*. Foreward by Stanley L. Engerman. Westport CT: Greenwood Press, 2 vols., xxix, 2712 p.

This is the first comprehensive bibliography on the literature of slavery in the Western Hemisphere. Over 15,000 items which appeared between 1865 and 1980, including books, articles, theses, dissertations, review essays, and unpublished papers and manuscripts. Scholarship from anthropology, sociology, linguistics, fine arts, folklore, religion, and formal historiography is included. Citations are grouped into 25 subject areas, covering such topics as the Atlantic slave trade; the economics of slavery; the slave family; slavery in the North, the Midwest, the West, and the upper and lower South; black slavery among the Indians; slavery in Canada, the Caribbean, Central, and South America; conditions of slave life, including diet, clothing, medicine, and recreation; and slave resistance. An extensive subject index listing over 2,000 categories, and over 5,000 cross-references greatly facilitates the location of individual works. Subject and author indexes are included.

SUBJECT(S): Slavery--America--Bibliography.
Slavery--United States--Bibliography.

132. Thompson, Edgar T. *The Plantation: An International Bibliography.* Boston: G.K. Hall, 1983. xix, 194 p. SERIES: A Reference Publication in Anthropology.

An annotated bibliography of books and articles on the topic of plantations. The focus is on colonial America, and pre- and post-Civil War plantations in the United States. It also covers plantation societies throughout the western hemisphere and the world. One of the sections lists fiction having plantation themes or settings, and includes children's literature. An author index is included.

SUBJECT(S): Plantations--Bibliography.

133. Thompson, Lawrence Sidney, comp. *The Southern Black: Slave and Free: A Bibliography of Anti- and ProSlavery Books and Pamphlets, and of Social and Economic Conditions in the Southern States from the beginnings to 1950.* Troy, NY: Whitston Pub. Co., 1970. 576 p.

This bibliography cites pamphlets, books, travel accounts and letters, written from the seventeenth to the mid-twentieth century, arranged alphabetically by author. Most items cited are in English; some are in French and Spanish.

SUBJECT(S): Southern States--Bibliography.
Afro-Americans--Southern States--Bibliography.
Slavery--United States--Bibliography.

Slavery - Documents

This section cites selected document collections and indexes dealing with slavery. Document collections dealing with general Afro-American history are cited in the History - Documents section. Slave narrative and other documents written by slaves are cited in the Slave Narrative section.

134. Blassingame, John W. and Mae G. Henderson, eds. *Antislavery Newspapers and Periodicals: An Annotated Index of Letters, 1817-1871*. Boston: G.K. Hall, 1980-1984, 5 vols. SERIES: Reference Publications in Afro-American Studies.

Approximately 40,000 letters appearing in several antislavery journals are indexed in this five-volume work. About one-fifth of the column space in antislavery journals was devoted to correspondence submitted by people of all races. Slavery was the major issue, but many other topics also received attention, including women's rights, temperance, religion, agriculture, labor, the Civil War, diplomacy, interracial violence, prison reform, literature, music, and education. Volume I: 1817-1845, indexes *Philanthropists*, *Emancipator*, *Genius of Universal Emancipation*, *Abolition Intelligencer*, *African Observer*, and the *Liberator*. Volume II: 1835-1865, indexes the *Liberator*, *Anti-Slavery Record*, *Human Rights*, and the *Observer*. Volume III: 1836-1854, covers the *Friend of Man*, *Pennsylvania Freeman*, *Advocate of Freedom*, and *American and Foreign Anti-Slavery Reporter*. Volume IV: 1840-1860, indexes the *National Anti-Slavery Standard*. Volume V: 1861-1871, also indexes the *National Anti-Slavery Standard*. Data for each journal is provided, including motto, publication information, editors, contributing reporters, special features, and library locations. Under each journal the entries are presented in chronological order, and are accompanied by a brief annotation summarizing the letter's content, and providing the names of writer and recipient, and full journal citation. Indexes of correspondents are included.

SUBJECT(S): Afro-American newspapers--Indexes.
Afro-American periodicals--Indexes.
American periodicals--Indexes.
Newspapers--Sections, columns, etc.--Letters to the editor.
Social problems--Indexes.

135. Breeden, James O., ed. *Advice Among Masters: The Ideal in Slave Management in the Old South*. Westport, CT: Greenwood Press, 1980. xxvi, 350 p. SERIES: Contributions in Afro-American and African Studies, no. 51.

This collection of documents contains over one hundred treatises and opinions on slave management by slave owners. These rare documents provide information on the concerns and interests of the slave-owner class. They are arranged by subject and cover nearly every facet of slave management and the master-slave relationship, including plantation discipline, food, housing, slave marriages, religious life, and health care for the slaves. Originally published in Southern agricultural journals during the Antebellum era, the documents are reprinted here in full or in part. Diagrams, tables, bibliographical notes, bibliography, and an index are included.

SUBJECT(S): Slavery--United States--Condition of slaves--Sources.
Plantation life--Southern States--History--Sources.

136. Catterall, Helen Honor (Tunnicliff), ed. *Judicial Cases Concerning American Slavery and the Negro.* New York: Octagon Books, 1968. 5 vols.

"Instances of every sort of complication or situation that could arise from the institution of slavery" are contained in this compendium of thousands of court records. Hundreds of manumission records are also included. Material is arranged chronologically under each state. Each volume contains an index of the subjects and names mentioned in cases.

SUBJECT(S): Slavery in the United States--Cases.
Slavery in Canada--Cases.
Slavery in Great Britain--Cases.
Slavery in Jamaica--Cases.
Afro-Americans--Legal status, laws, etc.

137. Donnan, Elizabeth. *Documents Illustrative of the History of the Slave Trade to America.* 4 vols. Washington, D.C.: Carnegie Institution, 1930-35. SERIES: Carnegie Institution of Washington, no 409. Reprint. New York: Octagon Books, 1965.

This extensive collection of documents provides basic source material for the study of the slave trade to to Maryland, Virginia, South Carolina, and Louisiana, the major ports to which slaves were shipped. Legal, economic, and personal documents, and slave ship manifests are included. These documents provide details relating to the slave trade which are generally not available elsewhere. The documents are grouped by colony or state, and each section contains an introduction on the general characteristics of the slave trade, as well as the problems involved in its documentation. The documents are accompanied by explanatory footnotes. There also are charts throughout the book which summarize the statistical data.

SUBJECT(S): Slave-trade--United States--Sources.
Slave-trade--History--Sources.

138. Rose, Willie Lee. *A Documentary History of Slavery in North America*. New York: Oxford University Press, 1976. xvi, 537 p.

A selection of documents which illustrate the historical development of slavery in the United States. Includes travelers' accounts, letters of slaves, fugitive slave narratives, songs and riddles, newspaper advertisements, legal cases, criminal trials, statutes, petitions, planters' diaries, and inventories. It includes a bibliographic introduction to sources in essay form and illustrations.

SUBJECT(S): Slavery--United States--History--Sources.

139. Windley, Lathan A., comp. *Runaway Slave Advertisements: A Documentary History from the 1730s to 1790*. Westport, CT: Greenwood Press, 1983. 4 vols.

This four-volume work is a sourcebook for the study of slavery and fugitive slaves in eighteenth-century Virginia, Maryland, North Carolina, South Carolina, and Georgia. When slaves successfully escaped, their owners would advertise for the reclamation of their lost property. These advertisements contain valuable data about the runaway slave population including sex, age, birthplace, height, stature, color, physical impairments, occupation, language, speech patterns, hobbies, deportment, literacy, how and why the slaves ran away, what they took with them, possible explanations slaves might give, and probable destinations.

SUBJECT(S): Fugitive slaves--Southern States--History--18th century--Sources.
Slavery--Southern States--History--18th century--Sources.
Southern States--Social conditions--18th century--Sources.

Slave Narratives

This section includes selected slave narrative collections and indexes to slave narratives. Works dealing primarily with the slave narrative as a literary form are cited in the Literature - General Surveys and Criticism section.

140. Blassingame, John W., ed. *Slave Testimony: Two Centuries of Letters, Speeches, Interviews, and Autobiographies*. Baton Rouge, LA: Louisiana State University Press, 1977. lxv, 777 p.

This is a collection of 111 letters written 1736 to 1864; eight speeches; 129 interviews conducted by journalists, scholars, and government officials; and 13 autobiographies. The slaves who provided these testimonies lived under a variety conditions or circumstances: as domestic servants and field hands, some were docile and others were rebels, some had kind masters and some masters were inhumane. These items were selected with the intent of revealing the mind of the slave, his private world, how he survived day to day, and the configuration of his culture and family life. Bibliographical references, and name and subject indexes are included.

SUBJECT(S): Slaves--United States--Biography.
Slavery--United States--History--Sources.

141. Botkin, Benjamin Albert, ed. *Lay My Burden Down: A Folk History of Slavery*. Chicago, IL: University of Chicago Press, 1968, 1945. xxi, 298 p.

An integrated selection of excerpts and complete narratives from the slave narrative collection of the Federal Writer's Project. They attempt to answer the questions: What does it mean to be a slave? What does it mean to be free? and How does it feel? They range in coverage from the last half of the eighteenth century to the anti-slavery periods and provide a broad basis for interpretation due to their variation in style and treatment. Photographs, a list of informants and interviewers, and a name-subject index are included.

SUBJECT(S): Slavery in the United States--Condition of Slaves.
Slaves.
Slave Narratives.
Afro-Americans--Biography.

142. Jacobs, Donald Martin, ed. *Index to the American Slave*. Westport, CT: Greenwood Press, 1981. xviii, 274 p. SERIES: Contributions in Afro-American and African Studies, no. 65.

This is an invaluable index to the three-series edition of *The American Slave: A Composite Autobiography*, edited by George P. Rawick. It provides a road map through the more than 20,000 pages of slave narratives presented in that work. The Slave Identification File provides an alphabetical listing of the 3,500 interviewees. A subject index lists specific citations under more than 100 subject categories ranging from "Family (separations)" and "Slave Surveillance" to "Indian Relatives" and "Political Participation." A name index by states is also included.

SUBJECT(S): Slaves--United States--Biography--Indexes.
Slavery--United States--Indexes.
American Slave: A Composite Autobiography--Indexes.

143. Rawick, George P.,ed. *The American Slave: A Composite Autobiography*. Westport, CT: Greenwood Publishing Co. Basic Set: 19 vols., 1972; Supplement: Series 1, 12 vols., 1977; Supplement: Series 2, 10 vols., 1979 SERIES: Contributions in Afro-American and African Studies, nos. 11, 35, and 49.

This massive work of over 20,000 pages in 41 volumes is a word-by-word record of 3,500 interviews with thousands of former slaves of the antebellum South. It constitutes the most valuable primary source materials available to students of American slavery. The interviews were conducted during the Depression by the Works Progress Administration. The index, (edited by Donald M. Jacobs) is published separately. The first volume of Series 1 (1972) is *Sundown to Sunup*, a sociological study of slave communities. The following volumes contain interviews with slaves from throughout the Southern States. In addition there is a volume of interviews concerning religious conversions and experiences.

SUBJECT(S): Slaves--United States--Biography.
Slavery--United States.

144. Starobin, Robert S., comp. *Blacks in Bondage: Letter of American Slaves*. New York: Viewpoints, 1974. xviii, 196 p.

This collection of slaves' letters reveals their daily life and inner thoughts. Included are letters to masters and mistresses from slave drivers, managers, house servants, artisans, hirelings, and field hands. Several letters are from one slave to another. Some of the letters relate to plantation routine, others to slave resistance. Bibliographical notes are included.

SUBJECT(S): Slavery in the United States--Personal narratives.

Slavery - Texts

145. Aptheker, Herbert. *American Negro Slave Revolts*. Forward by John Bracey. New York: International Publishers, 1983. 411 p.

A comprehensive and outstanding study on resistance to slavery in the United States. An extensive bibliography, and a name-subject index are included.

SUBJECT(S): Slavery--United States--Insurrections, etc.
Afro-American--History--to 1983.

146. Berlin, Ira. *Slaves Without Masters: The Free Negro in Antebellum South*. New York: Pantheon Books, 1974. xxi, 423 p.

An important study of free blacks in South from the 1600s to the Civil War. Includes tables and statistical data on the slave, free black, and white populations. Includes bibliographical references and manuscript sources are listed. An index is also included.

SUBJECT(S): Afro-Americans--History--to 1863.
Freedmen in the Southern States.

147. Blassingame, John W. *The Slave Community: Plantation Life in the Antebellum South*. Rev. ed. New York: Oxford University Press, 1979. xviii, 414 p.

The first edition of this important study was published in 1970. It is based primarily on selected ex-slave autobiographies, and was the first major work to attempt to arrive as an understanding of the institution of slavery from the perspective of the slaves. It thereby made a substantial contribution toward establishing an alternative methodology in slave studies involving the use of slave-produced documents as primary resources. A bibliography and an index are included.

SUBJECT(S): Slavery--Southern States.
Plantation life--Southern States.

148. Craton, Michael, ed. *Roots and Branches: Current Directions in Slave Studies*. Michael Craton. Toronto: New York: Pergamon Press, 1979. 292 p.

An important collection of papers presented by scholars at a conference entitled "Slave Studies," held in Waterloo, Ontario, in March 1979. Several disciplines were represented, including history, anthropology, economics, and sociology. The papers are valuable both for their content and for their numerous bibliographical references. Each paper is followed by one or more critical commentaries presented by participating conference scholars. Use of this work as a reference tool is hampered by the lack of an index and bibliography.

SUBJECT(S): Slavery--History--Congresses.

149. Curtin, Philip D. *The Atlantic Slave Trade: A Census*. Madison: University of Wisconsin Press, 1969 xix, 338 p.

This classic work brings together previously published information on the number of Africans brought across the Atlantic. It attempts to answer the questions: How many? When? From what parts of Africa? and To what destinations in the New World? It provides a comprehensive review and interpretation of the literature, and contains quantitative data on the slave trade, from the fifteenth through the nineteenth centuries. The slave trade of Spanish, English, French, and other North European colonies is covered. One chapter is devoted to mortality rates. An appendix presents a linguistic inventory of African language, and the locations in Africa where the languages were spoken. There are numerous maps and statistical tables. Bibliographical notes, a bibliography, and an index are included.

SUBJECT(S): Slave-trade--History

150. Davis, David Brion. *The Problem of Slavery in the Age of Revolution, 1770-1823*. Ithaca, NY: Cornell University Press, 1975. 576 p.

A sequel to the author's *Problem of Slavery in Western Culture*, this work focuses on the Anglo-American experience. There is a special emphasis on the ideological functions and implications of the British and American anti-slavery movements. It includes a calendar of events associated with slavery, the slave trade, and emancipation from 1770-1823. It also includes bibliographical notes and index.

SUBJECT(S): Slavery

151. Davis, David Brion. *The Problem of Slavery in Western Culture*. Ithaca, NY: Cornell University Press, 1966. 505 p.

This Pulitzer prize-winning classic attempts to systematically trace the origins of anti-slavery thought. It provides: a survey of representative attempts to conceptualize the moral and historical problem of slavery; a comparative analysis of slave systems in the Old World; a response to slavery in European thought from antiquity to the eighteenth century (excluding the question of black slavery in America); early attitudes toward American slavery and the problems and conditions which might have aided or impeded the rise of anti-slavery thought; and the early protest against black slavery in the eighteenth century. Generally, this study extends to the early 1770s, with less focus on the late-eighteenth and nineteenth centuries. Bibliographical notes and an index are included.

SUBJECT(S): Slavery
Slavery and the church.

152. Engerman, Stanley L., and Eugene D. Genovese., eds. *Race and Slavery in the Western Hemisphere: Quantitative Studies*. Princeton, NJ: Princeton University Press, 1975. xv, 556 p. SERIES: Quantitative Studies in History.

A collection of papers originally presented at a conference held at the University of Rochester, March 9-11, 1972, sponsored by the History Advisory Committee of the Mathematical Social Science Board. Presents a new theoretical and methodological orientation based upon the analysis of quantitative data. Some of the papers contain data which revise and correct some of the data presented by Curtin in his *Atlantic Slave Trade: A Census*. The papers are grouped into four sections covering the slave trade, social and demographic aspects of slave populations, the slave and free person of color in the urban enviroment, and post emancipation response. Contributing authors are in the fields of history, economics, sociology, and anthropology. Includes illustrations, bibliographical notes, and an index.

SUBJECT(S): Slavery--America--Congresses.
Slave-trade--Congresses.
America--Race relations--Congresses.

153. Fogle, Robert William and Stanley L. Engerman. *Time on the Cross.* Boston: Little, Bown, 1974. 2 vols.

An important, though controversial, study on the economic aspects of slavery based on the techniques of econometric history or "cliometrics". It argues that slavery was an efficient and profitable capitalistic enterprise; that slaves were more productive than free laborers; and that the material conditions of slaves compared favorably with those of the free industrial workers; and the institution of slavery was therefore not so brutal or inhumane as was popularly thought. Volume I contains findings, interpretations, and conclusions, and Volume II contains discussions of evidence and methods. Both conclusions and methods have been severely criticized by a number of other historians of slavery.

SUBJECT(S): Slavery in the United States--Economic aspects.

154. Foner, Philip S. *History of Black Americans: From Africa to the Emergence of the Cotton Kingdom.* Westport, CT: Greenwood Press, 1975. 680 p. SERIES: Contributions in American History, no. 40.

The first of a three part comprehensive and near encyclopedic history of blacks in America during the entire era of slavery through the Civil War. (See also *History of Black Americans: From the Emergence of the Cotton Kingdom to the Eve of the Compromise of 1850*, and *History of Black Americans: From the Compromise of 1850 to the End of the Civil War*, cited below by same author.) This volume covers African pre-history and the rise of slavery and the slave trade in the United States, to the rise of the cotton industry around 1820. Slavery and race relations in the Caribbean are also discussed. An extensive and highly useful bibliography is included. An index is also included.

SUBJECT(S): Afro-Americans--History.

155. Foner, Philip S. *History of Black Americans: From the Emergence of the Cotton Kingdom to the Eve of the Compromise of 1850.* Westport, CT: Greenwood Press, 1983. viii, 656 p. SERIES: Contributions in American History, no. 102.

A comprehensive history of slaves and free blacks from 1820, covering the emergence of Garrisonian abolitionism and the antislavery movement to 1848. An important chapter on American historians and Antebellum slavery provides an chronological review of slavery studies literature and outlines the contributions of noted historians. An extensive and highly useful bibliography is included. An index is also included.

SUBJECT(S): Afro-Americans--History.

156. Foner, Philip S. *History of Black Americans: From the Compromise of 1850 to the End of the Civil War*. Westport, CT: Greenwood Press, 1983. viii, 539 p. SERIES: Contributions in American History, no. 103.

This history of black Americans focuses on the contribution of blacks during the critical period from the Compromise of 1850 to the end of the Civil War. An extensive and highly useful bibliography is included. An index is also included.

SUBJECT(S): Afro-Americans--History.

157. Genovese, Eugene D. *From Rebellion to Revolution: Afro-American Slave Revolts in the Making of the Modern Wold*. Baton Rouge: LA, Louisiana State University Press, 1979. xxxvi, 173 p. SERIES: Louisiana. State University and Agricultural College. Walter Lynwood Fleming Lectures in Southern History.

SUBJECT(S): Slavery--America.
Slavery--United States--Insurrections, etc.
Maroons.

158. Genovese, Eugene D. *Roll, Jordan, Roll: The World the Slaves Made*. New York: Pantheon Books, 1974. xxii, 823 p.

This important history of slavery argues that slaves, as an objective social class, laid the foundations for a separate black national culture while enormously enriching American culture as a whole. Bibliographial notes and a list of manuscript collections cited are included. A subject index and a name index are also included.

SUBJECT(S): Slavery in the United States--Condition of Slaves.

159. Gilmore, Al-Tony, ed. *Revisiting Blassingame's The Slave Community: The Scholars Respond*. Westport, CO: Greenwood Press, 1978. xvi, 206 p. SERIES: Contributions in Afro-American and African Studies, no. 37.

An collection of critical essays by eminent scholars responding to the first edition (1972) of John W. Blassingame's *The Slave Community*. An essay by Mary Francis Berry, "The Slave Community: A Review of Reviews," provides a comprehensive summary of the numerous reviews which appeared on Blassingame's book in scholarly journals. Blassingame himself responds to the critics response in an essay entitled "Redefining the Slave Community: A Response to the Critics." Other contributors are George P. Rawick, Eugene D. Genovese, Earl E. Thorpe, Leslie Howard Owens, Stanley Engerman, John Henrik Clarke, and James D. Anderson. An index and brief biographical sketches on the contributors are included.

SUBJECT(S): Blassingame, John W., 1940- The slave community--Addresses, essays, lectures
Plantation life--Southern States--Addresses, essays, lectures.
Slavery--Southern States--Addresses, essays, lectures.

160. Miller, Randall M., ed. *The Afro-American Slaves: Community or Chaos?* Malabar, FL: R.E. Krieger Pub. Co., 1981. 146 p.

A multidisciplinary collection of articles by noted scholars on the dynamics and success of the slaves' struggle to build a cultural and social community. These concerns are examined in the areas of agricultural production, folk culture, speech, food choice and selection, clothing, arts, and crafts. The contributors include Peter H. Wood, Eugene D. Genovese, Lawrence W. Levine, Herbert Gutman, Gladys-Marie Fry, Thomas L. Webber, John W. Blassingame, and Charles W. Joyner. It includes a highly useful selection of suggestions for further reading in the form of a bibliographical essay.

SUBJECT(S): Slavery--United States--History--Addresses, essays, lectures.
Afro-Americans--History--To 1863--Addresses, essays, lectures.

161. Toplin, Robert Brent. *Freedom and Prejudice: The Legacy of Slavery in the United States and Brazil.* Westport, CT: Greenwood Press, 1981. xxvi, 134 p.

This important collection of essays contrasts and compares slavery and its consequences in the United States and Brazil. Those interested in comparative race relations will benefit most from this work.

SUBJECT(S): Slavery--United States.
Slavery--Brazil.
United States--Race relations.
Brazil--Race relations.

162. Woodson, Carter Godwin. *Free Negro Heads of Families in the United States in 1830, Together with a Brief Treatment of the Free Negro.* Washington, D.C.: The Association for the Study of Negro Life and History, Inc., 1925. lviii, 296 p.

The names, ages, and number of family members of free Negroes are listed in this work, following an introductory chapter on free

Negroes during slavery. An index to names is included.

SUBJECT(S): Afro-Americans--Directories.
Afro-Americans.

163. Woodson, Carter Godwin. *Free Negro Owners of Slaves in the United States in 1830, Together with Absentee Ownership of Slaves in the United States in 1830*. New York: Negro Universities Press, 1973, c1924. viii, 78 p.

Following the introductory chapters on free black slave owners and on absentee slave ownership, the names of slave owners and the number of slaves owned are listed by state.

SUBJECT(S): Slavery--United States.
Afro-Americans--Directories.

SOCIAL SCIENCES

Anthropology

164. Herskovits, Melville J. *The Anthropometry of the American Negro*. Columbia University Contributions to Anthropology, vol. 11. New York: Columbia University Press, 1930. 283 p.

One of the very few and perhaps the most comprehensive, anthropometric studies of the physical form of blacks in the United States. Conducted in the 1920s, this study was based on a sample of some 3,378 males and 2,281 females. It covers a wide range of measurements including those of height, head, face, shoulders, hands, arms, etc. Some inquiry was also made to determine the extent to which members of the sample were racially mixed, though this data is considered inconclusive. Data on a number of other ethnic or racial groups is also presented for comparative purposes. Numerous statistical tables and graphs, and a short bibliography of references is included.

SUBJECT(S): Anthropometry--United States.
Afro-Americans.

165. Herskovits, Melville J. *The Myth of the Negro Past*. Boston, Beacon Press, 1958. xxix, 368 p. SERIES: Beacon Paperback no. 69.

This classic and revisionist study confirms the survival of African traditions in black cultures in the Americas, and reveals the presence of a distinctive Afro-American culture in the United States. Extensive treatment is given to religion, language, domestic life, folklore, music, the nature of the acculturation process, and the parallels between Afro-American culture in the United States and other black cultures in the Western Hemisphere. Throughout, there are critical assessments of major works on blacks in the United States written by other authors prior to 1941. An extensive bibliography and index are included.

SUBJECT(S): Black race.

166. Posnansky, Merrick. "Towards an Archaeology of the Black Diaspora." *Proceedings of the Ninth International Congress for the Study of the Pre-Columbian Cultures of the Lesser Antilles, Santa Domingo, 1981*. Montreal: Center de Recherches Caribes, University de Montreal, 1983, pp. 443-50.

This article underscores the need for archaeologists and historians of the black diaspora of the new world to take into account the findings of African archaeology. The article also cites and provides a review of some of the research which has been conducted in the newly emerging field of archaeology of the black diaspora in the new world. A bibliography of references is included.

SUBJECT(S): Blacks--Antiquities.
Archaeology.
Afro-American--Antiquities.

167. Schuyler, Robert L. *Archaeological Perspectives on Ethnicity in America*: *Afro-American and Asian American Culture History*. Farmingdale, NY: Baywood Pub. Co., 1980. x, 147 p. SERIES: Baywood Monographs in Archaeology, no 1.

A collection of essays and reports on the results of archaeological investigations in Afro-American and Asian American cultural history. This relatively new and promising area in ethnic studies research provides additional data and insights into diet, social relations, degrees of acculturation, and basic economic patterns apart from written sources. Part I contains a group of eight articles relating to Afro-Americans, including an annotated bibliography of pertinent literature (pp. 76-85). Biographical sketches of the authors are also included.

SUBJECT(S): Afro-Americans--Antiquities--Addresses, essays, lectures.
Chinese Americans--Antiquities--Addresses, essays, lectures.
United States--Antiquities--Addresses, essays, lectures.

168. Szwed, John F., and Roger D. Abrahams. *Afro-American Folk Culture*: *An Annotated Bibliography of Materials from North*, *Central*, *and South America*, *and the West Indies*. Philadelphia: Institute for the Study of Human Issues, 1978. 2 vols. SERIES: American Folklore Society. Bibliographical and Special Series, vols. 31-32.

An exceptionally useful and comprehensive bibliography of Afro-American folk-culture in North, South, and Central America, and the Caribbean. Books, periodical articles, bibliographies, and some marginal materials such as pamphlets and phonograph records are cited. Some foreign language materials are also included. It does not include unpublished items such as dissertations or manuscripts. The focus is on the expressive and symbolic aspects of the lives of ordinary blacks (values, symbols, language, "small" behaviors), rather than on the conditions under which blacks have had to exist or on the lives of exceptional persons. Most of the works cited were written before 1974. A wide range of topics are covered, including African influences, carnivals and festivals, sects and cults, conjuring, witchcraft, black magic, dance, dialect, dress and costume, folklore, Gullah and Sea Island culture, literature, medicine, minstrelsy, music, names, and naming practices, proverbs, slavery, songs, tales, and tale telling. An extensive general subject index and geographical locale index are included.

SUBJECT(S): Folk-lore, Black--America--Bibliography. Blacks--America--Bibliography.

169. Whitten, Norman E., and John F. Szwed, eds. *Afro-American Anthropology: Contemporary Perspectives*, Forward by Sidney W. Mintz. New York: Free Press, 1970. X, 468 p.

A collection of twenty-two essays which attempt to update Afro-American studies in anthropology since the publication of Melville J. Herskovit's *Myth of the Negro Past* (1941). It brings anthropological theoretical and methodological perspectives to bear on some of the persistent problems in research relating to the family, kinship, ethnicity, economics, bilingualism and code-switching, unconventional politics, adaptations to marginality, and building black identities. It Includes recent studies of blacks in regions previously unexplored, including the Ecuadorian Andes, Colombia, Panama, Honduras, and the coastal rain forest; as well as areas previously studied; including Haiti, Guyana, Brazil, and the United States. An extensive bibliography of references cited, an index, and biographical sketches of the contributors are included.

SUBJECT(S): Black race--Addresses, essays, lectures.

Black Nationalism

170. Bracey, John H., Jr.,August Meier, and Elliott Rudwick, eds. *Black Nationalism in America*. New York: Bobbs-Merrill Company, Inc., 1970. 564 p.

This is the first collection of historical documents devoted exclusively to black nationalism. The introduction by the editors is one of the few essays which attempts to show the pattern of black nationalism throughout the course of American history. The documents were selected to show the persistence of black nationalism in American life, define the varieties of black nationalism, and to illustrate the thought the positions of those who were well known as nationalists as well as those with more subtle nationalist strains. The documents span a chronological period dating from the 1700s, with an essay by Richard Allen, to the late 1960s, with an interview with Huey P. Newton. A bibliography and a name-title-subject index are included.

SUBJECT(S): Afro-American--Collections.

171. Davis, Lenwood G., comp. *Malcolm X: A Selected Bibliography*. Westport, CT: Greenwood Press, 1985. vii, 157 p.

This first booklength bibliography cites works by and about

Malcolm X, including books, manuscripts, articles, and pamphlets. Eight appendices list dissertations and theses; obituaries, memorials, tributes and honors; poems; book reviews; audiovisual materials; records; namesakes, sceenplay, and broadside; and documentaries and a filmstrip. Bibliography and an index are included.

172. Hall, Raymond L. *Black Separatism in the United States*. Hanover, NH: Published for Dartmouth College by the University Press of New England, 1978. x, 306 p.

This work provides a historical overview of black separatism as a subcatecory of black nationalism. The role which individuals and organizations played is highlighted. The period covered ranges from the 1600s to the 1970s. Bibliographical notes, a bibliography, and a name-title-subject index are included.

SUBJECT(S): Afro-Americans--Race identity.
Black nationalism--United States.

173. Hill, Robert A., ed. *The Marcus Garvey and Universal Negro Improvement Association Papers*. Berkeley, CA: University of California Press, 1983. 2 vols.

A comprehensive survey of all presently available historical manuscripts and letters pertaining to the life and work of Marcus Mosiah Garvey as well as the popular worldwide organization he founded and led. Arranged in chronological order, Vol. I contains documents beginning with the earliest mentions in 1827 of the Garvey family in Jamaica and closes with Garvey's address at Carnegie Hall, August 25, 1919. Vol. II covers from August 25, 1919 to the UNIA's national convention of August 1920. These first volumes are part of a projected set of ten volumes: the first six are to focus on the United States: volumes seven and eight on Africa: and volumes nine and ten on the Caribbean.

SUBJECT(S): Garvey, Marcus, 1887-1940.
Universal Negro Improvement Association--History--Sources.
Black Power--United States--Sources.
Afro-Americans--Race Identity--History--Sources.
Afro-Americans--Civil Rights--History--Sources.
Afro-Americans--Correspondence.

174. Jenkins, Betty Lanier, and Susan Phillis. *Black Separatism: A Bibliography*. Westport, CT: Greenwood Press, 1976. xxv,163 p.

An annotated bibliography of references to the literature on the movement among some black Americans for complete separation from white society. Part I covers the separation versus integration controversy. Part II covers the institutional and psychological dimensions, and provides references to material on separatist thought in identity, education, politics, economics, and religion.

Name and title indexes are included.

SUBJECT(S): Black nationalism--United States--Bibliography.

Civil Rights and Legal Status

175. Avins, Alfred., comp. *The Reconstruction Amendments' Debates: The Legislative History and Contemporary Debates in Congress on the 13th, 14th, and 15th Amendments*. Richmond: Virginia Commission on Constitutional Government, 1967. xxxii, 764 p.

This work contains the texts of House and Senate debates on Reconstruction issues from 1865 to 1875. Also are included some debates from before the Civil War, 1849 to 1866. Debates are grouped according to the number of the Congressional session. There is a table of cases and authorities, a subject index, and House and Senate member indexes.

SUBJECT(S): United States Constitution. 13th amendment.
United States Constitution. 14th amendment.
United States Constitution. 15th amendment.
Civil rights--United States.

176. Bell, Derrick A., Jr. *Race, Racism, and American Law*. 2d ed. Boston: Little, Brown, 1980. xxvii, 685 p. SERIES: Law School Casebook Series.

This book deals with racism initiated by whites against blacks. It is intended to facilitate discussion and understanding of the role the law has played, both in the systematic subordination of black rights, and in the ongoing process by which the law has been utilized to ease or eliminate racial badges of servitude. It attempts to convey a clear understanding of current legal rules, and provide a basis for discussing new and potentially more effective attacks on racially biased policies. The book is organized into sections and chapters which deal with a wide range of topics relating to racial issues and the law, including slavery; interracial sex and marriage; the use of public facilities; voting rights; protest tactics, such as boycotts and sit-ins; educational equality and desegregation; housing; and employment. Within each section, cases and issues are summarized and the author's views set forth. Judicial opinions are not presented in whole or edited form, and no attempt is made to present a definitive version of the laws under discussion. Rather, the focus is on the legal issues within a given situation; a review of the precedents which the courts have used to resolve these issues; the exploration of new questions raised by these judicial efforts at resolution; and suggestions that substantive change may require relief which may be different or opposite to current policies and precedents. There are numerous footnotes throughout this book to the texts of pertinent legal cases, books, and articles. A table of legal cases and a general index are included. A companion volume, entitled *Civil Rights: Leading Cases*, contains edited versions of major case opinions of the Supreme Court on racial discrimination.

SUBJECT(S): Afro-Americans--Civil rights--Cases.
Afro-Americans--Legal status, laws, etc.--Cases.

177. Bell, Derrick A. Jr., ed. *Civil Rights--Leading Cases*. Boston: Little, Brown, 1980. 476 p.

This work contains a selection of edited opinions in major Supreme Court cases concerning race. It enables a more detailed examination of those cases which are summarized and discussed in the author's companion to this work, the second edition of *Race, Racism, and American Law*. The actual language of the Supreme Court is used, and the opinions are presented in chronological order to provide a sense of how the law has developed. An alphabetical table is also provided for quick reference.

SUBJECT(S): Afro-Americans--Legal status, laws, etc.--Cases.
Race discrimination--Law and legislation-- United States--Cases.

178. Bundy, Mary Lee and Irvin Gilchrist, eds. *The National Civil Rights Directory: An Organizations Directory. College Park, MD: Urban Information Interpreters*, 1979. iii, 183 p.

A directory of national and local civil rights organizations which attempt to mitigate racial discrimination in housing, education, employment, government programs, the media, the professions, and justice system and other areas. Citizen and professional, Asian, Black, Chicano, Native American, and Puerto Rican civil rights organizations are included. Other civil rights related organizations dealing with prisoners' rights, tenants rights, welfare rights, and poverty related groups organized around self determination issues are also listed. National organizations are listed by title in a single alphabet. Local organizations are listed by state. For each entry address and telephone number, objectives, activities, publications, and organization information is provided. An index guide to special types of organizations provides access to entries relating to black organizations, the organizations of other ethnic groups, as well as those organizations involved in civil rights endeavors in specific areas such as education, employment, health care, hunger, prisoners, students, etc. A list relevant periodial publications, and a bibliography are included.

SUBJECT(S): Civil rights--United States--Directories.

179. Burke, Joan Martin. *Civil Rights: A Current Guide to the People, Organizations, and Events*. 2nd ed. New York: Bowker, 1974. 266 p.

This guide contains an alphabetized, annotated list of people and organizations active in the civil rights movement. Appendices contain: a lists of Congressional voting records on civil rights acts; a list of federal and state agencies with civil rights responsibilities; a civil rights chronology; a list of leading black elected officials; a directory of civil rights resources; and a selected bibliography. An index is included.

SUBJECT(S): Civil rights--United States--Handbooks, manuals, etc.

180. Hill, George H. *Civil Rights Organizations and Leaders: An Annotated Bibliography*. New York, NY: Garland Publishing, Inc., 1985. 300 p.

This work cites materials relating to major civil rights organizations and leaders from 1910 to 1984. Books, dissertations, and over 1,500 articles are cited. Protests, conferences, court cases, economic development, publications, awards presentations of local chapters, and national organizations such as the NAACP and PUSH are covered. Information is provided on the presidents and directors of national organizations and other prominent civil rights leaders, including Ralph Abernathy, Benjamin Hooks, Jesse Jackson, John Jacobs, James Weldon Johnson, Vernon Jordan, Joseph Lowery, and Whitney Young. Martin Luther King, who is covered in other works, is excluded. Author and subject indexes are included.

SUBJECT(S): Civil rights--Bibliography.

181. Martin, J. Paul, ed. Center for the Study of Human Rights, Columbia University. *Human Rights: A Topical Bibliography*. Boulder, CO: Westview Press, 1983. xii, 299 p.

This unannotated bibliography cites books and articles drawn from law, the social sciences, and philogophy. The citations are grouped into subjects, covering philosophical and theoretical works, national and international perspectives, and specific rights issues. A list of organizations and an author index is included.

SUBJECT(S): Civil rights--Bibliography.

182. Murray, Pauli. ed. *States' Laws on Race and Color, and Appendices Containing International Documents, Federal Laws and Regulations, Local Ordinances and Charts*. Cincinnati: Woman's Division of Christian Service, Board of Missions and Church Extension, Methodist Church, 1950, x, 746 p.

States' laws on racial segregation and civil rights, in effect before the civil rights movement, are listed in this work. Rules applying to Indians and foreigners are also included. Laws on public accommodations, advertisements, housing, education, military practices, and legal protection are listed under each state. An appendix includes pertinent federal government and United Nations documents. An index of laws arranged by state is included.

SUBJECT(S): Afro-Americans--Legal status, laws, etc.
Race discrimination--United States.

183. Squires, Gregory D. *Affirmative Action: A Guide for the Perplexed*. East Lansing: Institute for Community Development, Continuing Education Service, Michigan State University, 1977. vii, 204 p.

Affirmative action is defined and summarized. The history of major legislative acts is discussed, and case studies which illustrate affirmative action are presented. Sources of information and assistance in undertaking action, and a directory of civil rights agencies are included.

SUBJECT(S): Affirmative action programs--United States.
Civil rights--United States.
Civil rights--United States--Directories.

Criminology and Juvenile Delinquency

184. Christianson, Scott, ed. *Index to Minorities and Criminal Justice: An Index to Periodicals and Books Relating to Minorities and Criminal Justice in the United States*. 1981 Cumulative Index. Albany, NY: Center on Minorities and Criminal Justice, School of Criminal Justice, State University of New York at Albany, 1981. 247 p.

This subject and author index cites books, government reports, monographs, unpublished dissertations, scholarly papers, selected court cases, and articles in over 400 periodicals. The fields covered include, criminal justice, criminology, sociology, psychology, law, history, medicine, philosophy, political science, social work, Afro-American studies, ethnic studies, and journalism.

SUBJECT(S): Minorities--United States--Indexes.
Criminal justice, Administration of-- United States--Indexes.

185. Davis, Lenwood G. *The Administration of Criminal Justice: An Exploratory Bibliography*. Monticello, IL: Council of Planning Librarians, 1975. 35 p. SERIES: Council of Planning Librarians. Exchange Bibliography, no. 814.

An unannotated bibliography of reports and studies, government documents, periodicals, books, and articles. A reprint of the *Omnius Crime Control and Safe Streets Act* of 1968 is included.

SUBJECT(S): Criminal justice, Administration of--United States--Bibliography.

186. Davis, Lenwood G. *Crime in the Black Community: An Exploratory Bibliography*. Monticello, IL: Council of Planning Librarians, 1975. 27 p. SERIES: Council of Planning Librarians. Exchange Bibliography, no. 852.

This brief unannotated bibliography includes reports, studies, government documents, dissertations, theses, books, and articles, published between the late-nineteenth century and the early 1970s. Lynching, police racism, and black police are some of the subjects covered.

SUBJECT(S): Afro-American criminals--Bibliography.

187. Davis, Lenwood G. *Deviant Behavior in the Black Community: An Exploratory Survey*. Monticello, IL: Council of Planning Librarians, 1976. 15 p. SERIES: Council of Planning Librarians. Exchange Bibliography, no. 1057.

An unannotated list of articles and books relating to black crime and delinquency. Materials on drug abuse, alcohol abuse, gangs, aggressive behavior, suicide, homicide, crime rates, and other topics relating to black criminology are cited. Many of the books cited include pertinent chapters or passages, but are not devoted exclusively to black crime.

SUBJECT(S): Afro-Americans--Psychology--Bibliography.
Deviant behavior--Bibliography.

188. Dorton, Eleanor. *Juvenile Delinquency in the Black Community*. Monticello, IL: Council of Planning Librarians, 1975. 16 p. SERIES: Council of Planning Librarians. Exchange Bibliography, no. 804.

An unannotated bibliography of books, articles, anthologies, bulletins, programmed materials, reviews, and cumulative indexes from *Crime and Delinquency Abstracts*. While most items cited were published in the 1960s, items published from 1900 to 1975 are cited.

SUBJECT(S): Juvenile delinquency--Bibliography.
Afro-American criminals--Bibliography.

Economics, Employment, and Business

189. Cantor, Milton, ed. *Black Labor in America*. Introduction by Herbert G. Gutman. Westport, CT: Greenwood Press, 1970. xii, 170 p. SERIES: Contributions in Afro-American and African Studies, no. 2.

A collection of articles which contain important and original research on the history of the black worker, with a focus on the the period from emancipation to 1945. The introduction provides an overview on the topic. Bibliographical notes and an index are included.

SUBJECT(S): Afro-Americans--Employment--History.
Afro-Americans--History--1877-1964.

190. Davis, Lenwood G. *Blacks in Public Administration: A Preliminary Survey*. Monticello, IL: Council of Planning Librarians, 1976, 1975. 13 p. SERIES: Council of Planning Librarians. Exchange Bibliography, no. 973.

This brief, unannotated bibliography cites books and articles on blacks in public administration, on the federal, state, and local level. Colleges, universities and other public institutions are included. Most items cited were written in the 1960s and 1970s.

SUBJECT(S): Civil service--United States--Minority employment--Bibliography.
Afro-Americans--Employment--Bibliography.

191. Foner, Philip S., and Ronald L. Lewis. *The Black Worker: A Documentary History from Colonial Times to the Present*. Philadelphia: Temple University Press, 1978-1984. 8 vols.

The eight volumes in this series focus on black workers in urban and industrialized areas and encompass the entire history of Afro-American labor. Announcements, letters, speeches, and other writings are included. Each volume provides an introduction and notes which place the documents in their historical context, and an author-title-subject index. Volume I, "Black Workers to 1869", has material on black mechanics, artists and craftsmen in the North and South. Volume II covers the national labor movements of the 1870s. Volume III covers the Knights of Labor. Volume IV contains material on the American Federation of Labor and the railway brotherhoods. Volume V is a documentary history of Afro-American labor from 1900 to 1919. Volume VI covers the era of post-war prosperity and the great depression 1920-1936. Volume VII covers from the founding of the CIO to the AFL-CIO merger, 1936 to 1955. Volume VIII covers the black worker since the AFL-CIO merger, 1955 to 1980.

SUBJECT(S): Afro-Americans--Employment.
Afro-Americans--Economic conditions.
United States--Race relations.
Trade-Unions--United States--Afro-American membership.

192. Hill, George H. *Black Business and Economics: A Selected Bibliography*. New York: Garland Pub. Co., 1985. xvi, 351 p. SERIES: Garland Reference Library of Social Science, vol. 267.

This bibliography cites 2,600 items on black involvement in American business and the economic conditions of blacks, 1900 to 1983. Books, government documents, dissertations, theses, and journal, magazine, and newspaper articles are included. Topics covered include banking, capitalism, consumerism, general business, income, insurance, labor and A. Phillip Randolph, management, marketing and advertising, organizations and clubs, personalities, and business development.

SUBJECT(S): Afro-American business enterprises--Bibliography.
Afro-Americans in business--Bibliography.
Afro-Americans--Employment--Bibliography.

193. Gagala, Kenneth L., ed. *The Economics of Minorities: A Guide to Information Sources*. Detroit: Gale Research Co., 1976. x, 212 p. SERIES: Economics Information Guide Series, vol. 2. SERIES: Gale Information Guide Library.

This guide to economics cites materials relating to blacks, Indians, and Spanish Americans, published 1965 to 1874. Well over half of the materials relate to blacks.

SUBJECT(S): Afro-Americans--Economic conditions--Bibliography.
Indians of North America--Economic conditions--Bibliography.
Hispanic Americans--Economic conditions--Bibliography.

194. Gibson, D. Parke. *$70 Billion in the Black: America's Black Consumers*. New York: MacMillan, 1978. 311 p.

A study on black American consumption patterns, including suggestions on how maketing campaigns may be designed to successfully reach blacks. Appendices provide data on minority consumer expenditures and income. An extensive bibliography on advertising and marketing to the black consumer is included.

SUBJECT(S): Afro-Americans as consumers.

195. Minority Business Enterprise. United States. Office of Minority Business Enterprise. *Minority Business Enterprise: A Bibliography*. Washington, D.C., 1973. iii, 231 p.

An annotated bibliography of 1,413 items focusing primarily on Afro-Americans. Chicanos, Asian Americans, and American Indians are also included. Books, bibliographies, articles, reports, speeches, handbooks, directories, and periodicals are cited. A subject index is included.

SUBJECT(S): Minority Business Enterprises--United States--Bibliography.
Business Enterprises--United States--Bibliography.

196. National Minority Business Campaign. *Try Us*. Minneapolis: National Minority Business Campaign. 1972-.

Updated periodically, this is the nation's oldest national directory providing current information on minority-owned businesses. It is designed to assist corporate and government buyers expand their purchases of goods and services from minority vendors. Businesses which provide sales or services on a national or regional level, and are at least half owned by minorities (Blacks, Hispanics, Native American, Asians) are listed. Entries are grouped in categories according to type of business, then by state in alphabetical order. An extensive index lists over 3,000 keywords to help users locate products and services. An alphabetical listing of firms is included. Continues: *National Black Business Directory*.

SUBJECT(S): Minority Business Enterprises--United States--Directories.
Business enterprises--United States--Bibliography.

197. Pinto, Patrick R., and Jeanne O. Buchmeier. *Problems and Issues in the Employment of Minority, Disadvantaged, and Female Groups: An Annotated Bibliography*. Minneapolis: Industrial Relations Center, University of Minnesota, 1973. 62 p. SERIES: Minnesota. University. Industrial Relations Center. Bulletin 59.

This annotated bibliography cites 548 works published between 1965 and 1972. The following subjects are covered: legal facets; topics in reference to disadvantaged groups in general; topics specific to blacks and other minority groups (Chicanos, women, the young, the elderly and the handicapped); staffing; training; compensation; unions; and miscellaneous topics. Reference works, books, government documents, and periodicals are cited.

SUBJECT(S): Discrimination in employment--United States--Bibliography.
Minorities--Employment--United States--Bibliography.
Women--Employment--United States--Bibliography.

198. Pressley, Milton M. *A Selected Bibliography of Readings and References Regarding Marketing to Black Americans*. Monticello, IL: Council of Planning Librarians, 1974. 36 p. SERIES: Council of Planning Librarians. Exchange Bibliography, no. 671.

This brief bibliography lists books and articles on advertising, buying and selling patterns, and the economic status of blacks. Most items cited were written between 1954 and 1974. There are no annotations or indexes.

SUBJECT(S): Afro-Americans as consumers--Bibliography.
Marketing--United States--Bibliography.

199. Schneider, Stephen A. *The Availability of Minorities and Women for Professional and Managerial Positions, 1970-1985*. Philadelphia: Industrial Research Unit, Wharton School, University of Pennsylvania, 1977. xviii, 280 p. SERIES: Manpower and Human Resources Studies, no. 7. SERIES: Wharton School. Industrial Research Unit. Studies, no. 55.

This work provides statistics on past and possible future involvement of women and minorities in a variety of professions, including engineering, accounting, business and management, physics, chemistry, law, dentistry, and medicine. Women, blacks, Spanish, and Japanese are covered. An author-title-subject index is included.

SUBJECT(S): Professions--United States--Supply and demand.
Women in the professions--United States.
Minorities in the professions--United States.

Housing and Urban Conditions

200. Clark, Thomas A. *Blacks in Suburbs, A National Perspective*. Foreword by George Sternlieb. New Brunswick, NJ: Rutgers University, Center for Urban Policy Research, 1979. xiii, 127 p.

A highly informative analysis incorporating substantial quantitative data. One chapter provides a close examination of selected metropolitan areas, including Los Angeles, San Francisco, Washington D.C., Atlanta, Houston, Chicago, Detroit, Boston, Philadelphia, and New York. Bibliographical notes, a bibliography, and an index are included.

SUBJECT(S): Afro-Americans--Housing.
Afro-Americans--Economic conditions.
Afro-Americans--Social conditions--1964-1975.
Afro-Americans--Social conditions--1975-Suburbs--United States.
Migration, Internal--United States.

201. Darden, Joe T. *Race, Housing, and Residential Segregation: A Selected Bibliography of Basic References*. Chicago, IL: CPL Bibliographies, 1982. vi, 34 p. SERIES: Council of Planning Librarians. Exchange Bibliography, no. 96.

An unannotated bibliography of works (mostly empirical studies) grouped into four categories: the pattern of residential segregation in the United States, the pattern of residential segregation outside the United States, the process of discrimination in housing, and anti-discrimination housing policies and laws.

SUBJECT(S): Discrimination in housing-- United States--Bibliography.
Race discrimination--United States--Bibliography.
United States--Race relations--Bibliography.

202. Davis, Lenwood G. *Blacks in the Cities, 1900-1974: A Bibliography*. 2d ed. Monticello, IL: Council of Planning Librarians, 1975. 82 p. SERIES: Council of Planning Librarians. Exchange Bibliography, nos. 787-788.

An unannotated bibliography covering history, politics, economics, poverty, and crime. Reference works, periodicals, bibliographies, newspapers, reports, governments documents, books, and articles are cited. In addition, this work contains a reprint of the *National Sickle Cell Program*, and the *Omnibus Crime Control and Save Streets Act* of 1968.

SUBJECT(S): Afro-Americans--Bibliography.

203. Davis, Lenwood G. *Ecology of Blacks in the Inner City: An Exploratory Bibliography*. Monticello, IL: Council of Planning Librarians, 1975. 80 p. SERIES: Council of Planning Librarians. Exchange Bibliography, nos. 785-786.

An unannotated bibliography focusing on the ecological concerns of urban blacks, including housing, overcrowding, poverty, and racism. Books, articles, government documents, bibliographies, newspaper articles, reports, pamphlets, and speeches are cited. Most items cited were written during the 1960s and 1970s, but some are from the turn of the century through the 1940s.

SUBJECT(S): Afro-Americans--Social conditions--Bibliography.
Slums--United States--Bibliography.
Cities and towns--United States--Bibliography.

204. Siegel, Judith A. *Racial Discrimination in Housing*. Monticello, IL: Council of Planning Librarians, 1977. 14 p. SERIES: Council of Planning Librarians. Exchange Bibliography, no. 1201.

An unannotated bibliography of books, periodical articles, unpublished material, and reference works. Most items cited were written between 1957 to 1977. Topics covered include segregation, integration, government activity, housing quality, and economic effects. Case studies are included.

SUBJECT(S): Discrimination in housing--United States--Bibliography.
Race discrimination--United States--Bibliography.

Linguistics

205. Brasch, Ila Wales. *A Comprehensive Annotated Bibliography of American Black English*. Baton Rouge: Louisiana State University Press, 1974. xii, 289 p.

A comprehensive annotated bibliography of the monographs, periodicals, and conference papers presented on black English. Topics covered include research into black English, general studies, pedagogy, general interest works of a popular nature, folklore, slave narratives, pertinent literary works, related materials about non-American black English, and works that present black English as a facet of being "culturally disadvantaged." Entries are arranged in a single alphabet by author rather than by subject and the lack of an index makes it difficult to identify works by topic.

SUBJECT(S): English language--United States--Dialects--Bibliography.
Afro-Americans--Language--Bibliography.
Creole dialects, English--Bibliography.

206. Dillard, J. L. *Black English: Its History and Usage in the United States*. New York: Random House, 1972 xiv, 361 p.

A classic work which investigates the ways in which black English differs from other varieties of American English. There are chapters on the structure and history of black English, pidgin English, and Afro-American dialect. It also includes illustrations, a glossary, and an appendix on the pronunciation of black English. An extensive bibliography and an index are also included.

SUBJECT(S): Afro-Americans--Language.
Language.
Afro-Americans--United States.

207. Labov, William. *Language in the Inner City: Studies in the Black English Vernacular*. Philadelphia: University of Pennsylvania Press, 1972 xxiv, 412 p.

A classic and highly technical exploration of the language, culture, social organization, and political situation of black youth in the inner cities of the United States. Chapters deal with the structure of black English vernacular, the vernacular in its social setting, and the uses of black English vernacular. A bibliography and an index are included.

SUBJECT(S): Black English.
Intercultural education--United States.

208. Labov, William. *The Study of Black English*. Champaign, IL: National Council of Teachers of English, and Washington, D.C.: Center for Applied Linguistics, 1969 73 p.

An important text on the distinguishing aspects and features of black English research.

SUBJECT(S): English-languages in the United States--Dialects.

209. Smitherman, Geneva. *Talkin and Testifyin: The Language of Black America*. Boston: Houghton Mifflin, 1977. 291 p.

An outstanding introduction to black English. Chapters cover the history of black English structure; sounds and structure of present-day black English; works and concepts in black English, past and present; the African world view and Afro-American oral tradition; black modes of discourse; black-white language attitudes; and social policy and educational practice. A selected glossary of black semantics, a bibliography, and an index are included.

SUBJECT(S): Black English.

210. Vass, Winifred Kellersberger. *The Bantu Speaking Heritage of the United States*. Foreword by Baruch Elimelech. Los Angeles: Center for Afro-American Studies, University of California, 1979. xi, 122 p. SERIES: Afro-American Culture and Society, vol. 2.

A study dealing with African cultural survivals in American English, folklore, folksongs, folktales, and place names in the United States. Revealing an intimate knowledge of American language and culture on the one hand, and African languages and culture on the the other, the author identifies aspects of language and culture in America that are African in origin. Each chapter contains numerous bibliographical notes. A vocabulary list of words of possible Bantu origin is also included.

SUBJECT(S): English language--Foreign words and phrases--Bantu.
United States--Civilization--Afro-American influences.

211. Wolfram, Walter A., and Nona H. Clarke, eds. *Black-White Speech Relationships*. Washington: D.C.: Center for Applied Linguistics, 1971. xiii, 161 p. SERIES: Urban Language Series, no. 7.

A collection of essays on several facets of Afro-American speech, including the study of the Gullah dialect, continuity and change in black English, and black/white speech patterns. Each article includes bibliographical references.

SUBJECT(S): Creole dialects, English.
English language--United States.

Politics and Politicians

212. Abramson, Paul R. *The Political Socialization of Black Americans: A Critical Evaluation of Research on Efficacy and Trust*. New York: Free Press, 1977. xi, 195 p.

This work provides a review of research on the political socialization of black children. The research indicates that black children feel politically less powerful, and have less trust for political leaders than white children. It also examines four basic theoretical explanations for these research findings. A bibliography and an index are included.

SUBJECT(S): Afro-American children.
Political socialization.
Afro-Americans--Psychology.

213. Christopher, Maurine. *Black Americans in Congress*. rev. and enl. ed. New York: 1976. xvi, 329 p.

This work provides biographies of black Congressional members from those first elected during Reconstruction to 1976. Drawings and photographs are included.

SUBJECT(S): Afro-Americans--Biography.
Legislators--United States.

214. Garrett, Romeo B. *The Presidents and the Negro*. Peoria, IL: Association for the Study of Afro-American Life and History, 1982. viii, 325 p.

This work documents what United States Presidents, from Washington to Carter, said and did on matters relevant to Afro-Americans. The Presidents are discussed in chronological order and each section concludes with references.

SUBJECT(S): Presidents--United States--Racial attitudes.
Afro-Americans--History.
United States--Race relations.

215. Joint Center for Political Studies. *Profiles of Black Mayors in America*. Washington, D.C.: The Center for Political Studies, 1977. xvi, 245 p.

This work contains one-page profiles of 150 black mayors, who were serving in the United States as of November 1975. Also included are a chapter which provides historical perspectives on black mayors, appendices, statistical references, and an index.

SUBJECT(S): Afro-American mayors--Biography.

216. *National Roster of Black Elected Officials*. Washington, D.C.: Joint Center for Political Studies. 1969-.

Periodically updated, this roster lists several thousand black elected officials at local, state, and federal levels. The titles, addresses, and terms of office are given for officials elected during the year preceding 1978, for those holding two offices concurrently, for black women officials, and for officials elected between 1969 and 1978. Names are arranged alphabetically by state, and then by level of office. There is an alphabetical index of names.

SUBJECT(S): Afro-Americans--Politics and suffrage--Directories--Periodicals.
United States--Registers--Periodicals.
Afro-Americans--Directories.
United States--Officials and employees--Directories.

217. Sinkler, George. *The Racial Attitudes of American Presidents from Abraham Lincoln to Theodore Roosevelt*. Garden City, NY: Doubleday & Company, 1971. xiii, 413 p.

This work documents the racial views of United States Presidents from Abraham Lincoln to Theodore Roosevelt. The Presidents are discussed in chronological order. A bibliography and an index are included.

SUBJECT(S): Presidents--United States--Racial attitudes.

218. Storing, Herbert J. *What Country Have I? Political Writings by Black Americans*. New York: St. Martin's Press, 1970. x, 235 p.

This collection contains the major political writings of black figures from Augustus Washington, in the mid-nineteenth century, to contemporary writers such as James Baldwin. In each section, there is a short introduction and suggestions for further reading. A bibliography and a subject index are also included.

SUBJECT(S): Afro-Americans--History--Sources.
Afro-Americans--Politics and suffrage--Addresses, essays, lectures.

219. Walton, Hanes. *The Study and Analysis of Black Politics: A Bibliography*. Metuchen, NJ: Scarecrow Press, 1973. xviii, 161 p.

This is the first systematic and comprehensive effort to bring together the literature of the past eighty years on the political behavior of black Americans. It lists articles from scholarly and popular journals, new books as well as reissues of out-of-print works, pamphlets, newspapers, papers presented at meetings of professional associations, and unpublished masters theses and doctoral dissertations. There are two appendices: the first lists all major articles in the *New York Times* covering black Republicans in the South from 1900 to 1956; the second contains an essay on political science education in black colleges. An author index is included.

SUBJECT(S): Afro-Americans--Politics and suffrage--Bibliography.

220. Walton, Hanes. *Black Politics: A Theoretical and Structural Analysis*. Philadelphia: Lippincott, 1972. xvii, 246 p. SERIES: The Lippincott Series in American Government.

This book explores black politics North and South, from the colonial period through the early 1970s, and sets forth some theoretical insights and generalizations about black political activity. The author documents the black struggle for political power; and demonstrates that the black presence in America, generally viewed as powerless, has actually wielded tremendous influence and has altered basic political philosophy and practices. Included is a systematic and fairly comprehensive bibliography. A name and subject index are also included.

SUBJECT(S): Afro-Americans--Politics and suffrage.

221. Williams, Darrell Fisher. *The Political Economy of Black Community Development: A Research Bibliography*. Monticello, IL: Council of Planning Librarians, 1973. 46 p. SERIES: Council of Planning Librarians. Exchange Bibliography, no. 457.

This brief bibliography focuses on the political economy of the black community. Books, periodicals, reports, papers, government documents, and unpublished material are cited. Topics covered include the content and methodology of literature on black economics; historical perspectives; economic disparity and the political economy of black underdevelopment; and black economic development. Entries do not include annotations, and there is no index.

SUBJECT(S): Afro-Americans--Economic conditions--Bibliography. Community development--United States--Bibliography.

Race and Ethnic Relations

This section includes selected works dealing with relations between Afro-Americans in the United States and whites and other minorities, relations with black Africans in or from Africa, and racism. The literature pertinent to black relations with other minorities is quite limited, though black/Jewish and historical studies relating to black/American Indian relations are fairly well represented.

222. Blakely, Allison. *Russian and the Negro*. Washington, D.C.: Howard University Press, 1986. 208 p.

This is the first work to present a comprehensive study of blacks in Russian history from ancient times, and with a global perspective. It looks at the presence of individuals of black African decent in Imperial and Soviet Russia, and at Russian attitudes toward Africa and people of African descent. A bibliography and index are included.

SUBJECT(S): Blacks--Relations with Russians.

223. Cassity, Michael J. *Chains of Fear: American Race Relations Since Reconstruction*. Westport, CT: Greenwood Press, 1984. xxxv, 253 p. SERIES: Grassroots Perspectives on American History, no. 3.

This work examines an extensive collection of historical documents which shed light on the events and forces which shaped the development of race relations throughout the history of the United States. The introduction and the documents selected stress the element of fear. The evolution of race relations is placed in the context of a developing scarcity consciousness created by a possessive market society and the social and psychological dislocation engendered by the process of modernization. An index is included.

SUBJECT(S): Afro-Americans--History.
Slavery--United States--History.
United States--Race relations.

224. Cassity, Michael J. *Legacy of Fear: American Race Relations to 1900*. Westport, CT: Greenwood Press, 1984. SERIES: Grassroots Perspectives on American History, no. 4.

This is a unique collection of documents which sheds light on the historical events and social forces that shaped the development of race relations from the seventeen century to 1900. The documents are drawn from the everyday experiences of both blacks and whites. As a companion to his *Chains of Fear*, the author emphasizes the element of fear as a central factor in race relations.

SUBJECT(S): Race relations.

225. Center for Minority Group Mental Health Programs. *Bibliography on Racism*. Washington, D.C.: DHEW Publication, 1972, 160 p.

An annotated bibliography of journal articles on racism, published through 1971. A large portion of the entries relate directly to Afro-Americans. Lengthy abstracts provide a full summary of article contents or research findings. An author index and a subject index are included.

SUBJECT(S): Race relations--Abstracts.
Race relations--Bibliography.
Mental hygiene--Bibliography.
Mental hygiene--Abstracts--Racism.

226. Davis, Lenwood G. comp. *Black-Jewish Relations in the United States 1752-1984: A Selected Bibliography*. Westport, CT: Greenwood Press, 1984. xvii, 134 p. SERIES: Bibliographies and Indexes in Afro-American and African Studies, no. 1

The first book-length bibliography on the relationship between blacks and Jews in the United States. It provides a historical and bibliographical overview, and shows how this relationship has changed over a period of more that two centuries. Sources of information on the opinions and views of black leaders, such as Booker T. Washington, W.E.B. DuBois, Malcolm X, Marcus Garvey, Martin Luther King, Jr., James Baldwin, are included. Special attention is given to the Jewish support of black civil rights and the role of Jews in the founding of the NAACP, the National Urban League, and other organizations. Sources on black anti-Semitism, Jewish racism, and black anti-Zionism, and pro-Arabism are also cited. An index is included.

SUBJECT(S): Afro-Americans--Relations with Jews.

227. Davis, Lenwood G. and Janet L. Sims-Wood, comps., with the assistance of Marsha L. Moore. *The Ku Klux Klan: A Bibliography*. Westport, CT: Greenwood Press, 1984. xi, 643 p.

A comprehensive compilation of research materials on the history and activities of the Ku Klux Klan. More than 10,000 books, pamphlets, theses and dissertations, periodical and newspaper articles, government documents, and official Klan publications are cited. The newspaper section comprises nearly seventy-five percent of the book. An index is included.

SUBJECT(S): Ku Klux Klan--Bibliography.
Ku Klux Klan (1915-)--Bibliography.

228. Fisher, William Harvey. *The Invisible Empire: A Bibliography of the Ku Klux Klan*. Metuchen, NJ: Scarecrow Press, 1980. ix, 202 p.

A selectively annotated bibliography of dissertations, manuscript/archival collections, government documents, monographs, and articles on the Klu Klax Klan from 1866 to 1978. Newspaper articles are generally omitted, but some citations to articles in underground newspapers of the 1960s and early 1970s are included. Government documents are included is they are major committee reports. An author and subject indexes are included.

SUBJECT(S): Ku-Klux Klan--Bibliography.
Ku Klux Klan (1915-)--Bibliography.

229. Helmreich, William B., comp. *Afro-Americans and Africa: Black Nationalism at the Crossroads*. Westport, CT: Greenwood Press, 1977. xxxiii, 74 p. SERIES: African Bibliographic Center. Special Bibliographic Series, new ser., no. 3.

An annotated bibliography of books and articles written between 1960 and 1973 which deal with the opinions, attitudes, and relationships of Afro-Americans toward Africa. An index is included.

SUBJECT(S): Afro-Americans--Bibliography.
Afro-Americans--Attitudes and Relations with Africa.
Africa--Bibliography.

230. Jakle, John A. *Ethnic and racial minorities in North America: A Selected Bibliography of the Geographical Literature*. Assisted by Cynthia A. Jakle. Monticello, IL: Council of Planning Librarians, 1973. 71 p. SERIES: Exchange Bibliography, nos. 459-460.

Afro-Americans are one of forty-six groups covered in this bibliography, which centers on spatial and territorial issues of various ethnic groups. Seventeen pages of entries are on Afro-

Americans. Books, periodicals, and theses, published from the turn of the century to the present, are included. There are no annotations or indexes.

SUBJECT(S): Minorities--United States--Bibliography.
Minorities--Canada--Bibliography.

231. Jacobs, Sylvia M. *The African Nexus: Black American Perspectives on the European Partitioning of Africa, 1880-1920*. Westport, CT: Greenwood Press, 1981. xiv, 311 p. SERIES: Contributions in Afro-American and African Studies, no. 55.

This work attempts to assess the extent and possible impact of the views and attitudes of black Americans on the European partitioning of Africa in the late nineteenth and early twentieth centuries. It focuses primarily on the responses of black intellectuals. The ideas and attitudes presented and discussed by region in Africa. Bibliographical notes, bibliography, and an index are included.

SUBJECT(S): Public opinion--United States.
Afro-Americans--Attitudes.
African--Colonization--Public opinion.

232. Kinloch, Graham C. *Race and Ethnic Relations: An Annotated Bibliography*. New York, NY: Garlard Publishers, Inc., 1984. 278 p.

An extensive bibliography of the social science literature on race and ethnic relations in the United States and worldwide, 1960 to 1980. The citations are grouped into five sections: general bibliographies and research trends; theory and methodology; race and ethnic relations in other societies; and a list of major organizations and publications. Author and subject indexes are included.

SUBJECT(S): Race relations--Bibliography.

233. Lieberson, Stanley. *A Piece of the Pie: Blacks and White Immigrants Since 1880*. Berkeley: University of California Press, 1980. xiii, 419 p.

Explores the causes of the economic gap between blacks and European immigrants since 1880. Government policies and black participation in government, legal and political issues, education history, residential segregation, and occupational trends are examined. Bibliography, and author and title indexes are included.

SUBJECT(S): Minorities--United States.
Afro-Americans--Social conditions.
Afro-American--Economic conditions.
United States--Ethnic relations.

234. Littlefield, Daniel F., Jr. *Africans and Creeks: From the Colonial Period of the Civil War*. Westport, CT: Greenwood Press, 1979. xiii, 286 p. SERIES: Contributions in Afro-American and African Studies, no. 47.

A study of Africans among the Creeks from the early eighteenth century until the Civil War. The emphasis is on the colonial contacts between the two peoples, the development of the institution of African slavery among the Creeks, the relationship between Africans and Creeks during the Red Stick War of 1813-14, and the years leading up to the Creeks removal from Alabama and Geogia to the West (Arkansas) in the 1820s. There is also an account of the institution of slavery in the West, of slaving activities in the Western Creek Nation, and of the involvement of the Creeks and their blacks in the Civil War. Bibliographical notes, a bibliography, an index, maps are included.

SUBJECT(S): Creek Indians--Slaves, Ownership of.
Afro-Americans--Relations with Indians.
Indians of North America--Slaves, Ownership of.

235. Littlefield, Daniel F., Jr. *Africans and Seminoles: From Removal to Emancipation*. Westport, CT: Greenwood Press, 1977. x, 278 p. SERIES: Contributions in Afro-American Studies, no. 32.

A well documented study which supports the thesis that the development of Seminole antipathy for blacks was more the result of pressure from Indian neighbors than from an acquired racial prejudice. Includes maps, bibliography, and index.

SUBJECT(S): Seminole Indians--Slaves, Ownership of.
Afro-Americans--Relations with Indians.
Slavery--Indian Territory.
Indians of North America--Indian Territory--Slaves, Ownership of.

236. Littlefield, Daniel F., Jr. *The Cherokee Freedmen: From Emancipation to American Citizenship*. Westport, CT; Greenwood Press, 1978. xii, 281 p. SERIES: Contributions in Afro-American and African Studies, no. 40.

A well documented history of black freedmen participation in the Cherokee nation. Emphasis is placed on the freedmen's struggle to establish their rights to citizenship in the Cherokee nation and to lands and tribal funds; and the Cherokee nation's 40 year struggle to define the social, political, and legal status of the freed blacks among them is presented in great detail. Includes maps, illustrations, photos, bibliograpahy, and an index.

SUBJECT(S): Cherokee Indians--Slaves, Ownership of.
Afro-Americans--Indian Territory--Relations with Indians.
Freedmen--Indian Territory.

237. Littlefield, Daniel F., Jr. *The Chickasaw Freedmen: A People Without a Country*. Westport, CT: Greenwood Press, 1980. xii, 248 p. SERIES: Contributions in Afro-American and African Studies, no. 54.

An account of the social and economic life of the freed Chickasaw blacks. Includes illustrations, bibliography, and index.

SUBJECT(S): Chickasaw Indians--Slaves, Ownership of.
Indians of North America--Oklahoma--Slaves, Ownership of.
Freedmen--Oklahoma.
Afro-Americans--Oklahoma--History.
Oklahoma--Race relations.

238. Moikobu, Josephine Moraa. *Blood and Flesh: Black American and African Identifications*. Westport, CT: Greenwood Press, 1981. xiii, 226 p. SERIES: Contributions in Afro-American and African Studies, no. 59.

This unique work examines the degree to which African and Afro-American students interact and identify social and culturally. A bibliography is included.

SUBJECT(S): Afro-Americans--Relations with Africans.
Afro-Americans--Race identity.
Afro-American college students--New York (State)--Case studies.
African students--New York (State)--Case studies.

239. Obudho, Constance E. *Black-White Racial Attitudes: An Annotated Bibliography*. Westport CT: Greenwood Press, 1976. xii, 180 p.

An outstanding annotated bibliography of books, articles, and dissertations produced between 1950 and 1974. Entries are arranged by subject. Racial attitudes in children, youth, adults, and related aspects of racism are covered. Annotations clearly and fully describe the content of each work. Author and subject indexes are included.

SUBJECT(S): Attitude (Psychology)--Bibliography.
Blacks--Race identity--Bibliography.
United States--Race question--Bibliography.

240. Purdue, Theda. *Slavery and the Evolution of Cherokee Society, 1540-1866*. Knoxville, TN: University of Tennessee Press, 1979. xiv, 207 p.

An important, well documented study on black slavery in and the evolution of Cherokee society from the first black-Cherokee contacts during the colonial period to the Civil War. Includes bibliographical notes, a bibliographical essay, and a bibliography. Maps and an index are also included.

SUBJECT(S): Cherokee Indians--Slaves, Ownership of.
Indians of North America--Slaves, Ownership of.
Afro-Americans--Relations with Indians.
Slavery--United States.

241. Shankman, Arnold *Ambivalent Friends: Afro-Americans View the Immigrant*. Westport, CT: Greenwood Press, 1982. xiv, 198 p. SERIES: Contributions in Afro-American Studies, no. 67.

Focusing on the South and the West, 1800 to 1935, this work deals with black attitudes toward five immigrant groups: Chinese, Japanese, Mexicans, East Indians, and Jews. Makes extensive use of black newspaper and journal sources. Tables and bibliography are included.

SUBJECT(S): Afro-Americans--Attitudes.
Minorities--United States--Public opinion.
Public opinion--United States.
United States--Foreign population--Public opinion.
United States--Emigration and immigration--Public opinion.

242. Weisbord, Robert G. and Stein, Arthur. *Bittersweet Encounter: The Afro-American and the American Jew*. Westport, CT: Greenwood Press, 1970. xxvii, 242 p. SERIES: Contributions in Afro-American and African Studies, no. 5.

A careful evaluation of black-Jewish relations in the United States, which places the controversy in perspective. The major black-Jewish confrontations of recent years are summarized.

SUBJECT(S): Afro-Americans--Relations with Jews.

Race and Ethnic Relations - Mulattoes and Miscegenation

For works dealing with interracial mating and marriage, see Interracial Mating section under Family and Related Studies.

243. Mencke, John G. *Mulattoes and Race Mixture: American Attitudes and Images, 1865-1918*. Ann Arbor, MI: UMI Research Press, 1979. xiii, 269 p. SERIES: Studies in American History and Culture, no. 4.

This work discusses and provides insight into mulatto related attitudes, images and problems. It includes chapters on mulatto images in turn-of-the century Afro-American fiction and in fiction by white authors, and contains discussions of and useful citations to fiction in which mulattoes are depicted. Bibliographical notes, bibliography, and an index are included.

SUBJECT(S): Mulattoes--United States.
Afro-Americans in literature.
United States--Race relations.

244. Reuter, Edward Byron. *The Mulatto in the United States, Including a Study of the Role of Mixed-blood Races throughout the World.* Boston: R.G. Badger, the Gorham Press, 1918. 417 p. Reprint: Greenwood Press, Westport, CT.

A classic study of mulattoes in the United States. Includes the names of hundres of mulattoes of the early twentieth century.

SUBJECT(S): Mulattoes--United States.
Miscegenation.
United States--Race relations.

245. Williamson, Joel. *New People: Miscegenation and Mulattoes in the United States.* New York: Free Press, 1980. xvi, 221 p.

This work outlines the history of miscegenation and mulattoes in the United States from the seventeen through the twentieth centuries, and is the first to attempt to cover the full range of this topic since Edward Byron Reuter's *The Mulatto in the United States, Including a Study of the Role of Mixed-blood Races throughout the World.* Bibliographical notes and an index are included.

SUBJECT(S): Mulattoes--United States.
Miscegenation--United States.
United States--Race relations.

Sociology

246. Blackwell, James E., and Morris Janowitz, comps. *Black Sociologists: Historical and Contemporary Perspectives.* Chicago: University of Chicago Press, 1974. xxii, 415 p. SERIES: The Heritage of Sociology.

A collection of essays providing an introduction, assessment, and interpretation of the life and work of black sociologists. Bibliographical notes and an index are included.

SUBJECT(S): Afro-American sociologists--United States--Congresses.

247. Center for Black Studies, University of California, Santa Barbara. *Selected Works of Black Sociologists*. Santa Barbara, CA: The Center, 1977. iii, 89 p.

This bibliography lists books, pamphlets, periodical articles, articles in books, and some unpublished materials. Represented are works by: Kelly Miller, 1863-1939; Monroe Nathan Work, 1866-1945; William Edward Burghardt Du Bois, 1868-1963; George Edmund Haynes, 1975-1960; Charles Spurgeon Johnson, 1893-1956; Edward Franklin Frazier, 1894-1962; and Oliver Cromwell Cox, 1901-1974. Its use is hampered by a lack of an index and because the works listed under each author are not alphabetized by title nor grouped according to topic.

SUBJECT(S): Afro-Americans--Bibliography.
Afro-Americans--Social conditions--Bibliography.
Afro-Americans Economic conditions--Bibliography.

248. Ladner, Joyce A., ed. *The Death of White Sociology*. New York: Vantage Books, A Division of Random House, 1973. 476 p.

An collection of writings by some of the nation's outstanding black social scientists. These works attempt to define the emerging field of black sociology, and to establish basic premises, guidelines, concerns, and priorities. The editor maintains that black sociology is a reaction to, and revolt against, the biases of "mainstream" bourgeois, liberal sociology; and constitutes a positive step toward incorporating the experiences of Afro-Americans in the general discipline of sociology.

SUBJECT(S): Afro-Americans--Social conditions--Research--United States.
Sociology--History--United States.
Afro-American Sociology.
Black Sociology.

249. Staples, Robert. *Introduction to Black Sociology*. New York: McGraw-Hill, 1976. xi, 338 p.

An important reference for the study of black sociology. Chapters are devoted to the nature of black sociology; race and racism; culture and personality; community institutions; the family; religion; social class; crime and delinquency; majority groups; and social movements and change. Each chapter includes extensive bibliographic references for further study. An index is included.

SUBJECT(S): Blacks--Social conditions--1964-Sociology.

250. Thompson, Daniel C. *Sociology of the Black Experience*. Westport, CT: Greenwood Press, 1974. x, 261 p.

Bibliography and an index are included.

SUBJECT(S): Afro-Americans--Social conditions.
Afro-Americans--Civil rights.
Afro-American--Families.

Statistics, Demography, and Migration

251. *American Statistics Index*. Washington: Congressional Information Service, 1973-.

An annual guide to the statistical publications of the United States government. Monthly up-date supplements are issued. Cites statistical sources on population by region and ethnic group, housing, education, economics, legal activities, energy, defense, etc. The subject index cites materials on Afro-Americans under "Black Americans." A separate volume contains abstracts of the materials indexed. Full texts of the documents cited are available on microfiche or in paper form.

SUBJECT(S): United States--Statistics--Bibliography.
United States--Statistics--Abstracts.
Statistics--Bibliography.
Statistics--Abstracts.
United States--Government publications-- Bibliography.

252. Bianchi, Suzanne M. *Household Composition and Racial Inequality*. New Brunskwick, NJ: Rutgers University Press, 1981. xvi, 199 p.

A revised doctoral dissertation on the household income of black and white Americans, and the implications of racial differences for the economic well-being of each race. Statistical tables and figures are dispersed throughout. Chapter topics are: defining the household and measuring economic well-being; changing living arrangements of blacks and whites; changing sources of household income of blacks an whites; changing employment and earnings of householders; and economic well-being of blacks and whites - issues and implications. An appendix contains data on poverty thresholds, family budgets, and household economic need. Illustrations, bibliographical notes, a bibliography, and an author-title-subject index are included.

SUBJECT(S): Family--United States--Statistics.
Afro-American families--Statistics.
Single-parent family--United States--Statistics.
Households--United States--Statistics.
Income distribution--United States--Statistics.
Family size--Economic aspects--United States--Statistics.

253. *Black People and the 1980 Census: Proceedings From a Conference on the Population Undercount*. Held at the University of Chicago, November 30 - December 1, 1979, Chicago, Illinois. Chicago, IL: Chicago Center for Afro-American Studies and Research, 1980.

The purpose of this conference was to point out the significance of the census and the harmful impact of the repeated census undercount of blacks and other minorities. This published transcript of the proceedings constitutes virtually the only major work available on this vital topic. Included are the papers of a large number of professionals and academicians from a wide variety of fields. Many of the papers include statistical tables, charts, maps, and bibliographical references. A selected bibliography accompanies one of the papers, pp. 164-170, and may serve as a useful reference to some of the pertinent literature. The resolutions of the conference are also presented. A subject index, and a list of the many tables and charts scattered throughout this document are omitted --features which would have greatly enhanced access to the wide range of data and information contained in this work.

SUBJECT(S): Afro-Americans--Social conditions--1975- --Congresses.
Afro-Americans--Economic conditions--Congresses.
Census undercounts--United States--Congresses.
United States--Census, 20th, 1980--Congresses.

254. Center for Afro-American and African Studies, The University of Michigan. *Black Immigration and Ethnicity in the United States: An Annotated Bibliography*. Westport, CT: Greenwood Press, 1985. iii, 176 p. SERIES: Bibliographies and Indexes in Afro-American Studies, no. 2.

A comprehensive survey of the scholarly literature relating to black Caribbean and African immigration of recent decades and its impact on the composition of the black population in the United States. It provides an overview of the subject, reviews related research, identifies gaps in the literature, and encourages discussion on policy issues. A total of 1,049 items are listed, including books, periodical articles, government documents, and dissertations. Approximately half of the citations are annotated. An index is included.

255. Hall, Charles E. United States. Bureau of the Census. *Negroes in the United States*,1920-32. Prepared under the supervision of Z. R. Pettet. Washington: U.S. Govt. Print. Off., 1935. 845 p.

SUBJECT(S): Afro-Americans--Statistics.

256. Johnson, Daniel M. and Rex R. Campbell. *Black Migration in America: A Social Demographic History*. *Studies in Social and Economic Demography*. Durham, NC: Duke University Press, 1981. viii, 190 p.

A study on the causes and consequences of black migration. It begins with the forced migration of the slave trade era and ends with the 1970s. Although no bibliographies are included, there are numerous bibliographical notes. Maps, tables, diagrams and an index are included.

SUBJECT(S): Afro-Americans--Population.
Migration, Internal--United States.
United States--Population.

257. Jones, Marcus E. *Black Migration in the United States with Emphasis on Selected Central Cities*. Saratoga, CA: Century Twenty One Pub., 1980, ix, 138 p.

An investigation of black migration within the United States from a geographical perspective. Covers the Antebellum period through the middle-1970s. Central cities include those with black populations of 50,000 or more. Includes many charts and graphs, and an extensive bibliography.

SUBJECT(S): Afro-Americans--Social conditions.
Afro-Americans--Economic conditions.
Migration, Internal--United States.
Rural-urban migration--United States.
United States--Social conditions.

258. Momeni, Jamshid A. *Demography of the Black Population in the United States: An Annotated Bibliography with a Review Essay*. Westport, CT: Greenwood Press, 1983. xxi, 354 p.

This important and unique bibliography is intended to encourage and facilitate research on the black population and its social, economic, and political impact on American society. The 650 entries are accompanied by lengthy annotations providing a summary of the work's contents. An introductory essay provides a synthesis of important developments in black demography over the past century. Entries are grouped by subject covering several topics, including: fertility, nuptiality, and family; fertility outside marriage; fertility regulation, including abortion, sterilization, and genocide; health and mortality; migration, urbanization, and ecology; population growth, composition, and spacial distribution; and vital rates. Tables, figures, and an author index are included.

SUBJECT(S): Afro-Americans--Population--Bibliography.

259. Price, Daniel O. *Changing Characteristics of the Negro Population*. U.S. Department of Commerce, Bureau of the Census. Washington D.C.: U.S. Government Printing Office, 1969. 259 p.

Examines major changes in the Negro population, as reflected in census data since 1870, with emphasis on the period, 1940-1960. Chapters are devoted to population distribution and redistribution, occupational changes and distribution, education, marital patterns and household composition. It frequently includes variations by sex as well as comparisons with whites. Data presented are derived from the decennial census of the population. Includes numerous tables and charts, and a subject index.

SUBJECT(S): Afro-Americans--moral and social conditions
Afro-Americans--employment.

260. Reid, John. "Black America in the 1980s." *Population Bulletin*. vol. 37, no.4, 1982, 39 p. Washington, D.C.: Population Reference Bureau.

This small, highly readable volume provides a review of demographic and socioeconomic trends in the black population through 1982, and assesses changes in the status of blacks relative to whites, since the publication of the 1962 edition of Gunnar Myrdal's classic, *An American Dilemma*. It contains statistical data and discussion addressing the following areas: population growth, composition, and distribution; fertility and family planning; mortality; migration; family and marital status; education; employment and occupation; and income and poverty. Charts, tables, bibliographical references, and a selected bibliography are included.

SUBJECT(S): Population--Periodicals.

261. Ross, Frank Alexander, and Louis Venable Kennedy *A Bibliography of Negro Migration*. New York: B. Franklin, 1969. 251 p. SERIES: Burt Franklin Bibliography and Reference Series, no. 270.

Originally published in 1934 and reprinted in 1969, this bibliography contains books, pamphlets, articles, bibliographies, and manuscripts on the migration of blacks in the United States between 1865 and 1932. Chronological, subject,and geographical indexes are included.

SUBJECT(S): Afro-Americans--Bibliography.
Afro-Americans--Social conditions-- Bibliography.
Afro-Americans--Employment--Bibliography.
Bibliography--Bibliography--Afro-Americans.

262. *Statistical Abstract of the United States*. Washington D.C.: U.S. Department of Commerce, Social and Economic Statistics Administration, Bureau of the Census, 1878-.

Published annually since 1878, this is the standard summary of statistics on the social, political, and economic organization of the United States. It is designed to serve as a volume for statistical reference and as a guide to other statistical publications. It contains data selected from both government and private sources. Emphasis is given to national data, but many tables present data for regions, states, and some metropolitan areas and cities. The data included is generally for the most recent year or period available. Although there is no section which deals exclusively with blacks, the use of the term "Black Population" in the index will refer the reader to data directly related to blacks on various topics.

SUBJECT(S): Statistics--Periodicals.
United States--Statistics.

263. United States. Bureau of the Census. *Negro population, 1790-1915*. Washington: U.S. Govt. Print. Off., 1918; New York: Kraus Reprint, 1969. 844 p.

Included in this collection of published and formerly unpublished materials by the Census Bureau statistics for population per square mile, breakdowns by counties, and total populations from each census from 1790 to 1910. Also included is statistical information on all facets of Afro-American life, from 1790-1915. Diagrams, charts, and narrative introductions are arranged in the following seven sections: growth and geographical distribution, migratory displacement and segregation, physical characteristics, vital statistics, educational and social statistics, economic statistics, and general statistics. A subject index is included.

SUBJECT(S): Afro-Americans--Statistics.

264. United States. Bureau of the Census. *The Social and Economic Status of the Black Population in the United States, 1790-1978*. Current Population Reports: Special Studies: Series P-23: no. 80. Washington U.S Government Printing Office, 1980. 271 p.

An historical overview of changes in the demographic, social, and economic characteristics of the black population in the United States, 1790 to 1978. It focuses on changes in population distribution, income levels, labor force, employment, education, family composition, mortality, fertility, housing, voting, public office holdings, armed forces personnel, and other major aspects of life. Most data presented are from the Bureau of the Census. Data was also gathered from other federal agencies and private sources. Numerous charts, graphs, and tables are included. There are appendices which provide data sources for tables, definitions and explanations, and one which discusses the sources and reliability of data presented.

SUBJECT(S): Afro-Americans--Economic conditions-- Statistics. Afro-Americans--Social conditions-- Statistics.

HUMANITIES

Art

265. Cederholm, Theresa Dickason. *Afro-American Artists: A Bio-bibliographical Directory.* Boston: Trustees of the Boston Public Library, 1973. 348 p.

This highly useful and comprehensive bio-bibliography provides basic biographical information on Afro-American artists from the eighteenth century to 1973. Dates, education, works by, and literature about the artists are included. There is also an unannotated bibliography of books, newspapers, magazines, and catalogs.

SUBJECT(S): Afro-American artists--Bio-bibliography-- Directories.

266. Christensen, Eleanor Ingalls. *The Art of Haiti.* Philadelphia: Art Alliance Press, 1975. 76 p.

Haitian art and sculpture, from pre-colonial times to the present, is discussed and illustrated in color and black and white. The history of the Centre de Art, the first major Haitian art museum, is also given. There are two appendices: the first is a chronological history of the Centre de Art, and the second is a collection of brief biographies of over one hundred twentieth century Haitian artists. Includes a bibliography and an author-title-subject index.

SUBJECT(S): Art, Haitian--History.
Primitivism in art--Haiti.

267. Davis, Lenwood G., and Janet L. Sims. *Black Artists in the United States: An Annotated Bibliography of Books, Articles, and Dissertations on Black Artists, 1779-1979.* Westport, CT: Greenwood Press, 1980. xiv, 138 p.

An annotated bibliography on black art and artists in the United States. Entries are grouped into the following six sections: major books dealing exclusively with black art; general books which deal only in part with black art; major articles of ten or more pages; general articles, including those from art journals and popular black periodicals such as *Jet* and *Ebony*, and older black periodicals such as *Opportunity* and *Crisis* dissertations; and a list of black art works in the national archives. An index is included.

SUBJECT(S): Afro-American art--Bibliography.
Afro-American artists--Bibliography.

268. Dover, Cedric. *American Negro Art*. Greenwich, CT: New York Graphic Society, 1960. 186 p.

This classic work on black art contains a collection of short essays on the interrelationship between black art and history, from ancient times to the present, and examples of black art. Of particular interest are examples from nineteenth century Afro-American painters living abroad. Reproductions are in black and white and color. A bibliography and an index are included.

SUBJECT(S): Afro-American art.
Art, American.

269. Driskell, David C. *Two Centuries of Black American Art: Exhibition, Los Angeles County Museum of Art, The High Museum of Art, Atlanta, Museum of Fine Arts, Dallas, The Brooklyn Museum*. Los Angeles: Los Angeles County Museum of Art; New York: Alfred Knopf, 1976. 221 p.

This work is based on an exhibition of Afro-American art at the Los Angeles County Art Museum held in 1976. It describes and illustrates the work of black American artists from 1720 to the 1970s. Although it focuses primarily on paintings, some drawings and sculpture are included. A bibliography and index of artists are also included.

SUBJECT(S): Afro-American art--Exhibitions.

270. Ferris, William, ed. *Afro-American Folk Art and Crafts*. Boston, MA: G.K. Hall, 1983. 436 p. SERIES: Perspectives on the Black World.

This work presents artists' and scholars' views of black folk arts and crafts. It provides a fascinating look into the life and works of black quilt makers, sculptors, instrument makers, basket makers, builders, blacksmiths, and potters. Autobiographical narratives by individual artists -edited from taped interviews- are followed by scholarly studies on their art. Photos of the artists' work appear throughout the book and in an introductory photo essay. It also includes annotated bibliographies to previous scholarship, and an annotated list of documentary films.

SUBJECT(S): Afro-American folk art--Addresses, essays, lectures.
Afro-American art industries and trade--Addresses, essays, lectures.

271. Holmes, Oakley N., Jr., comp. *The Complete Annotated Resource Guide to Black American Art: Books, Doctoral Dissertations, Exhibition Catalogs, Periodicals, Films, Slides, Large Prints, Speakers, Filmstrips, Video Tapes, Black Museums, Art Galleries, and Much More*. Spring Valley, NY: Black Artists in America, 1978. *iii, 275 p.*

This work is intended to serve the casual as well as the specialist user. In addition to materials indicated in the title, it also includes a list of speakers available to lecture on Afro-American art, and a chronological listing of exhibitions, books, and films.

SUBJECT(S): Afro-American arts--Bibliography.

272. Igoe, Lynn Moody, and James Igoe. *250 Years of Afro-American Art: An Annotated Bibliography*. New York: Bowker, 1981. xxv, 1266 p.

This comprehensive, annotated bibliography contains 25,000 citations on art work, art history, and documentation on the life and works of 3,900 Afro-American artists. Artists of fine arts and crafts are included. Citations cover books, periodicals, newspapers, exhibition catalogs, announcements, fliers, and dissertations. Primary sources, such as diaries and letters are also included. Scholarly publications, popular resources, and children's books are cited. In addition, citations on blacks from black periodicals, such as *Crisis*, *Opportunity*, and *Phylon*, are included and listed alphabetically under the periodical title. Citations from major art periodicals such as *Art Journal*, *Art Digest*, and others are also included. Although most items cited are in English, some are in Spanish, Italian, French, Dutch, German, Latin, Polish, and Danish.

SUBJECT(S): Afro-American art--Bibliography.

273. Lewis, Samella S. *Art: African American*. New York: Harcourt Brace Jovanovich, 1978. x, 246 p.

This work is useful for its historical survey of Afro-American art and its biographical sketches of the artists. Covers the period from 1619 through 1978. Numerous reproductions in black and white and color are included. It also included a bibliography citing books, exhibition catalogs, and periodical articles. An index is included.

SUBJECT(S): Afro-American art.

274. Lewis, Samella S., and Ruth G. Waddy, eds. *Black Artists on Art*. rev. ed. Los Angeles: Contemporary Crafts; Pasadena, CA: distributed by Ward Ritchie Press, 1976. 2 vols.

First published in 1969 and reprinted in 1976, this two volume work is "intended to introduce the works and thoughts" of a number of contemporary Afro-American artists. It contains photographic reproductions in color and black and white and biographical sketches of 147 artists.

SUBJECT(S): Afro-American art.
Afro-American artists.

275. Livingston, Jane, and John Beardsley. *Black Folk Art in America, 1930-1980*. Jackson: University Press of Mississippi: Center for the Study of Southern Culture, 1982. 186 p.

A catalog of the first major exhibition of Afro-American folk art, a generally neglected and little known art form. It includes three essays, which define and describe Afro-American folk art, provide a historical overview of origins and early manifestations from the slave era, and discuss the spiritual and imaginative aspects of this unique and important contribution to American culture. It also includes brief biographies, descriptions, and reproductions of the works of twenty folk artists from 1930-1982. A selected bibliography is also included.

SUBJECT(S): Afro-American art--Exhibitions.
Primitivism in art--United States-- Exhibitions.
Ethnic art--United States--Exhibitions.

276. Locke, Alain LeRoy, ed. *The Negro in Art: A Pictorial Record of the Negro Artist and of the Negro Theme in Art*. Washington, D.C.: Associates in Negro Folk Education, 1940. 224 p.

This classic and well illustrated study of black artists and their works depicts blacks in art from seventeenth century Europe to twentieth century America. Black ritualistic and folk art are also discussed. Critical notes and a bibliography are included.

SUBJECT(S): Afro-American artists.
Afro-Americans in literature and art.

277. Price, Sally, and Richard Price. *Afro-American Arts of the Suriname Rain Forest*. Los Angeles: Museum of Cultural History, University of California; Berkeley: University of California Press, 1980. 237 p.

This study attempts to present the art of the Maroons of the Suriname Rain Forest, within the framework of Maroon life and aesthetic values. It interprets the artistry and aesthetics of the Maroons from an ethnographic and ethnoaesthetic perspective, and traces the development of aesthetic ideas and artistic forms over time. Photographs and drawings are included. A bibliography of references cited, and a name-subject index are also included.

SUBJECT(S): Arts, Maroon--Exhibitions.
Maroons--Suriname--Exhibitions.

278. Rodman, Selden. *The Miracle of Haitian Art*. Garden City, NY: Doubleday, 1974. 95 p.

Described as a guide for the intelligent traveller and collector of Haitian art, this is one of the few works available in English on black Haitian sculptors and painters. Art, produced between the 1940s to the early 1970s, is discussed as an expression of native folk beliefs. Black and white and color reproductions are included. Bibliographical references are also included.

SUBJECT(S): Art, Haitian.

279. Sagay, Esi. *African Hairstyles: Styles of Yesterday and Today*. New Hampshire: Heinemann Educational Books Inc, 1983. xii, 108 p.

One of the very few works dealing with the art of hairdressing. It provides an overview of the traditional African hairstyles, and categorizes them by region. It also discusses, in detail, the black hairstyles of today, and provides instructions on cornrowing and hair threading. Exceptionally well illustrated throughout. A brief bibliography is included.

SUBJECT(S): Hairdressing-Africa-History.
Hairdressing of Blacks.

280. St. Louis Public Library. *An Index to Black American Artists*. St. Louis, 1972. 50 p.

Produced by the Art and Architecture Department of the St. Louis Public Library, this index lists artists, galleries, and schools. For each artist: dates, type of art work, latest address (as of 1972), and references to written material are included. It includes a selected bibliography.

SUBJECT(S): Afro-American artists--United States--Indexes.
Afro-American art--United States--Indexes.

281. Stebich, Ute, ed. *Haitian art*. New York: Brooklyn Museum: Exclusively distributed by H. N. Abrams, 1978. 176 p.

One of the few works in English available on Haitian artists. Over fifty artists and their works are discussed, and over 200 color and black and white illustrations are included. Following a chronology of Haitian art, there are essays on voodoo and art, and on the African origins of Haitian art. Brief biographies of the painters and sculptors are given. A selected bibliography and an index to lenders is included.

SUBJECT(S): Art, Haitian--Exhibitions.

Dance

The published literature relevant to Afro-American dance is not extensive, and bibliographical control over the existing literature is not well developed. There are no book bibliograhies or other references sources devoted to Afro-American dance or dancers. In addition to the items cited below, the subject index lists several items under the heading Dance which contain additional information on black dance and/or provide citations to relevant monogaphs, dissertations, or articles. Relevant materials may also be identified through use of the current journal abstracting and indexing services which cover the humanities.

282. Aschenbrenner, Joyce. *Katherine Dunham: Reflections on the Social and Political Contexts of Afro-American Dance*. With notations of the Dunham method and technique by Lavinia Williams. NY: CORD Inc., 1981. xiii, 164 p. SERIES: Dance Research Annual, no. 12.

This work includes an extensive list of bibliographical references, and numerous illustrations.

SUBJECT(S): Dunham, Katherine.
Afro-Americans--Dancing.

283. Emery, Lynne Fauley. *Black Dance in the United States from 1619 to 1970*. Forward by Katherine Dunham. 1st ed. Palo Alto, CA: National Press Books, 1972. x, 370 p.

One of the few works on black dance, this comprehensive history incorporates accounts of slaves, slave owners, travelers, critics' reviews and other sources. Although the focus is on the United States there is also a chapter on dance in the Caribbean, from 1518 to 1970. The dance steps, dancers, and the social aspects are discussed. Drawings and photographs are included. There is bibliography and an author-title-subject index.

SUBJECT(S): Afro-Americans--Dancing.

284. Goines, Margaretta Bobo. "African Retentions in the Dance of the Americas," *Dance Research Monograph*, 1, (1971-1972), pp. 209-229. New York: Committee on Research in Dance, 1973.

This is a report on research in progress. It provides a survey of African cultural survivals in black American dance. The emphasis is on Latin America and the Caribbean areas, with three pages devoted to dance in the United States. Bibliographical notes are included.

SUBJECT(S): Blacks--Dancing.
Afro-Americans--dancing.

285. Sterns, Marshall Winslow and Jean Stearns. *Jazz Dance*. Ney York: Schirmer Books, 1979. xvi, 464 p.

SUBJECT(S): Dancing--United States--History.
Jazz dance--History.

Folklore

286. Abrahams, Roger D. *Deep Down in the Jungle: Negro Narrative Folklore from the Streets of Philadelphia*. Chicago: Aldine Publishing Co., 1970. 278 p.

A pioneering, in depth study of black ghetto folklore. It contains a wide range of black urban folktales with analysis and interpretations.

SUBJECT(S): Folk-Lore--Afro-American
Afro-Americans--Philadelphia.

287. Brewer, John Mason., comp. *American Negro Folklore*. New York: Quadrangle/New York Times Book Co., 1968. xviii, 386 p.

An anthology of folktales, religious and secular songs, personal experiences, superstitions, proverbs, rhymes, riddles, names, and children's rhymes and songs. Illustrative drawings and an author-title-subject index are included.

SUBJECT(S): Folk-lore, Afro-American.

288. Courlander, Harold, comp. *A Treasury of Afro-American Folklore: The Oral Literature, Traditions, Recollections, Legends, Tales, Songs, Religious Beliefs, Customs, Sayings, and Humor of Peoples of African Descent in the Americas*. New York: Crown Publishers, 1976. xx, 618 p.

An anthology of folktales, songs, rhymes, and stories, from Latin America, the Caribbean, and the United States. Included are several African folktales, after which many Afro-American folktales are patterned. Also included are photographs of sculpture, pottery and dance. A bibliography and index are included.

SUBJECT(S): Folk-lore, Black--America.

289. Dance, Daryl Cumber. *Shuckin and Jivin: Folklore from Contemporary Black Americans*. Bloomington: Indiana University Press, 1978. xxii, 390 p.

An anthology of Afro-American folktales dictated by Virginian informants. These, however, are not found exclusively in Virginia, but are found widely scattered throughout the country. They are derived from many sources, and some can be traced to early African, European, and Asian origins. Some are of white American and American Indian influence. Brief biographies of most of the major informants are included. Annotations give information about the collection of each tale and indicate printed sources. The tales are grouped together by motifs dealing with: heaven and hell; ghosts; conjuring; religion; self-degrading; white women and black men; women; marital infidelity; ethnic jokes; cruelty of whites; outsmarting whitey; the bad nigger; miscellaneous animal tales; and miscellaneous risque tales. There is no index.

SUBJECT(S): Afro-Americans--Virginia--Folklore.
Afro-American tales--Virginia.
Afro-Americans--Folklore.
Afro-American tales.

290. Dorson, Richard Mercer, comp. *American Negro Folktales*. Greenwhich, CT: Fawcett Publications, 1970. 378 p. SERIES: A Fawcett Premier Book, no. 357.

An anthology of folktales collected in Michigan, Arkansas, and Mississippi in the early 1950s. There is an introductory chapter on black folktales and story tellers. The stories have animal, religious, lying, protest, witchcraft, and other themes. There is a brief index of motifs and a index of tale types. A short bibliography is included.

SUBJECT(S): Afro-American tales.

291. Dorson, Richard Mercer, ed. *Negro Folktales in Michigan*. Westport, CT: Greenwood Press, 1974. xiv, 245 p.

An anthology of black folktales collected in several predominately black communities in Michigan in the 1950s. Most tales were transported from the South by black immigrants to Michigan, but many contain elements which may be traced to peoples and locales world wide, which were adopted by Afro-American blacks. It also includes chapters on the communities and storytellers, who served as the author's sources, and on the art of storytelling. The tales are grouped into chapters by type: "Animal and Bird Stories," "Old Marster and John," "Colored Man," "Horrors," "Hoodoos and Two-Heads," "Spirits and Hants," "Witches and Wonders," "The Lord and the Devil," "Preachers," "Liars and Irishmen," and "Fairy Tales." Bibliography, notes are included. An index of informants, an index of motifs, and an index of tale types are also included.

SUBJECT(S): Afro-American tales.
Tales, American--Michigan.

292. Dundes, Alan, comp. *Mother Wit from the Laughing Barrel: Readings in the Interpretation of Afro-American Folklore*. New York: Garland, 1981. xiv, 674 p. SERIES: Critical Studies on Black Life and Culture. vol. 7.

A collection of writings from widely scattered sources on the meaning, significance, and interpretation of black American folklore. It contains illustrative excerpts of folktales with critical and theoretical writings dealing with: attitudes and relationships between folklore and a sense of group identity; origins of black folklore; folk speech with special reference to traditional names and slang; important forms of traditional word play such as "signifying," and "playing the dozens"; custom and belief, folk song; narrative forms which include folktales, legends, and memorates; and an analysis of traditional humor. Bibliographical notes, and a bibliographical essay for further reading are also included.

SUBJECT(S): Afro-American folk-lore--Addresses, essays, lectures.
Afro-American--Social life and customs--addresses, essays, lectures.

293. Fry, Gladys-Marie. *Night Riders in Black Folk History*. Knoxville, Tenn.: University of Tennessee Press, 1975. xi, 251 p.

An outstanding study on white manipulation of beliefs, relating to conjuring, witches, and ghosts, as a means of controlling the black population during the slavery and post-slavery eras. These means of controlling blacks were originally practiced by masters and overseers dressed as ghosts. Later, psychological control was extended to the system of mounted patrols (or "patterollers") to monitor slave movement in antebellum days. Subsequently, such methods were practiced by the Ku Klux Klan of the Reconstruction era. To their black victims, these groups were known as the "night riders." This book documents such practices from the reminiscences, genealogical data, legends of oral tradition, and on data gathered through interviews with black informants in Washington, D.C. It includes a section devoted to a survey of historical source material on black intellectual thought and a section devoted to field work methodology. It also includes biographies of the informants, illustrations an extensive bibliography of works cited or consulted, and a name-title-subject index.

SUBJECT(S): Slavery--United States--Condition of slaves.
Afro-Americans--Southern States.
Afro-American folklore.
Southern States--Race relations.

294. Harris, Joel Chandler, ed. *Uncle Remus, His Songs, and His Sayings*. Introductions by Robert Hemenway. New York: Penguin Books, 1982. 222 p. SERIES: Penguin American Library.

A collection of Uncle Remus folktales, proverbs, songs, and twenty-one character sketches based on stories which Harris, a white journalist, heard as a child.

SUBJECT(S): Afro-Americans--Folklore.
Tales--United States.
Folklore, Afro-American.
Animals--Fiction.

295. Haywood, Charles. *A Bibliography of North American Folklore and Folksong*. 2d rev. ed. New York: Dover Publications, 1961. 2 vols., xxx, 1301 p.

Part III of volume I of this annotated bibliography, (pp. 430-560) is devoted to "The Negro." The materials cited includes bibliographies, general studies and collections, and periodicals. Specific titles in black folklore and folksong, including spirituals, work songs, social songs, blues, and minstrelsy, are also cited. Creole and West Indies folklore and folk song are also included. Maps are included.

SUBJECT(S): Folklore--United States--Bibliography.
Afro-Americans--Folklore--Bibliography.
Indians of North America--Folklore--Bibliography.
Folk-songs--United States--Bibliography.
Afro-Americans--Songs and music--Bibliography.
Indians of North America--Music--Bibliography.

296. Hughes, Langston, and Arna Bontemps. *The Book of Negro Folklore*. New York: Dodd, Mead, 1958. 624 p.

An anthology of Afro-American folklore, including folktales, traditional poetry, spirituals, and rhymes, on both secular and religious subjects. Also included are selected blues lyrics, contemporary songs, and prose written in a folk-like manner. There are no indexes or illustrations. Generally, the table of contents provides adequate access by subject and/or theme.

SUBJECT(S): Afro-American--Folklore.

297. Hurston, Zora Neale. *Mules and Men*. Preface by Franz Boas; introduction by Robert Hemenway; illustrations by Miguel Covarrubias. Bloomington: Indiana University Press, 1978, c1935. Reprint of the edition published by Lippincott (Philadelphia), with a new introduction. xxviii, 291 p.

A pioneering and classic work intended to alter the popular conception of Southern black folk. The theme of this work is that the folklore of the black south is an expressive system of great social complexity and profound aesthetic significance. The work refutes the pathological view of an uneducated, rural, black people, and subordinates the economic and social deprivation approach to achieve a cultural perspective. Included are seventy folktales, a series of voodoo rituals, and a glossary of folk speech. An appendix includes folk songs with music scores, conjure formulas, root prescriptions, and personal accounts of Ms. Hurston's collecting experiences.

SUBJECT(S): Afro-Americans--Louisiana--Folklore.
Afro-Americans--Florida--Folklore.
Tales--Louisiana.
Tales--Florida.
Voodooism--Louisiana.
Afro-Americans--Florida.
Afro-Americans--Louisiana.
Afro-American songs.

298. Levine, Lawrence W. *Black Culture and Black Consciousness: Afro-American Folk Thought from Slavery to Freedom*. New York: Oxford University Press, 1978. xx, 522 p. SERIES: Galaxy Books, no 530.

This work attempts to present a history of the thought of black Americans, with a focus on orally transmitted expressive culture, from the Antebellum era to the end of the 1940s. Sources used are black folksongs, folktales, proverbs, aphorisms, jokes, verbal games, and "Toasts" (a long narrative oral poem). This study serves a dual purpose: to help establish the contours of Afro-American folk thought in the United States; and to call to the attention of other historians, the importance of a body of sources which, until recently, they had chosen to ignore. Bibliographical notes and a name-subject index are included.

SUBJECT(S): Afro-Americans-Folklore.

299. Puckett, Newbell Niles. *Folk Beliefs of the Southern Negro*. Montclair, NJ: Patterson Smith, 1968. xiv, 644 p. SERIES: Patterson Smith Reprint Series in Criminology, Law Enforcement, and Social Problems Publication, no. 22.

Originally a doctoral dissertation on acculturation. It contains approximately 10,000 folk beliefs of southern blacks, shows the origin of the beliefs whenever possible, and indicates some of the general principles governing the transmission and content of folklore in general. The folk beliefs are presented and discussed in chapters devoted to burial customs, ghosts, and witches; voodooism and conjuration; minor charms and cures; taboos; prophetic signs or omens; and Christianity and superstition. It includes a bibliography of references cited, and an analytic index which allows the identification of folk beliefs by subject or theme.

SUBJECT(S): Afro-American folklore.
Voodooism--United States.

300. Puckett, Newbell Niles. *Popular Beliefs and Superstitions: a Compendium of American Folklore : from the Ohio Collection of Newbell Niles Puckett*. Edited by Wayland D. Hand, Anna Casetta, Sondra B. Thiederman. Boston, MA: G.K. Hall, 1981. 3 vols., lviii, 1829 p.

Described as the "greatest collection of folk beliefs and superstitions for any single area of the world," this monumental three-volume work contains over 36,000 entries from 87 ethnic groups. Among the such topics covered are: birth, death, folk medicine, love and marriage, friends and enemies, supernatural powers, ghosts, animals, and numbers. Nearly 6,000 of the sayings are of black origin. Volume I contains an introductory essay, which places the folk beliefs and superstitions contained in these volumes within a world wide context, discusses other major collections of folklore, and provides background information on the compilation of this work. Volume I also contains a selected, representative bibliography, which includes major state and regional collections, and smaller collections of folk beliefs and superstitions, ethnic materials, and books and articles on special topics. Volume III consists of an ethnicfinding list and a subject index, both of which are exceptionally well constructed and highly effective identification and retrieval aids. Through the ethnic-finding list, one can identify and locate the nearly 6,000 entries which are of Afro-American origin as well as determine the subjects to which these entries relate.

SUBJECT(S): Puckett, Newbell Niles--Library--Collected works.
Folklore--Ohio--Collected works.
Superstition--Ohio--Collected works.
Ohio--Social life and customs--Collected works.

301. Robinson, Beverly. *Aunt (Ant) Phyllis*. Los Angeles: The Woman's Graphic Center, 1982. 42 p.

This work provides an overview of the life of Mrs. Phillis Carter, a Southern African American Woman deemed important by her community. It is the result of several in depth interviews and is a contribution to what may be termed "representative folklore." Unlike the traditional folkloric field work, which focuses on capturing a specific genre from an informant (e.g., music, folk art, and narratives), this work reveals the versatility of the individual, thereby eliciting several genres of one's collective knowledge. It includes a selected bibliography and a biographical sketch of the author.

SUBJECT(S): Afro-Americans--Georgia--Biography.
Georgia--Biography.
Afro-American folklore.

302. Spalding, Henry d., ed. and comp. *Encyclopedia of Black Folklore and Humor*. 2nd ed. Middle Village, NY: Jonathan David Publishers, 1978. 589 p.

A compendium of humorous folktales, anecdotes, folk songs, rhymes, proverbs, and superstitions derived chiefly from the folklore of black oral traditions dating from the arrival of slaves in the new world to modern times. An attempt is made to retain the original black English speech patterns. The works are grouped into sections covering various genres or themes, ie., slavery, emancipation, secular and religious parables, folksongs, poetry, and each section is prefaced by introductory and critical material. The 1972 edition includes an addenda containing soul food recipes and a bibliography, while the 1978 edition integrates the recipes throughout the text.

SUBJECT(S): Afro-American wit and humor.

303. Waters, Donald J. *Strange Ways and Sweet Dreams: Afro-American folklore from the Hampton Institute*. Boston: G.K. Hall and Twayne Publishers, 1983. 439 p.

A collection of proverbs, riddles, conventional superstitions, sermons, conjuring practices, and folktales collected by members of the Hampton Folklore Society in the late-nineteenth century. A comprehensive introduction provides a framework for studying much of the material collected in this volume.

SUBJECT(S): Afro-American--Southern States--Folklore.
Afro-American--Southern states--social life and customs.

Music

304. Berry, Lemuel, Jr. *Biographical Dictionary of Black Musicians and Music Educators*. s.l.: Educational Books Publishers, 1978. 389 p.

This work contains biographical sketches of composers, musicians, conductors, educators, singers, instrumentalists, publishers, scholars, directors, musicologists, and music critics from the late 1800s. Entries include the individual's most recognized achievements, birth and death dates, and other information when known. A brief bibliography and is included. Several appendices provide partial lists of professional and college choirs, conductors, and directors.

SUBJECT(S): Afro-American musicians--Biography.
Music teachers--United States--Biography.

305. Charters, Samuel Barclay. *Jazz: New Orleans, 1885-1963: An Index to the Negro Musicians of New Orleans*. rev. ed. New York: Oak Publications, 1963. 173 p.

This index provides biographical information on New Orleans jazz musicians. Entries are grouped in sections according to time periods. Each section contains an introduction, biographies, descriptions of brass bands and orchestral groups, and addenda. A discography and additional source material in an appendix are included. Indexes of musicians, bands, halls, caberets and theatres, tune titles, and the addenda sections are also included.

SUBJECT(S): Jazz musicians.
Jazz music.
Jazz music--Bibliography.
Music--Louisiana--New Orleans.

306. Davidson, Celia Elizabeth. *Operas by Afro-American Composers: A Critical Survey and Analysis of Selected Works*. 1980. 521 leaves. (On Microfilm) SERIES: Catholic University of America. Studies in Music, no. 76.

SUBJECT(S): Afro-American musicians--Biography.
Opera--United States--History and criticism.

307. Davis, Stephen. *Reggae Bloodlines: In Search of the Music and Culture of Jamaica*. rev. ed. Garden City, NY: Anchor Press, 1979. 216 p.

This work provides a brief history of Jamaica, and its people, with an emphasis on its music, and its national spirit, and the Brotherhood of Rastafari. It includes interviews with reggae master musicians as well as reports on Jamaican politics. Many photographs are included. It also includes a brief list of further readings and a Jamaican discography.

SUBJECT(S): Reggae music.
Jamaica--Social conditions.

308. De Lerma, Dominique-Rene. *Bibliography of Black Music*. Westport, CT: Greenwood Press, 1981-1984. 4 Vols. SERIES: Greenwood Encyclopedia of Black Music.

This four-volume bibliography cites an exceptionally wide range of works relating to black music. Works published in the United States and abroad, in English, and in foreign languages, are included. Volume I: "Reference Materials" includes citations to catalogs of library and museum collections, encyclopedias, bibliographies, discographies, directories, dissertations and theses, periodicals, lexicons, etymologies, and iconographies. Volume II: "Afro-Americans Idioms" cites general histories; works relating to minstrelsy, spirituals and earlier folk music; ragtime; musical theater; concert music; band music; blues; gospel music; rhythm and blues and other popular music; and jazz. Volume III: "Geographic Studies" cites over 5,000 items under geographic areas, including forty-three African countries and culture groups; twenty-nine countries in South America and the Caribbean, twenty areas in the United States, the District of Columbia, and Mexico. Volume III also includes an index of authors, co-authors, and editors. Volume IV: "Theory, Education, and Related Studies" covers literature on instruments, performance practice, theory, education, interdisciplinary studies on music and the social sciences, business, economics, and related arts, and liturgy, with concluding sections on women's and children's music.

SUBJECT(S): Music, Black--Bibliography.
Afro-Americans--Music--Bibliography.

309. De Lerma, Dominque-Rene. *The Black-American Musical Heritage: A Preliminary Bibliography*. Music Library Association, 1969. 451 p. SERIES: Explorations in Music Librarianship, no. 3.

A list of nineteenth and twentieth century monographs, theses, articles, and dissertations arranged alphabetically by author, Most are in English, and a few in Portuguese and German. An index of subject, names, and places is included.

SUBJECT(S): Music libraries.

310. Feather, Leonard G, and Ira Gitler. *The Encyclopedia of Jazz in the Seventies*. Introduction by Quincy Jones. New York: Horizon Press, 1976. 393 p.

This encyclopedia contains biographies and photographs of famous jazz personalities, a tabulation of results from an annual poll in *Down Beat* on the best records and performances, an essay on jazz education, and a list of films related to jazz.

SUBJECT(S): Music--Bio-bibliography.
Jazz musicians--Biography.
Jazz music--Discography.

311. Feather, Leonard G. *The Encyclopedia of Jazz in the Sixties*. New York: Horizon Press, 1966. 312 p.

Brief biographies of jazz performers comprise the major part of this work. For each musician, a biography, a selected discography, and address are given. There is also a section of comments by jazz performers on the work of other jazz musicians. Poll tabulations from *Down Beat* for 1960-1966, on the best performers and performances, are listed, as are similar poll results from *Playboy*. Photographs of famous jazz personalities are included. A bibliography and a list of important jazz recordings of the 1960s are also included.

SUBJECT(S): Music--Bio-bibliography.
Jazz musicians.
Jazz music--Discography.

312. Floyd, Samuels A. and Marsha J. Reisser. *Black Music in the United States: An Annotated Bibliography of Selected Reference and Research Materials*. Millwood, New York: Kraus International Publications, 1983. 234 p.

This bibliography of research materials is designed for the inexperienced layman as well as the mature black music specialist. It cites a wide range of materials, including guides; materials on research methodology; bibliographies; discographies; periodical indexes; dictionaries and encyclopedias; histories; collective biographies; collections of printed music; archive repositories in several states; and materials relating to folk music, spirituals, minstrelsy, ragtime, blues, jazz, and gospel music. An an author-subject-title index is included.

SUBJECT(S): Afro-Americans--Music--Bibliography.
Music--United States--Bibliography.

313. Futrel, Jon , et. al. *The Illustrated Encyclopedia of Black Music*. Edited by Ray Bonds. New York: Harmony Books, 1982.

A well illustrated, beautifully produced work containing over 650 critical biographies of important rhythm and blues, soul, reggae, disco and funk performers, producers, song writers, and important persons in the industry. Entries are grouped into separate alphabetical sections by decade. It is the first encyclopedia to chronicle the contributions of black popular musicians over the past forty years.

SUBJECT(S): Afro-American musicians--Biography.
Musicians, Black--Biography.

314. Handy, D. Antoinette. *Black Women in American Bands & Orchestras*. Metuchen, NJ: Scarecrow Press, 1981. xii, 319 p.

This work provides a historical overview of black orchestras and blacks in orchestras in the United States. This is followed by chapters which contain overviews and biographical profiles of black women in the following specific areas: orchestra leaders; string players; wind and percussion players; keyboard players; administrators; and musicians of the younger generation. A bibliography, an index of biographical profiles, and a general index are included.

SUBJECT(S): Afro-American women musicians.

315. Harris, Sheldon. *Blues Who's Who: A Biographical Dictionary of Blues Singers*. New Rochelle, NY: Arlington House, 1979. 775 p.

This work contains biographies of 571 blues singers from 1900 to 1977. Each entry includes brief biographical data, a detailed listing of career credits, and quotes from periodicals, magazines or other sources which describe or assess the performer's work. A selected bibliography lists books, periodicals, magazines, and record companies. There are film, radio, television, and theater indexes which list performances and programs in which singers in this book participated. There is also an index of songs written by the singers, and a name and place index. Photographs of the singers are included.

SUBJECT(S): Blues (Songs, etc.)--United States--Bio-bibliography.

316. Jackson, Irene V. *Afro-American Religious Music: A Bibliography and a Catalogue of Gospel Music*. Westport, CT: Greenwood Press, 1979. xiv, 210 p.

This pioneering bibliography focuses on the music of established black churches and denominations in the United States, as well as black cults in the Caribbean and South America. Entries on West African music are also included, especially that music associated with religious rituals. The catalogue lists the Library of Congress's holdings of black gospels copyrighted between 1938 and 1965. Gospels are listed by composer or author, and each entry includes the name of the arranger, author, publishing company, and copyright year. A subject index is included.

SUBJECT(S): Spirituals (Songs)--Bibliography.
Gospel music--Bibliography.
Afro-Americans--Music--Bibliography.

317. Johnson, James Peter, comp. *Bibliographic Guide to the Study of Afro-American Music*. Washington, D.C.: Howard University Libraries, 1973. 24 p. SERIES: Howard University Libraries Consciousness IV. Bibliographic Series.

A guide to music related histories, biographies, autobiographies, bibliographies, discographies, indexes, abstracts, encyclopedias, dictionaries, periodicals, and pictorial sources. Most items cited were produced from 1953 to 1973.

SUBJECT(S): Afro-American music--Bibliography.
Music--United States--Bibliography.

318. Kennington, Donald, and Danny L. Read. *The Literature of Jazz: A Critical Guide*. 2d ed., rev. Chicago: American Library Association, 1980. xi, 236 p.

This critical guide to jazz covers literature written from the turn of the century to the late 1960s. Eight chapters cover the background, history and analysis of jazz, reference works, periodicals, jazz in literature, and organizations related in some way to jazz in the United States and Europe. Each chapter has a narrative section followed by a bibliography. There is an appendix on jazz in films, and an index of books, periodicals, and films. A subject-author index is also included.

SUBJECT(S): Jazz music--Bibliography.

319. Lovell, John. *Black Song: The Forge and the Flame: The Study of How the Afro-American Spiritual Was Hammered Out*. New York: MacMillan, 1972. xviii, 686 p.

This important work analyzes the history, form, and content of spirituals, and discusses the influence of spirituals on other forms of music. One of the chapters lists publications and performances of spirituals in foreign countries. Inludes illustrations, source notes and an extensive bibliography. An author-title-subject index is also included. included.

SUBJECT(S): Spirituals (Songs)--History and criticism.
Gospel music--Bibliography.
Afro-Americans--Music--Bibliography.

320. Meadows, Eddie S. *Jazz Reference and Research Materials: A Bibliography*. New York: Garland Publishing, 1981. xii, 300 p. SERIES: Critical Studies on Black Life and Culture, vol. 22. SERIES: Garland Reference Library of the Humanities, vol. 251.

An annotated bibliography of books, articles, masters theses and doctoral dissertations written on, or about, specific jazz styles and jazz musicians from the turn of the century through 1978. It is divided into two parts: one dealing with jazz and its performance, and the other consisting of reference materials such as bibliographies, dictionaries, technical materials, anthologies, autobiographies, and discographies. There are subject and name indexes for each section.

SUBJECT(S): Jazz music--Bibliography.

321. Nanry, Charles. *The Jazz Text*. New York: Van Nostrand Reinhold, 1979. x, 276 p.

An important general introduction to jazz aimed at music students and performers. The text includes photos and biographical information on some of the major jazz figures, brief lists of some of their recordings, biographical information sources, and discography references. A brief bibliography and an index are included.

SUBJECT(S): Jazz music.

322. Odum, Howard Washington and Guy Benton Johnson. *Negro Workaday Songs*. Chapel Hill, NC: Univeristy of North Carolina Press, 1926. xii, 278 p.

A collection of simple, beautiful work songs, with explanatory notes and commentary. Included are blues workaday sorrow songs, songs of the lonesome road, bad man ballards, jamboree songs, songs of jail, the chain gang, policemen, construction camps, women's songs of men, and folk minstrel type songs. A bibliography and an index to songs is included.

SUBJECT(S): Afro-American songs--History and criticism.
Afro-American songs.

323. Placksin, Sally. *American Women in Jazz: 1900 to the Present: Their Words, Lives, and Music*. New York: Seaview Books, 1982. xvii, 332 p.

This work provides biographical information on a representative group of women of all races who have played important roles in jazz, from 1900 to 1982. The biographies are grouped by decade. Included are illustrations, bibliographical footnotes, a selected discography, and a selected bibliography. An index is also included.

SUBJECT(S): Jazz musicians--United States.
Jazz music--United States--History and criticism.
Women musicians--United States.
Women composers--United States.

324. Roach, Mildred. *Black American Music, Past and Present*. rev. ed. Boston: Crescendo Pub. Co., 1976. vii, 199 p.

This survey of Afro-American music and composers traces the development of black music from the slave era through the 1970s. It is well illustrated with photographs and excerpts of music scripts. Biographical sketches of composers are included. Bibliographical notes on readings and recordings, a list of musical terms, a chronological list of composers, and an index are also included.

SUBJECT(S): Afro-Americans--Music--History and criticism.

325. Rust, Brian A., comp. *Jazz Records: 1897-1942*. rev. ed. London: Storyville Publications and Co., 1970. 2 vols.

This two-volume discography lists individuals and groups alphabetically, and is a quick and useful source of information on early jazz recordings. For each; names, dates, and recordings are given. Special features are noted, such as a 1925 record in which Louis Armstrong introduces the members of his band. A name and title index are included.

SUBJECT(S): Jazz music--Discography.

326. Skowronski, JoAnn. *Black Music in America: A Bibliography*. Metuchen, NJ: Scarecrow, 1981. ix, 723 p.

This bibliography lists books and articles about black music and black musicians in the United States, from colonial times through 1979. It is divided into three sections: selected musicians and singers, general references, and reference works. Entries are numbered consecutively throughout the book, and within each section the items are listed chronologically by publication date and under each musician's name. An author index is included.

SUBJECT(S): Afro-Americans--Music--History and criticism--Bibliography.
Afro-American musicians--Bibliography.
Music--United States--Bibliography.

327. Southern, Eileen. *Biographical Dictionary of Afro-American and African musicians*. Westport, CT: Greenwood Press, 1982. xii, 478 p. SERIES: Greenwood Encyclopedia of Black Music.

This dictionary draws together widely dispersed and, in many instances, previously unpublished information on more than 1,500 musicians of African descent, born between 1642 and 1945. A few exceptional individuals born after 1945 are also included. Most individuals listed are, or were, professional musicians. Others who have made important contributions to black music history, such as concert promoters, patrons, and critics are also included. The biographical sketches give an objective account of the individual's professional life; dates of birth and death; education; details of career arranged in chronological order; representative compositions or performances; a bibliography; and, when possible, a discography.

SUBJECT(S): Afro-American musicians--United States--Bio-bibliography.
Musicians--Africa--Bio-bibliography.

328. Standifer, James A. *Source Book of African and Afro-American Materials for Music Educators*. Washington: Contemporary Music Project, 1972. xvii, 147 p. SERIES: Contemporary Music Project, no. 7.

A collection of bibliographies for teachers and students of music. In addition to bibliographies on the development and types of African and Afro-American music, there is a discography and a list of names of black composers and performers. There are also classroom exercises intended to give students experience in performing and understanding African and Afro-American music.

SUBJECT(S): Music, African--Bibliography.
Afro-American music--Bibliography.

329. Taft, Michael. *Blues Lyric Poetry: A Concordance*. New York: Garland Publishing, Inc., 1984. 3 vols. SERIES: Garland Reference Library of the Humanities, vol. 362.

A concordance to the over 2,000 blues lyrics contained in the companion work *Blues Lyric Poetry: An Anthology*, by the same author. It analyzes all formal lyrics rather than only printed texts, and each word appears in alphabetical order and within the context of its sung line in a key word format. Through the use of this work, the formulas, themes, and linguistic structures of the blues reveal themselves in clear patterns.

SUBJECT(S): Blues (Songs, etc.)--Texts--Concordances.
American poetry--Afro-American authors--Concordances.
American poetry--20th century--Concordances.

330. Taft, Michael. *Blues Lyric Poetry: An Anthology*. New York: Garland Publishing, Inc., 1984. xxvii, 379 p. SERIES: Garland Reference Library of the Humanities, vol. 361.

This anthology includes over 2,000 blues lyrics, written and sung by black performers, and commercially recorded from 1920 to 1942. Included are songs by over 350 singers, representing the entire range of the blues, from down-home or country blues to vaudeville songs. These recordings were originally aimed at the black record-buying public. These songs are now highly regarded as one of the most sophisticated and complex forms of folk and popular poetry to emerge during twentieth-century America by folklorists, ethnomusicologists, scholars of black and American studies, literary scholars, blues and jazz fans, and modern song writers. Each song has been personally transcribed by the author, and includes the title, place, date, and other discographical information. The entries are arranged chronologically by recording date of each song. Also included is a concordance of blues titles, which serves as an index of titles and a finding list for themes in the blues songs. This anthology also serves as a text source for *Blues Lyric Poetry: A Concordance*, by the same author.

SUBJECT(S): American poetry--Afro-American authors.
American poetry--20th century.
Blues (Songs, etc.)--Texts.
Afro-Americans--Music.

331. Tischler, Alice. *Fifteen Black American Composers: A Bibliography of Their Works*. Detroit: Information Coordinators, 1981. 328 p. SERIES: Detroit Studies in Music Bibliography, no. 45.

This work contains biographical sketches and a bibliography on the following fifteen black American composers: Edward Boatner, Margaret Bond, Edgar Rogie Clark, Arthur Cunningham, William Levi Dawson, Roger Dickerson, James Furman, Adolphus Hailstark, Robert A. Harris, Wendell Logan, Carman Leroy Moore, Dorothy Moore, John Price, Noah Francis Ryder, and Frederick Charles Tillis. The bibliographies consists primarily of the works composed by the composers. A title index, and an index by type of work are included. A publisher's address for each composer is appended.

SUBJECT(S): Afro-American composers--Bio-bibliography.

332. Tudor, Dean and Nancy Tudor *Black Music*. Littleton, CO: Libraries Unlimited, 1979. 262 p. SERIES: American Popular Music on Elpee.

An evaluative, annotated survey and buying guide to nearly 1,300 black music recordings.

SUBJECT(S): Afro-Americans--Music--Discography.
Music, Popular (Songs, etc.)--United States--Discography.

333. Tudor, Dean and Nancy Tudor. *Jazz*. Littleton, CO: Libraries Unlimited, 1979. 302 p. SERIES: American Popular Music on Elpee.

An evaluative, annotated guide to jazz recordings.

SUBJECT(S): Jazz music--Discography.
Sound recordings--Collectors and collecting.

334. Turner, Patricia. *Afro-American Singers: An Index and Preliminary Discography of Long-Playing Recordings of Opera, Choral Music, and Song*. Minneapolis: Challenge Productions, 1977. xvi, 255 p.

This index covers singers, choral groups, and composers. It is arranged by type of composition, i.e. popular, classical, and religious. For each person or group, a bibliography listing all their long-playing records and excerpts from their reviews are given. An index by type of singer, and a brief bibliography are included.

SUBJECT(S): Vocal music--Discography.
Afro-American singers--Discography.

335. White, Evelyn Davidson. *Choral Music by Afro-American Composers: A Selected, Annotated Bibliography*. Metuchen, NJ: Scarecrow Press, 1981. v, 167 p.

This bibliography of choral music by Afro-American composers consists of a list of composers and arrangers, an annotated list of compositions, a title index, a selected collection of Negro spirituals, and biographical sketches. The appendix contains a select reading list, a select discography, and the addresses of the composers' publishers.

SUBJECT(S): Choruses--Bibliography.
Afro-Americans--Music--Bibliography.

Philosophy

336. Harris, Leonard, ed. *Philosophy Born of Struggle: An Anthology of Afro-American Philosophy from 1917*. Dubuque, IA: Kendall/Hunt Publishing Company, 1983. xxi, 316 p.

An important collection of essays by blacks in a relatively neglected field. An introductory essay by the editor provides a historical overview on Afro-American philosophy and philosophers. The remaining essays are grouped into three sections. The first section, "Philosophy Experienced," contains articles that offer perspectives on what is, or should be, the nature of American philosophy; explore the life and works of particular thinkers; and argue for a given approach to the doing of philosophy. The second section, "Experience Explained," explores viable ways of elucidating the social and intellectual character of Afro-American situations and forms of legitimation associated with theories of oppression and liberation. The third section, "Experience Interpreted," contains articles that look at a body of texts and cultural patterns and tell us what they mean and how they should be understood. The works of many black authors are represented, including: Broadus N. Butler, Robert C. Williams, Alain L. Locke, John H. McClendon, Cornel West, Lucius T. Outlaw, William T. Fontaine, Bernard R. Boxill, Angela Y. Davis, Cornelius L. Golightly, Johnny Washington, Berkley B. Eddins, Essie A Eddins, Laurence Thomas, Howard McGary, Jr., Maulana Karenga, William R.

Jones, Houston A Baker, Jr., Albert G. Mosley, Thomas F. Slaughter, Jr., and Leonard Harris. The final chapter, by the editor, consists of an extensive, select, bibliography of works, primarily by Afro-American social philosophers.

SUBJECT(S): Afro-American--Addresses, essays, lectures.
Afro-American philosophy--Addresses, essays, lectures.

Religion

337. Austin, Allan D., ed. *African Muslims in Antebellum America: A Sourcebook*. Garlard Publishing, Inc., 1984. 759 p. SERIES: Critical Studies on Black Life and Culture, vol. 5.

This volume contains scattered historical and ethnographical materials relating to the presence black African Muslims brought to North America from 1730 to 1860. It provides substantial information on fifteen, and more modest information on 50 black individuals who were literate in Arabic and schooled in the Koran. It documents nearly all primary records, in both Arabic and English, by and about the Africans in question, and includes personal narratives, travelers' accounts, letters, and missionary reports. Secondary historical sources are also included. The material is well edited, annotated, and analyzed. An introduction places the subject in perspective. Illustrations and maps are included. A bibliography and an index are also included.

SUBJECT(S): Slaves--United States--Biography.
Afro-Americans--History--To 1863--Sources.
Muslims--United States--History--Sources.
Slavery--United States--History--Sources.
Slaves--America--Biography.
Slavery--America--History--Sources.
Muslims--America--History--Sources.

338. Burkett, Randall K., and Richard Newman eds. *Black Apostles: Afro-American Clergy Confront the Twentieth Century*. Boston: G. K. Hall, 1978. xvi, 283 p.

This work contains biographies of major Afro-American religious figures of the twentieth century. Included are Christians of the major denominations, individuals such as Father Divine, and Arnold J. Ford, and black rabbis. Each biography includes notes. An index is included.

SUBJECT(S): Afro-American clergy--Biography--Addresses, essays, lectures.

339. Leffall, Delores C., comp. *The Black Church: An Annotated Bibliography.* Washington, D.C.: Minority Research Center, 1973. 92 p. SERIES: Minority Group Series.

This bibliography on the black church is divided into several sections which cover: annotated books; unannotated books and unpublished documents; films; and articles in books and periodicals. An author index is included.

SUBJECT(S): Afro-American churches--Bibliography. Afro-Americans--Religion--Bibliography.

340. Lincoln, C. Eric. *The Black Muslims in America.* Rev. ed. Westport, CT: Greenwood Press, 1982. xxxi, 302 p. Foreword by Gordon W. Allport.

A history of the Black Muslims religious organization from its founding in Detroit in the 1930s.

SUBJECT(S): Black Muslims.

341. Rhoades, F. S. *Black Characters and References of the Holy Bible.* New York: Vantage Press, 1980. 94 p.

This work is designed to further knowledge of black characters, nations, and locales referred to in the Bible. The biblical citations are taken in chronological order, starting with the Old Testament, and continuing through the New Testament and the apostles. A list of biblical verses referring to blacks is included. Bibliographical notes, and a brief bibliography are also included.

SUBJECT(S): Blacks in the Bible.

342. Simpson, George Eaton. *Black Religions in the New World.* New York: Columbia University Press, 1978. 415 p.

This is a monumental and classic study of black religious belief and ritual in North, Central, and South America, and the Caribbean, from the beginning of the slave trade to the present. It explores the relation of black religion in the New World to African beliefs; traces the history of black-created cults, such as the Cuban Santeria and Haitian Vodun, which combine African and Christian elements; examines the role of black believers in the established Protestant and Roman Catholic churches, and contrasts them with black religious movements, such as Pentecostalism and the politically motivated Black Muslim, Rastafarian, and Garveyite cults. It is well documented, with copious bibliographic notes. An extensive bibliography, an index of names, and an index of subjects are included.

SUBJECT(S): Blacks--America--Religion.
Afro-Americans--Religion.
Cults--America.

343. Williams, Daniel T. *The Black Muslims in the United States: A Selected Bibliography*. Tuskegee, AL: Hollis Burke Frissell Library, Tuskegee Institute, 1964. 19 p.

An unannotated bibliography on Black Muslims in the United States. The preface contains an introductory overview on the topic. Also included is a reprint of the text of "The Muslim Program" outlining what the Muslims want and believe, as stated in *Muhammad Speaks*, January 17, 1964.

SUBJECT(S): Black Muslims--Bibliography.

344. Williams, Ethel L. *Biographical Dictionary of Negro Ministers*. 3rd ed. Boston: G.K. Hall, 1975. xix, 584 p.

This directory contains biographical information on over 1,400 black clergymen. The entries are arranged alphabetically. A geographical index and addresses of denominational headquarters are also included.

SUBJECT(S): Afro-American clergy--United States--Biography--Dictionaries.

345. Williams, Ethel L, and Clifton F. Brown, comps. *The Howard University Bibliography of African and Afro-American Religious Studies: With Locations in American Libraries*. Wilmington, DE: Scholarly Resources, 1977. xxi, 525 p.

This bibliography lists over 13,000 primary and secondary sources in the areas of African, Afro-Caribbean, and Afro-American religious studies. The entries are arranged in five major subject areas: African heritage, Christianity, and slavery; the black man and religious life in the Americas; the civil rights movement, 1954-1967; and the contemporary religious scene. The major churches, denominations, religious organizations are covered. Religious sects and smaller groups such as Black Jews, and Black Muslims are also covered. In addition, there are appendices which list major manuscript collections on black ministers, religious figures, and institutions; and citations providing biographical and autobiographical data on 6,000 black religious figures. Brief annotations are included only when the titles do not clearly indicate the contents of the works. Library location information is also included. An index is included.

SUBJECT(S): Afro-Americans--Religion--Bibliography-- Union lists.
Slavery--America--Bibliography--Union lists.
Afro-Americans--Civil rights--Bibliography-- Union lists.
Catalogs, Union--United States.
Africa--Religion--Bibliography--Union lists.

Speeches and Rhetoric

346. Boulware, Marcus Hanna. *The Oratory of Negro Leaders, 1900-1968*. Westport, CT: Negro Universities Press, 1969. Forward by Alex Haley. xxii, 312 p. SERIES: Contributions in Afro-American and African Studies, no. 1.

A history of Negro orators in the United States during the twentieth century. It acquaints the reader with black orators from 1900 to 1968; and attempts to describe the speech and persuasion techniques of politicians, preachers, labor leaders, lecturers, cultists, civil rights advocates, and militants. It is designed to demonstrate that effective public speaking is one of the gateways to leadership, and attempts to provide insight into the various types of speech making. It includes a an appendix of orators, a bibliography, a name index, and a subject index.

SUBJECT(S): Afro-American orators.
Afro-Americans--History--1877-1964.

347. Foner, Philip Sheldon, ed. and comp. *The Voice of Black America: Major Speeches by Negroes in the United States, 1797-1971*. New York: Simon and Schuster, 1972. xv, 1215 p.

This two-volume work contains the texts of speeches by black Americans and speeches by whites about blacks. The speeches are arranged by chronological period. Volume I covers 1797 to 1900. Volume II covers 1900 to 1973. Each address is prefaced by an introduction, which describes the context in which it was presented. An author-title-subject index is included. It contains much material not in print elsewhere.

SUBJECT(S): Afro-Americans--Addresses, essays, lectures.

348. Glenn, Robert W. *Black Rhetoric: A Guide to Afro-American Communication*. Metuchen, NJ: Scarecrow Press, 1976. x, 376 p.

A guide to the "content and communication of speeches and essays by Afro-Americans." The first of its four sections contains 40 bibliographies; the second lists 182 anthologies; the third section lists over 1,270 books and essays and is arranged by subject with references to the anthologies containing them. Section four lists over 2,400 speeches and essays arranged alphabetically by author, and a chronological index (1760-1973) of speeches and essays. An index to authors is included.

SUBJECT(S): Afro-Americans--Bibliography.

349. King, Anita, ed. and comp. *Quotations in Black*. Westport, CT: Greenwood Press, 1981. xviii, 344 p.

A compilation of over 1,100 quotations and proverbs by approximately 200 blacks. Many of the proverbs are of African or South American derivation. The quotes are listed by author in a chronological arrangement by date of birth, and a brief biographical sketch of each author is included. The proverbs are listed alphabetically by initial keyword, under region, country, and language. Author, and subject/keyword indexes are included.

SUBJECT(S): Quotations, Black.
Quotations, English--Africa, North.

350. McFarlin, Annjennette Sophie. *Black Congressional Reconstruction Orators and Their Orations, 1869-1879*. Metuchen, NJ: Scarecrow Press, 1976. ix, 333 p.

A survey of sixteen black Congressional reconstruction politicians, who served in the 41st to the 45th Congresses, 1869 to 1879. It provides brief biographical sketches and transcripts of their Congressional speeches. A brief bibliography accompany each entry, and some portraits of the congressman are included.

SUBJECT(S): United States. Congress--Biography.
Afro-Americans--Civil rights--Addresses, essays, lectures.
Afro-Americans--History--1863-1877--Sources.
Afro-Americans--Biography.

351. Scott, Robert Lee and Wayne Brockriede Wayne, comps. *The Rhetoric of Black Power*. Westport, CT: Greenwood Press, 1969. viii, 207 p.

The public statements of leaders such as Stokley Carmichael, Hubert Humphrey, and Martin Luther King, Jr. are analyzed with respect to the black power issue.

SUBJECT(S): Afro-Americans--Politics and suffrage.
Afro-Americans--Psychology.

Theater Arts

This section cites sources for plays, drama criticism, and to materials relating the history and criticism of Afro-American performance and involvement in the theatrical stage. Works dealing primarily with Afro-American participation in motion pictures, television, and other mass media are cited those sections.

352. Abramson, Doris E. *Negro Playwrights in the American Theater*. New York: Columbia University Press, 1969. xxii, 335 p.

This work examines representative black plays produced in the New York professional theater between 1925-1959, in Harlem, on Broadway, and off-Broadway theaters. Twenty plays, the work of seventeen playwrights, are considered. These plays are studied with the intention of assessing them as reflections of the persistent problems which blacks face in American society. The theaters in which the plays were produced are described, and the individual plays are analyzed for their reflection of the problems of blacks. The plays are discussed in groups according to decade. and each chapter contains a brief description of the Afro-American's position in the political-economic-social scene in the United States at the time. Conclusions at the end of each chapter show: the relationships between periods and plays; the development of black drama; and the continuing concern of black playwrights with the current and persistent problems. Bibliographical notes, and a bibliography are included. A name-title-subject index is also included.

SUBJECT(S): American Drama--Afro-American authors--history and criticism.
American drama--20th century--history and criticism.
Theatre--U.S.

353. Arata, Esther Spring, and Nicholas John Rotoli. *Black American Playwrights, 1800 to the Present*. Metuchen, NJ: Scarecrow Press, 1976. vii, 295 p.

An alphabetical list of 530 black playwrights. Included are citations to plays written by the playwrights and citations to criticism and reviews. Over 1,550 titles covering the eighteenth century to the present are cited. Awards received are also listed. A general bibliography and title index are included.

SUBJECT(S): American drama--Afro-American authors--Bibliography.
American drama--Afro-American authors--History and criticism--Bibliography.

354. Arata, Esther Spring. *More Black American Playwrights: A Bibliography*. Metuchen, NJ: Scarecrow Press, 1978. xiii, 321 p.

This work cites approximately 490 playwrights, 190 of which also appear in the 1976 edition of *Black American Playwrights, 1800 to the Present*. Information contained in the 1976 volume is not duplicated in this 1978 edition. The reader is referred to the 1976 edition for information already covered. As with the 1976 edition, this work includes an alphabetical listing of playwrights and their works, numerous criticisms and reviews, and a list of awards received. A general bibliography and title index are included.

SUBJECT(S): American drama--Afro-American authors-- History and criticism--Bibliography.
American drama--Afro-American authors--Bibliography.

355. Bogle, Donald. *Brown Sugar: Eighty Years of America's Black Female Superstars*. Designed by Joan Peckolick. New York: Harmony Books, 1980. 208 p.

This landmark study examines the personal and public lives of the most noted black females in all fields of entertainment from 1900 through the 1970s. Numerous photographs are included. Although highly readable and informative, thorough documentation is lacking. It is therefore difficult to identify, locate, and examine source documents. A brief bibliography and an index are included.

SUBJECT(S): Afro-American entertainers--Biography.
Women entertainers--United States--Biography.

356. Bullins, Ed, ed. *The New Lafayette Theater Presents: Plays with Aesthetic Comments by Six Black Playwrights*. Garden City, NY: Anchor Press/Doubleday, 1974. 301 p.

A collection of black revolutionary plays, and interviews with the playwrights.

SUBJECT(S): Black Dialectic Change and Experience.
Black Revolutionary Works.
American drama--Afro-American authors.

357. Bullins, Ed, comp. *New Plays from the Black Theatre: An Anthology*. New York: Bantam Books, 1969. xv, 304 p.

An anthology of eleven plays written by black playwrights. These new plays dramatize the black experience, and portray the life styles of blacks in the black community. The themes range from the revolutionary to the historical. An interview with Ed Bullins is included.

SUBJECT(S): American drama--Afro-American authors.
American drama--20th century.

358. Carter-Harrison, Paul, comp. *Kuntu Drama: Plays of the African Continuum.* New York: Grove Press, distributed by Random House, 1974. xiii, 352 p. SERIES: An Evergreen Book.

A collection of seven plays by black writers, assembled to reflect and objectify the African continuum--those concepts and beliefs identified in this work as common to African people the world over. It includes brief biographical notes on the playwrights, and an introduction by Paul Carter Harrison. Works by Leon Roomer, Aime Cesaire, Imamu Amiri Baraka, Adrienne Kennedy, Lennox Brown, Clay Ross, and Paul Carter Harrison are included.

SUBJECT(S): Drama--Black authors.

359. Craig, Evelyn Quinta. *Black Drama of the Federal Theatre Era: Beyond the Formal Horizons.* Amherst: University of Massachusetts Press, 1980. x, 239 p.

An analysis of the plays produced by black playwrights during the Federal Theater era. Biographical notes, a bibliography, and a name-title-subject index are included.

SUBJECT(S): American drama--Afro-American authors--History and criticism.
American drama--20th century--History and criticism.
Federal Theater Project.
Afro-American in Literature.

360. Haskins, James. *Black Theater in America.* New York: Thomas Crowell Junior Books, 1982. 184 p.

This work traces the story of the struggle of black performers in America in their quest for artistic freedom, while coping with such obstacles as slavery and segregation, from the pre-Civil War days to the present. It surveys drama, comedy, and music. Photographs, a selected bibliography, and a name-title index are included.

SUBJECT(S): Afro-American theater--History.

361. Hatch, James Vernon. *Black Image on the American Stage: A Bibliography of Plays and Musicals, 1770-1970.* New York: DBS Publications, 1970. xiii, 162 p.

The bibliography of plays and musical lists approximately 2,000 items. It attempts to include all major black American playwrights and their plays and musicals, as well as all important plays which contain black characters and themes. Entries are arranged alphabetically by author, within chronological periods, according to the decade in which the play was first produced. It includes lists of theses and dissertations, and books and bibliographies which were helpful in compiling this work. A title index and an author index are included.

SUBJECT(S): American drama--Afro-American authors-- Bibliography.

362. Hatch, James Vernon., and Omanii Abdullah. *Black Playwrights, 1823-1977: An Annotated Bibliography of Plays*. New York: Bowker, 1977. xxi, 319 p.

This annotated bibliography lists over 2,700 plays, by approximately 900 black authors. The work is intended for directors and producers in search of plays to meet their specific production requirements, and for scholars and researchers seeking historical data. While containing primarily stage plays, the bibliography also lists films, TV, and radio plays. The annotations include length, cast, place and date of production, and location sources. It also includes: bibliographies of books, anthologies, and dissertations on black theater; a list of taped interviews with theatrical personalities; awards given to black theater artists; and addresses of playwrights and agents. A title index is included.

SUBJECT(S): American drama--Afro-American authors--History and criticism--Bibliography.
American drama--Afro-American authors--Bibliography.
Drama--Black authors--Bibliography.

363. Hatch, James Vernon, ed. and comp. *Black Theater U.S.A.: Forty Five Plays by Black Americans, 1847-1974*. Ted Shine, consultant. New York: Free Press, 1974. x, 886 p.

An anthology of the full texts of forty-five plays covering several areas of black American life, including history, family life, and the lives of famous blacks. There are folk plays from the 1920s, and a section of plays by black women. Each is prefaced by an introduction. An author-title-subject index is included.

SUBJECT(S): American drama--Afro-American authors.

364. Hill, Errol, ed. *The Theater of Black Americans: A Collection of Critical Essays*. Englewood Cliffs, NJ: Prentice-Hall, 1980. 2 vols. SERIES: Twentieth Century Views. SERIES: Spectrum Book.

A collection of critical essays on the emergence and development of black theater in the United States. It discusses black theater as an art and industry, as an expression of culture, as a source of livelihood for the artists and craftsmen, as a medium of instruction, and a purveyor of entertainment. Volume I includes a discussion on the historical origins, rituals, and aesthetics of black theater as well as on some of the more important plays and playwrights. The essays in Volume II focus on black theater companies such as the LaFayette Players, the American Negro Theater, the Negro Ensemble Company, and the National Black Theater. Several essays are devoted to discussions on black theater audiences and the critics of black theater.

SUBJECT(S): Afro-American Theater--Address, essays, lectures.
Afro-American Theater Companies.

365. Hughes, Langston, and Milton Meltzer. *Black Magic: A Pictorial History of the Negro in American Entertainment*. Englewood Cliffs, NJ: Prentice-Hall, 1967. 375 p.

A comprehensive pictorial history of Afro-Americans in virtually every field of entertainment from the slave era through the mid-1960s. Numerous photographs, text, and an excellent names-subject index are included.

SUBJECT(S): Afro-American actors.
Entertainers--United States.

366. Jones, Bessie and Bess Lomax Hawes. *Step It Down: Games, Plays, Songs, and Stories from the Afro-American Heritage*. New York: Harper and Row, 1972. xxi, 233p.

This work was the result of the observations of Ms. Bessie Jones, a Negro woman born in Dawson, Georgia, around the turn of the century; and of the Sea Island Singers. It presents a collection of the games, plays, songs, and stories Ms. Jones learned while growing up. These categories of activities are presented in separate sections, each of which is preceded by a general introduction which provides historical background, special techniques of dance or musicianship, and statements on the relative ease or difficulty of the games which follow. It includes a note to parents and teachers, annotations providing additional sources of historical data, and sources for investigating individual songs or games more intensively. It also includes a selected bibliography, and a game index.

SUBJECT(S): Play--party.
Singing games, American.
Afro-American songs.

367. Keyssar, Helene. *The Curtain and the Veil: Strategies in Black Drama*. New York: B. Franklin, 1981. xiii, 302 p. SERIES: American Cultural Heritage, no. 1.

This critique of black drama focuses on American born playwrights, and highlights particular works of these artists. The chapters include discussions of Willie Richardson's *The Broken Banjo*, and

The Chip Woman's Fortune; Langston Hughes' *Emperor of Haiti*; Theodore Ward's *Big White Frog*; Lorraine Hansberry's *A Raisin In the Sun*; Imamu Amiri Baraka's *Dutchman*; and Ed Bullins' *In the Wine Time*. Also included is a bibliography listing anthologies, books on general history and criticism, theses and dissertations, articles and essays, and over 200 playwrights and their plays. An author-title-subject index is included.

SUBJECT(S): American drama--Afro-American authors--History and criticism.
American drama--Afro-American authors--Bibliography.

368. Locke, Alain Le Roy, and Gregory Montgomery, eds. *Plays of Negro Life: A source Book of Native American Drama*. Decorations and illustrations by Aaron Douglas. Westport, CT: Negro University Press, 1970. 430 p.

This anthology contains an introduction by Alain Locke, notes on the plays and authors, a chronology of the black theater from the early 1800s to the late 1920s, and a bibliography of Negro drama. Twenty plays by black and white authors are included which illustrate the development of "Dramas of Negro Life.," Illustrations are included.

SUBJECT(S): Afro-Americans--Drama.
American Drama.

369. Mapp, Edward. *Directory of Blacks in the Performing Arts*. Metuchen, NJ: Scarecrow Press, 1978. xv, 428 p.

Contains biographical and career information for over 850 American, African, West Indian, and Canadian blacks in television, theater, film, music, and dance. Also included is a directory of organizations, a bibliography, and a classified index (by profession) of those listed in the directory.

SUBJECT(S): Blacks in the performing arts--Directories.
Performing arts--Directories.

370. Mitchell, Loften. *Black Drama: The Story of the American Negro in the Theatre*. New York: Hawthorn Books, 1967. 248 p.

This work includes twelve essays on the history of black theater, with a focus on New York. The great stars of the black theater are discussed in great detail. Illustrations and a name-subject index are included.

SUBJECT(S): Afro-Americans in literature.
Theater--United States.
Afro-Americans--Moral and social conditions.
Afro-American actors.

371. Mitchell, Loften. *Voices of The Black Theatre*. Clifton, NJ: J.T. White, 1975. ix, 238 p.

This work provides an intimate portrait of twentieth century black theater through the individual recollections of eight influential black artists and performers. The contributors include: Eddie Hunter, Reginal M. Andrews, Dick Campbell, Abram Hill, Paul Robeson, Frederick O'Neal, Vinnette Carroll, and Ruby Dee. It includes brief biographical information on each contributor and a name-subject index.

SUBJECT(S): Afro-Americans in literature.
Theater--United States.
Afro-Americans--Moral and Social conditions.
Afro-American actors.

372. Patterson, Lindsay, ed. and comp. *Anthology of the Afro-American in the Theatre: A Critical Approach*. Cornwells Heights, PA: Publishers Agency, 1978. iv, 306 p. SERIES: International Library of Afro-American Life and History.

This collection of articles provides a historical and critical overview of blacks in theater. Drama, musicals, playwrights, actors, films, dance, radio, and television are covered. Numerous photographs, and biographical sketches of the contributors are included. A brief bibliography, and an index are also included.

SUBJECT(S): Afro-Americans in the performing arts.
Afro-American actors and actresses.
Afro-Americans--Social conditions.

373. Primus, Marc, ed. *Black Theatre: A Resource Directory*. New York: The Black Theatre Alliance, 1973, 28 p.

This directory is divided into four sections. The first lists over 150 black theater groups, mostly non-profit and professional. Section two list over fifty black directors and their addresses. Technicians and administrators are listed in section three. Section four lists over 200 playwrights and their works published since 1969 to 1973. Though dated, this work remains a useful source for students of black theater.

SUBJECT(S): Theater--United States--Directories.
American drama--Afro-American authors--Bibliography.

374. Reardon, William R., and Thomas D. Pawley, eds. *The Black Teacher and the Dramatic Arts; A Dialogue, Bibliography, and Anthology*. Westport, CT: Negro Universities Press, 1970. viii, 487 p. SERIES: Contributions in Afro-American and African Studies, no. 3.

A collection of material presented at a 1968 summer institute for black repertory theater at the University of California, Santa Barbara. Included are discussions on teaching theater to black students on the college and secondary school levels, and in the community. Also included are a bibliography of 1000 items written between 1908 and 1968; and an anthology of five plays, four of which are published here for the first time. Portraits are included.

SUBJECT(S): American drama--Afro-American authors.
College and school drama.
Afro-Americans in the performing arts--Bibliography.

375. Richardson, Willis, and Carter G. Woodson, eds. *Plays and Pageants from the Life of the Negroes.* Washington, D.C.: The Associated Publishers, Inc., 1930. 373 p. 373 p.

An excellent collection of simple and diverse plays by black authors for use in schools. Illustrations and brief biographical sketches of the writers are included.

SUBJECT(S): American drama--Afro-American authors.

376. Sampson, Henry T. *Blacks in Blackface: A Source Book on Early Black Musical Shows.* Metuchen, NJ: Scarecrow Press, 1980. x, 552 p.

This exceptionally important and useful work surveys the growth and development of the black musical theater from the mid-1800s to the late-1930s. Chapter I includes a chronology of black musical show productions. Other chapters are devoted to: the activities of some of the men who provided financial resources and built the theaters; the leading black show producers; the history of several famous black theaters; an extensive list, including synopses, of black shows produced from 1900 to 1940; and biographical data on many of the lead performers. Numerous photographs, poster reproductions, and tables are included. Appendix B is a fifty-six page list of black musical shows, not mentioned elsewhere in the book, arranged by date of production, and covering the years 1900 to 1940. A general index is included.

SUBJECT(S): Musical revue, comedy, etc.--United States.
Afro-American entertainers.

377. Seller, Maxine Schwartz, ed. *Ethnic Theatre in the United States.* Westport, CT: Greenwood Press, 1983. viii, 606 p.

A collection of scholarly essays on ethnic theater in the United States. Each article examines the amateur and professional history, as well as the social, educational, and political importance of ethnic theater to the community. The relationship of ethnic theater to the mainstream American theater is also discussed. The most significant individuals involved in ethnic theater are identified. Important primary and secondary literature is examined. Illustrations, bibliography, and an index are included.

SUBJECT(S): Ethnic theater--United States--Addresses, essays, lectures.

378. Tokson, Elliot H. *The Popular Image of the Black Man in English Drama, 1550-1688*. Boston: G.K. Hall, 1982. xii, 178 p. SERIES: Perspectives on the Black World.

This study describes the way English creative writers of the sixteenth and seventeenth centuries depicted black Africans introduced in their culture in the middle-1550s. It includes copious bibliographical notes, a bibliography, and an appendix listing black characters in plays, including those in which white characters were disguised as blacks. An index is included.

SUBJECT(S): English drama--Early modern and Elizabethan, 1500-1600-- History and criticism.
English drama--17th century--History and criticism.
Africans in literature.
Blacks in literature.
Slavery and slaves in literature.
Race awareness in literature.

379. Wittke, Carl Frederick. *Tambo and Bones: A History of the American Minstrel Stage*. New York: Greenwood Press, 1968. ix, 269 p.

This important volume traces the development of the minstrel. The origins of Negro minstrelsy, early minstrel shows, the prosperity and decline of minstrelsy, the technique of the American minstrel show, and the careers and work of prominent minstrel performers are examined.

SUBJECT(S): Minstrel Shows.

380. Woll, Allen L. *Dictionary of the Black Theater on Broadway, off-Broadway, and Selected Theaters*. Westport, CT: Greenwood Press, 1983.

A unique reference source for black theater. It provides a brief history of black theater, from "A Trip to Coontown" (1898), to "Dreamgirls" (1981). One major section provides documentation on over 300 shows from 1898 to 1981. Another section provides biographical information on those involved in black theater during the period covered. The appendices contain a chronology, a discography, a bibliography, a name index, a play/film index, songs index, and notes on the contributors.

SUBJECT(S): Afro-American actors and actresses--Dictionaries.
Afro-American entertainers--Dictionaries.
Afro-American Theater Companies.
Afro-Americans--Drama.
Afro-Americans--in the performing arts-- Dictionaries.

LITERATURE

Literature - General Bibliographies

381. French, W.P., M.J. Fabre, and A. Singh, eds. *Afro-American Poetry and Drama, 1760-1975: A Guide to Information Sources*. Detroit: Gale Research Co., 1979. ix, 493 p. SERIES: American Literature, English Literature, and World Literatures in English, vol. 17. SERIES: Gale Information Guide Library.

This bibliography is divided into two major parts covering poetry, 1760-1975; and drama, 1850-1975. The poetry section lists general bibliographies, reference works, critical studies, and anthologies. Works by individual poets, most of whom were born in the United States, are arranged chronologically. Biographical and critical works for each poet are also cited. The drama section contains lists of major library resources, useful periodicals, general bibliographies, anthologies, and selected historical and critical studies. The main portion of the drama section consists of a list of works by individual playwrights, born and/or living primarily in the United States, and arranged alphabetically within chronological periods. Unpublished plays as well as biographical and critical works are cited for each playwright.

SUBJECT(S): American literature--Afro-American authors--Bibliography.
American poetry--Afro-American authors-- Bibliography.
American drama--Afro-American authors-- Bibliography.

382. Inge, M. Thomas, ed. *Black American Writers: Bibliographical Essays*. New York: St. Martin's Press, 1978. 2 vols.

Intended to provide "appraisal of the best biographical and critical writings about America's seminal black writers," this two-volume work contains separate essays on black writers, from the eighteenth century through 1978. An effort was made to include all major black writers. Volume I covers the earliest writers of the eighteenth century through the Harlem Renaissance, and includes Jupiter Hammon, Phillis Wheatley, Benjamin Banneker, Davis Walker, Frederick Douglass, Booker T. Washington, W.E.B. Dubois, William Wells Brown, Charles Waddell Chesnutt, Martin R. Delany, Paul Laurence Dunbar, Sutton E. Griggs, Frances Ellen Watkins Harper, Frank J. Webb, Arna W. Bontemps, Countee Cullen, James Weldon Johnson, Claude Mckay, Jean Toomer, and Langston Hughes. Volume I also includes a chapter on slave narratives. Volume II covers Richard Wright, Ralph Ellison, James Baldwin, and Amiri Baraka. The bibliographical essays are comprehensive and contain the following: citations to and critical appraisals of works by the authors; biographical and critical writings about the authors; manuscripts and special sourses for additional study; and overviews on the current state of scholarly recognition of the lives and careers of the authors. A name index is included with each volume.

SUBJECT(S): American literature--Afro-American authors--Bio-bibliography.

383. Perry, Margaret. *The Harlem Renaissance: An Annotated Bibliography and Commentary*. New York: Garland Pub., 1982. xxxix, 272 p. SERIES: Critical Studies on Black Life and Culture, vol. 2.

A comprehensive annotated bibliography of works by and about black writers of the Harlem Renaissance, written 1919 to 1980. An introduction provides a detailed overview of the Renaissance period from the early-1920s to the early-1930s. Entries are arranged alphabetically by author in the following categories: bibliographical and reference materials; literary histories; general studies; and studies of several authors, including books, articles, parts of books, and book and drama reviews. Sections devoted to studies of individual authors such as Arna Bontemps, Countee Cullen, and Sterling Brown, cite archival materials and reviews of the authors' works published during the period. Also cited are articles, parts of books, stories by minor writers, editorials, films, filmstrips, and records, anthologies, library and other special collections materials with detailed descriptions of holdings, and dissertations. The major sources consulted are also listed. An author index and a title index are included.

SUBJECT(S): Afro-American arts--New York (N.Y.)--Bibliography.
Harlem Renaissance--Bibliography.

384. Turner, Darwin T, comp. *Afro-American Writers*. New York: Appleton-Century-Crofts, Educational Division, 1970. xvii, 117 p. SERIES: Goldentree Bibliographies in Language and Literature.

A bibliographic guide to drama, fiction, and poetry by Afro-Americans for graduate and undergraduate students. Works on art, music, journalism, folklore, and literary history and criticism are also included. An author-title-subject index is also included.

SUBJECT(S): American literature--Afro-American authors--Bibliography.
Afro-Americans--History--Bibliography.

385. Whitlow, Roger. *Black American Literature: A Critical History with a 1,520 Title Bibliography of Works Written by and about Black Americans*. rev. ed. Chicago: Nelson-Hall, 1976, 1973. xv, 287 p.

This work contains an introductory essay, and critical essays on major literary figures and their works, from 1746 to 1973. The bibliography contains 1,520 entries citing folklore, poetry, fiction, drama, anthologies, literary criticism, bibliographies, and social and historical commentary, arranged alphabetically by author. An index is also included.

SUBJECT(S): American literature--Afro-American authors-- History and criticism.
American literature--Afro-American authors--Bibliography.
Afro-Americans--Bibliography.

Literature - General Anthologies

386. Baraka, Imamu Amiri, and Amina Baraka, eds. and comps. *Confirmation: An Anthology of African American Women*. New York: Quill, 1983. 418 p.

This literary anthology contains the works of some forty-nine African American women. Included are works by established authors such as Gwendolyn Brooks and Alice Walker, and works by new writers published here for the first time. Although most of the items are poems, a few short stories, plays, and critical works are also represented. Brief biographical notes on the authors are included.

SUBJECT(S): Afro-American women--Addresses, essays, lectures.
Afro-American women--Literary collections.
American literature--Afro-American authors.
American literature--Afro-American (women) authors.
American literature--Twentieth century.
American literature--Women authors.

387. Barksdale, Richard, and Kenneth Kinnamon, comps. *Black Writers of America: A Comprehensive Anthology*. New York: Macmillan, 1972. xxiii, 917 p.

A comprehensive anthology of Afro-American literature covering the eighteenth century to 1972. Selections from speeches, essays, letters, political pamphlets, histories, journals, plays, stories, and poetry are included. For each writer there is a brief biography and critique. An author-title is included.

SUBJECT(S): American literature--Afro-American authors.
American literature--Afro-American authors--Bibliography.
American literature--Afro-American authors--History and criticism--Bibliography.

388. Bell, Roseann P., Bettye J. Parker, and Beverly Guy-Sheftall, eds. *Sturdy Black Bridges: Visions of Black Women in Literature*. Garden City, NY: Anchor Press/Doubleday, 1979. xxxi, 422 p.

An important collection of exemplary works in black women's literature, some written expressly for this book. Included are critical essays, interviews, poetry, fiction, and drama. Useful bibliographies devoted to Afro-American, African, and Caribbean women writers are included. Illustrations are also included.

SUBJECT(S): Women, Black, in literature--Addresses, essays, lectures.
Women authors, Black--Addresses, essays, lectures.
Women, Black--Literary collections.

389. Brown, Sterling Allen, Arthur P. Davis, and Ulysses Lee, eds. *The Negro Caravan*. 1941. Reprint. New York: Arno Press, 1969. xviii, 1082 p. SERIES: The American Negro, His History and Literature. SERIES: Afro-American Culture Series.

This anthology provides a comprehensive collection of Afro-American literature to 1940. Short stories, novels, poetry, folk literature, drama, speeches, pamphlets, letters, biographies, and essays are included. An appendix contains a chronology linking the literature with the period. An author-title index is included.

SUBJECT(S): American literature--Afro-American authors.

390. Butcher, Philip, ed. *The Ethnic Image in Modern American Literature, 1900-1950*. Washington, D.C.: Howard University Press, 1985. 2 Vols.

This two-volume literary anthology contains more than 200 works of poetry, drama, fiction, and non-fiction which portray the realities and stereotypes of ethnic groups in the United States. Among the authors included are: Truman Capote, Edna Ferber, John Steinbeck, Stephen Vincent Benet, Eudora Welty, Hart Crane, Countee Cullen, James Michener, Edna St. Vincent Millay, Norman Mailer, Richard Wright, Zora Neale Hurston, and H.L. Mencken. A sequel to *The Minority Presence in American Literature, 1600-1900*.

SUBJECT(S): American literature.
Minorities--United States--Literary collections.

391. Butcher, Philip, ed. *The Minority Presence in American Literature, 1600 to 1900*. Washington, D.C.: Howard University Press, 1977. 2 vols.

A comprehensive anthology of literary writings by major American authors, 1600 to 1900, depicting the experiences of Indians, Blacks, Chinese, and other large minority groups in the Unites

States. The authors represented include: Benjamin Franklin, Phillis Wheatley, Ralph Waldo Emerson, Walt Whitman, Bret Harte, and Theodore Dreiser. See also sequal, *The Ethnic Image in Modern American Literature, 1900-1950*.

SUBJECT(S): American literature.
Minorities--United States--Literary collections.

392. Cunard, Nancy, comp. *Negro: An Anthology*. 1934. Reprint. Edited and abridged, with an introduction by Hugh Ford. New York: F. Ungar Pub. Co., 1970. xxxii, 464 p.

Originally published in 1934, this anthology contains the works of 150 black and white authors. Included are poetry, essays, articles, and biographies of blacks in the United States, the West Indies, South America, Europe, and Africa. Much of the material was written by well-known known writers, including Langston Hughes and Zora Neal Hurston. There are several photographs, maps, and drawings. There are no bibliographies or indexes.

SUBJECT(S): Afro-Americans--Collections.

393. Emanuel, James A., and Theodore L. Gross *Dark Symphony: Negro Literature in America*. New York: Free Press, 1968. 604 p.

An anthology of short stories, novel excerpts, poems, and essays by thirty-four major black writers. Black writing in the United States from Frederick Douglass to 1968 is covered, with an emphasis on twentieth century works. Introductions to the major periods of black literature, and biographical sketches with critical commentary on each author are included. An extensive classified bibliography and an index are also included.

SUBJECT(S): American literature--Afro-American authors.

394. Harper, Michael S., and Robert B. Stepto, eds. *Chant of Saints: A Gathering of Afro-American Literature, Art, and Scholarship*. Urbana: University of Illinois Press, 1979. xviii, 486 p.

This anthology contains carefully selected works by or about black Americans who have worked in the forefront of literary and artistic creation in a wide variety of fields. Included are selections of poetry, interviews with novelists, essays on prose, music, and cultural history, and art. This book is intended to serve as a yardstick by which to measure the evolution of Afro-American literature and culture, and as a commentary on developments in these areas since the appearance of Alain Locke's, *The New Negro* in 1925.

SUBJECT(S): American literature--Afro-American authors.
American literature--Afro-American authors--History and criticism--Addresses, essays, lectures.
Afro-American arts.

395. Huggins, Nathan Irvin, ed. *Voices from the Harlem Renaissance*. New York: Oxford University Press, 1976. 438 p.

This anthology attempts to establish the cultural and artistic context of the Harlem Renaissance, and to provide a broad range of the works characteristic of the period. The selected works represent most of the major writers, including Alain Locke, James Weldon Johnson, Langston Hughes, Zora Neale Hurston, and many others.

SUBJECT(S): Afro-Americans--Literary collections.
American literature--Afro-American authors.
Afro-American arts--New York (City).
American literature--20th century.
Arts, Modern--20th century--New York (N.Y.).
Harlem Renaissance.
Harlem (New York, N.Y.).

396. Neal, Larry, and Imamu Amiri Baraka, comps. *Black Fire: An Anthology of Afro-American Writing*. New York, Morrow, 1968. xviii, 670 p.

This anthology includes essays, poetry, fiction and drama. These artistic and political works express the tension within black America. The compilers re-examine western politics, social, and artistic values in a quest for answers to problems which have continued to haunt the black community. Illustrations, and biographical sketches of each writer are included.

SUBJECT(S): American literature--Afro-American authors.
American literature--20th century.

397. Patterson, Lindsay, ed. and comp. *An Introduction to Black Literature in America, from 1746 to the Present*. Cornwells Heights, PA: Publishers Agency, 1978. xvii, 302 p. SERIES: International Library of Afro-American Life and History.

An anthology of poetry, essays, narratives, speeches, work songs, ballads, and lyrics to blues songs written between 1746 and 1978. Items are arranged chronologically. Brief essays on Afro-American literature, a bibliography, and an index are included.

SUBJECT(S): American literature--Afro-American authors.
American literature--Afro-American authors-- History and criticism.

398. Robinson, William Henry, comp. *Nommo: An Anthology of Modern Black African and Black American Literature*. New York: Macmillan, 1972. xvi, 501 p.

This anthology covers works by American and African blacks written between 1952 and 1972. Essays, stories, novel excerpts, drama, poetry are included which illustrate African and Afro-American political and literary themes. Biographical sketches of the authors are included. A bibliography of Afro-American and African literature, and an author-title-subject index are also included.

SUBJECT(S): American literature--Afro-American authors.
African literature (English).
French literature--Black authors.

Literature - General Anthology Indexes

399. Kallenbach, Jessamine S., comp. *Index to Black American Literary Anthologies*. Sponsored by the Center of Educational Resources, Eastern Michigan University. Boston: G. K. Hall, 1979. xvi, 219 p. SERIES: Bibliographies and Guides in Black Studies.

A unique and highly useful aid in locating works published in literary anthologies. Section I is an alphabetical listing by author, providing birth and death dates, the genres in which the author wrote, and citations to the anthologies or collected works in which their titles are found. Section II cites works listed by title.

SUBJECT(S): American literature--Afro-American authors--Indexes.

Literature - General Surveys and Criticism

This section contains bibliographies and reference texts relating to criticism and critical surveys of literature in its several forms. Critical works dealing specifically with fiction, poetry, or theatrical plays are cited in the Literature - Fiction, Literature - Poetry, and Theater Arts - Literature and Performance sections, respectively. Critical works dealing with slave narratives as a literary form are also included here. Slave narrative collections and works dealing with slave narratives from a historical point of view are cited in the History - Slave Narratives section.

400. Baker, Houston A., Jr. *The Journey Back*: *Issues in Black Literature and Criticism*. Chicago: University of Chicago Press, 1980. xvii, 198 p.

An important study which suggests an interdisciplinary approach to black literature and literary criticism. It proposes a critical "journey back" to the "word" in its cultural context through utilizing concepts and methods drawn from a number of intellectual disciplines, including linguistics, psychology, and anthropology. From this perspective, the author presents an assessment of eighteenth century black writers, and an analysis of the autobiographical element in the narrative of Southern slaves. Specific treatment is given to the works of Richard Wright, Ralph Ellison, James Baldwin, Amiri Baraka, and Gwendolyn Brooks. An awarness of black literature is presupposed. Biographical notes and index are included.

SUBJECT(S): American literature--Afro-American authors--History and criticism.

401. Baker, Houston, A., Jr. *Singers of Daybreak*: *Studies in Black American Literature*. Washington, D.C.: Howard University Press, 1974. xi, 109 p.

A collection of essays dealing with manifestations of the black creative spirit, life renewal, and regeneration. Authors discussed include Gwendolyn Brooks, Paul Lawrence Dunbar, Ralph Ellison, George Cain, and Jean Toomer. An awareness of black literature is presupposed. Bibliographical notes and a selected bibliography of criticism are included.

SUBJECT(S): American literature--Afro-American authors--Addresses, essays, lectures.

402. Bigsby, C.W.E. *The Second Black Renaissance*: *Essays in Black Literature*. Westport, CT: Greenwood Press, 1980. vi, 332p. SERIES: Contributions in Afro-American and African Studies, no. 50.

Social trends of the past quarter-century have produced another generation of black writers whose work C.W.E. Bigsby refers to as the second black renaissance. These essays provide a critical tour through the literature of this second black renaissance, beginning with Richard Wright, Ralph Ellison, and James Baldwin. Other novelests of the 1950s and 1960s are also considered, including John A. Williams and William Melvin Kelley. The poetry and drama of this period are also dealt with at length. An analysis of the black autobiography as a literary form is presented, and the problem of language for black writers attempting to reconstruct an ambiguous past and to define an identity distinct from that offered by American society is addressed. Bibliographical notes, bibliography, and index are included.

SUBJECT(S): American literature--Afro-American authors--History and criticism.
American literature--20th century--History and criticism.

403. Evans, Mari, ed. *Black Women Writers (1950-1980): A Critical Evaluation*. Garden City, NY: Anchor Press/Doubleday, c1983. xxviii, 543 p.

A collection of critical essays on fifteen nationally recognized black women writers, including Maya Angelou, Toni Cade Bambara, Gwendolyn Books, Alice Childress, Lucille Clifton, Mari Evans, Nikki Giovanni, Gayl Jones, Audre Lorde, Paule Marshall, Toni Morrison, Carolyn Rodgers, Sonia Sanchez, Alice Walker, and Margaret Walker. For each there appears a statement by the writer prepared in response to a list of questions designed to elicit the way in which she viewed her Self and society, her motivation for writing, and something of her methodology; two critical essays by noted literary critics; and a brief bio-bibliography.

SUBJECT(S): American literature--Afro-American authors--History and criticism.
American literature--Women authors--History and criticism.
American literature--20th century--History and criticism.

404. Fisher, Dexter and Robert B. Stepto, eds. *Afro-American Literature: The Reconstruction of Instruction*. New York: Modern Language Association of America, 1979. viii, 256 p.

An important collection of essays which focus on critical issues pertinent to designing advanced or intermediate courses in Afro-American literature. Various critical approaches and course designs are discussed with an emphasis on what is literary as opposed to sociological or ideological. Among the contributors are Robert B. Stepto, Melvin Dixon, Henry-Louis Gates, Jr., Sherley Anne Williams, Robert Hemenway, and Robert G. O'Meally. An awareness of black literature is presupposed. Bibliographical notes are included.

SUBJECT(S): American literature--Afro-American authors-- History and criticism--Congresses.
American literature--Afro-American authors--Study and teaching (Higher)--Congresses.
Afro-Americans--Study and teaching (Higher)--Congresses.

405. Foster, Frances Smith. *Witnessing Slavery: The Development of Ante-bellum Slave Narratives*. Westport, CT: Greenwood Press, 1979. xi, 182 p. SERIES: Contributions in Afro-American and African Studies, no. 46.

A study of the forms of slave narratives and the social context and literary traditions within which they developed. The colonial period through 1865, and the post-bellum influence of slave narratives is covered. Bibliographical notes, a bibliography, and an index are included.

SUBJECT(S): American prose literature--Afro-American authors--History and criticism.
Slavery and slaves in literature.
Slaves--United States--Biography.
Autobiography.

406. Gates, Henry Louis, Jr., ed. *Black Literature and Literary Theory*. London; New York: Metheun, 1984. 350 p.

An important collection of essays on black literature and literary theory by noted black writers and critics. Among the contributing authors are Sunday Anozie, Anthony Appiah, Huston A. Baker, Jr., Kimberly W. Benston, Barbara Johnson, Robert B. Stepto, Mary Helen Washington, Susan Willis, and Wole Soyinka. An awareness of black literature is presupposed. Bibliographical notes and an index are included.

SUBJECT(S): Afro-American authors--History and criticism--Addresses, essays, lectures.
African fiction (English)--Black authors--History and criticism--Addresses, essays, lectures.
African fiction (English)--Black authors--History and criticism--Addresses, essays, lectures.
Caribbean fiction (English)--Black authors--History and criticism-- Addresses, essays, and lectures.
Literature--History and criticism--Theory, etc.--Addresses, essays, lectures
Criticism--Addresses, essays, lectures.

407. Harris, Trudier. *From Mammies to Militants: Domestics in Black American Literature*. Philadelphia: Temple University Press, 1982. xvi, 203 p.

A survey of the literature by black writers which portrays black women as domestics and maids who work for white women and their families. The works of several authors are covered, including Charles Chestnut, Kristin Hunter, Toni Morrison, Richard Wright, William Melvin Kelley, Alice Childress, John A. Williams, Douglas Turner Ward, Babara Woods, Ted Shine, and Ed Bullins. Bibliographical notes, a bibliography, and an index are included.

SUBJECT(S): American literature--Afro-American authors--History and criticism.
American literature--20th century--History and criticism.
Domestics in literature.
Afro-Americans in literature.
Women in literature.
Race relations in literature.

408. Margolies, Edward. *Native Sons: A Critical Study of Twentieth-Century Negro American Authors*. Philadelphia: Lippincott, 1968. 210 p.

A critical discussion of major themes in modern Afro-American literature. The works of William Attaway, Richard Wright, Chester Himes, James Baldwin, Ralph Ellison, Malcolm X, William Demby, and LeRoi Jones are analyzed. A bibliography and author-title-subject index are included.

SUBJECT(S): American literature--Afro-American authors--History and criticism.
American literature--20th century--History and criticism.

409. Perry, Margaret. *Silence to the Drums: A Survey of the Literature of the Harlem Renaissance*. Westport, CT: Greenwood Press, 1976. xv, 193 p. SERIES: Contributions in Afro-American and African Studies, no. 18.

An analysis of the literature of the Harlem Renaissance. Novels, short stories, poetry, and the people who produced them are discussed. A chronology lists major events, publications, and lynchings, between 1917 and 1934. A bibliography, a bibliography of bibliographies, and an author-title-subject index are also included.

SUBJECT(S): American literature--Afro-American authors--History and criticism.
American literature--20th century--History and criticism.

410. Popkin, Michael, ed. and comp. *Modern Black Writers*. New York: Ungar, 1978. xx, 519 p. SERIES: A Library of Literary Criticism.

This work contains critical essays on eighty black writers of fiction, drama, and poetry of the United States, Latin America, and the Caribbean. The essays reprinted here originally appeared in books and periodicals. The writers are arranged alphabetically with critical excerpts arranged chronologically after each writer's name. It also includes a list of authors by country, a list of authors as critics, a list of periodicals used, and a list of all works mentioned in the critical selections. An index is also included.

SUBJECT(S): Literature--Black authors--History and criticism--Addresses, essays, lectures.

411. Sekora, John, and Darwin T. Turner, eds. *The Art of Slave Narrative: Original Essays in Criticism and Theory*. Macomb, IL: Essays in Literature Office, Western Illinois University, 1982. 149 p.

This work contains essays, in criticism and theory, on the slave narrative as a literary form. Emphasizing the antebellum narrative, it reveals the sources and affiliations of the narrative in United States literary history as well as in Latin America and the Caribbean traditions. It also notes the value of the narrative to the work of Ralph Ellison, Ernest Gaines, James Baldwin, and other contemporary black writers. Its use to instructors and students is enhanced by the presence of an essay on the use of the slave narrative in the classroom, and a selected checklist of critical works on the slave narrative.

SUBJECT(S): Afro-American Authors--History and Criticism.
Afro-Americans in Literature.
Autobiography.
Narration (Rhetoric).
Slaves--Biography.
Slavery and Slaves in Literature.

412. Southgate, Robert L. *Black Plots & Black Characters: A Handbook for Afro-American Literature.* Syracuse, NY: Gaylord Professional Publications, 1979. 456 p.

This unique work contains plot summaries of selected plays and long poems written from the eighteenth century through 1979. It includes "A Short Companion for Afro-American Literature and History" which serves as a dictionary of writers, events, movements, organizations, etc., which have been important in the history of Afro-American literature. An author bibliography lists creative, biographical, and critical works. A general bibliography arranged by topic cites anthologies, autobiographies, bibliographies, civil rights materials, and other materials.

SUBJECT(S): American literature--Afro-American authors--Handbooks, manuals, etc.
Afro-Americans--Handbooks, manuals, etc.
American literature--Afro-American authors-- Bibliography.
Afro-Americans--Bibliography.
Afro-Americans--Biography.

413. Stepto, Robert B. *From Behind the Veil: A Study of Afro-American Narrative.* Urbana: University of Illinois Press, 1979. xv, 203 p.

A pioneering study of the Afro-American narrative. The author asserts that Afro-American culture has its store of canonical stories or pre-generic myths, the primary one being the quest for freedom and literacy. One initially finds these themes conspicuously displayed in the early slave narrative. The author shows how these pre-generic myths evolved into literary genre through an examination of the slave narrative, and the works of later black writers such as W.E.B. Du Bois, Richard Wright, and Ralph Ellison. Presupposes an awareness of the literature. A bibliography and an index are included.

SUBJECT(S): American prose literature--Afro-American authors--History and criticism.
Narration (Rhetoric).
Autobiography.
Afro-Americans in literature.

Literature - Fiction

414. Barthold, Bonnie J. *Black Time: Fiction of Africa, the Caribbean, and the United States.* New Haven, CT: Yale University Press, 1981. x, 209 p.

This important work provides historical background on black fiction, focusing specifically on the black experience of time. It considers the characteristic themes and forms in black fiction, and relates them to the writers' manipulation of time. Seven representative novels are dealt with in detail, including: *Arrow of God* by Chinua Achebe, *In the Castle of My Skin* by George Lamming, *Cane* by Jean Toomer, *Blood on the Forge* by William Attaway, *Song of Solomon* by Toni Morrison, *Season of Anomy* by Wole Soyinka, and *Why Are We so Blest* by Ayi Kwei Armah. A bibliography of works cited and an index are included.

SUBJECT(S): Fiction--Black authors--History and criticism.
African fiction (English)--Black authors--History and criticism.
Caribbean fiction (English)--Black authors--History and criticism.
American fiction--Afro-American authors--History and criticism.

415. Berzon, Judith R. *Neither White Nor Black: The Mulatto Character in American Fiction.* New York, NY: New York University Press, 1978. viii, 280 p.

This work identifies the patterns and themes of the mulatto character in fiction by white and black authors and seeks to distinguish cultural myths from historical and social reality. Bibliographical notes, a bibliography, and an index are included.

SUBJECT(S): American fiction--History and criticism.
Mulattoes in literature.

416. Bruck, Peter, ed. *The Afro-American Novel Since 1960.* Amsterdam: Gruener, 1982.

This collection of critical essays is intended to reconstruct the social history underlying the contemporary Afro-American novel as well as the history of criticism, in order to redirect attention to the ideological forces that have dominated and at times hampered the reception of black fiction. A chronological checklist of Afro-American fiction covering 1945 to 1980 is included.

SUBJECT(S): American fiction--Afro-American authors--History and criticism.
American fiction--20th century--History and criticism.

417. Christian, Barbara. *Black Women Novelists: The Development of a Tradition, 1892-1976*. Westport, CT: Greenwood Press, 1980. xiv, 275 p. SERIES: Contributions in Afro-American and African Studies, no. 52.

One of the few works providing a historical and critical treatment of works by black women novelists. Covering the period 1860 to 1960, it attempts to identify and examine the origins of the literary tradition created by black women novelists, and traces the development of stereotypical images imposed on black women and the impact those images had on their works. It also examines in detail the works of Paule Marshall, Toni Morrison, and Alice Walker. A bibliography and index are included.

SUBJECT(S): American fiction--Afro-American authors--History and criticism.
American fiction--Women authors--History and criticism.
American fiction--20th century--History and criticism.
Afro-American women in literature.

418. Davis, Thadious, Trudier Harris, eds. *Afro-American Fiction Writers After 1955*. Detroit, MI: Gale Research Co., 1984. xiii, 350 p. SERIES: Dictionary of Literary Biography.

This work contains lengthy bio-bibliographical essays on the life and work of forty-nine black writers of fiction. Materials are arranged in chronological order under each author. The authors were selected in an attempt to capture the trends, hopes, political aspirations, and cultural affirmations of blacks from 1955 through the early 1980s. Included are well-known novelists James Baldwin, Ernest Gaines, and Toni Morrison; writers of children's literature such as Virginia Hamilton, Kristin Hunter, and Sharon Bell Mathis; science fiction writers Octavia Butler, and Samuel Delaney; and many lesser known authors. An appendix includes an essay by Darwin T. Turner on Afro-American literary critics and a select bibliography further reading. An index and photos are included.

SUBJECT(S): American fiction--Afro-American authors--History and criticism.
American fiction--20th century--History and criticism.
Afro-American novelists--Biography--Dictionaries.
Novelists, American--20th century--Biography--Dictionaries.
American fiction--20th century--Bio-bibliography.

419. Fairbanks, Carol and Eugene A. Engeldinger. *Black American Fiction: A Bibliography*. Metuchen, NJ: Scarecrow Press, 1978. vii, 351 p.

A bibliography of twentieth century black fiction arranged alphabetically by author. Novels, short fiction, book reviews, biographies, and critiques are cited. A general bibliography on black American literature, is also included.

SUBJECT(S): American fiction--Afro-American authors--Bibliography.

420. Houston, Helen Ruth. *The Afro-American Novel, 1965-1975: A Descriptive Bibliography of Primary and Secondary Material*. Troy, NY: Whitston Pub. Co., 1977. viii, 214 p.

An annotated bibliography of novels by fifty-six Afro-American writers written since 1964. For each novelist, there is a biographical sketch; a chronological list of novels written between 1964 and 1975, with plot summaries, and in some cases a comment on the writer's techniques; a list of critical books and articles by and about the author, with annotations providing a summary of content; and citations to novel reviews, with a brief quote to indicate the tenor of the review, and, in some instances, a summary of review content. A bibliography of sources consulted, an index of novel titles and short story anthologies, and an author index are included.

SUBJECT(S): American fiction--Afro-American authors--Bio-bibliography.
American fiction--20th century-- History and criticism--Bibliography.

421. Lee, Robert A., ed. *Black Fiction: New Studies in the Afro-American Novel Since 1945*. London: Vision Press, 1980. 254 p. SERIES: Vision critical studies.

SUBJECT(S): American fiction--Afro-American authors-- History and criticism--Addresses, essays, lectures.
American fiction--20th century--History and criticism-- Addresses, essays, lectures.

422. Margolies, Edward, and David Bakish. *Afro-American Fiction, 1853-1976: A Guide to Information Sources*. Detroit: Gale Research Co., 1979. xviii, 161 p. SERIES: American Literature, English Literature, and World Literatures in English, vol. 25. SERIES: Gale Information Guide Library.

This guide to fiction contains a checklist of 723 novels; a bibliography of 98 short story collections; secondary sources on major authors, including biographical and critical studies; and a chapter of bibliographies and general studies. An appendix lists works, chronologically, written between 1853 and 1976. Author, title, and subject indexes are included.

SUBJECT(S): American fiction--Afro-American authors--Bibliography.

423. Stadler, Prettyman Quandra, ed. *A Collection of Contemporary Black Fiction*. Washington, D.C.: Howard University Press, 198?

An anthology of short stories by seventeen outstanding contemporary fiction writers, including Toni Cade Bambara, Darrell Grey, Albert Murray, Louise Meriwether, Deloris Harrison, and LeRoi Jones (Amiri Baraka).

SUBJECT(S): American fiction--Afro-American authors.

424. Whiteman, Maxwell. *A Century of Fiction by American Negroes, 1853-1952: A Descriptive Bibliography*. Philadelphia, 1955. 64 p.

A comprehensive, annotated bibliography of fiction by Afro-Americans authors, intended and to serve as a "guide for teachers and students of American literature." Entries are arranged alphabetically by author. An introductory essay on Afro-American bibliography is included. A chronology of Afro-American literature is also included.

SUBJECT(S): American fiction--Afro-American authors--Bibliography.

Literature - Poetry

425. Chapman, Dorothy H. *Index to Black Poetry*. Boston: G. K. Hall, 1974. xxii, 541 p.

This highly useful index provides a comprehensive reference to black poems and poets through 1974. Poetry by and about blacks is indexed by title, first-line, author, and subject. Thirty-three anthologies and ninety-four books and pamphlets are indexed.

SUBJECT(S): American poetry--Afro-American authors--Indexes.

426. Deodene, Frank, and William P. French. *Black American Poetry Since 1944: A Preliminary Checklist*. Chatham, NJ: Chatham Bookseller, 1971. 41 p.

A checklist of first editions of all separately published books and pamphlets of poetry by Afro-American authors published between 1944 and 1971. A few anthologies are also listed.

SUBJECT(S): American poetry--Afro-American authors--Bibliography. American poetry--20th century--Bibliography.

427. Hughes, Langston, and Arna Bontemps. *The Poetry of the Negro, 1746-1949: An Anthology*. Garden City, NY: Doubleday, 1949. xviii, 429 p.

This anthology focuses primarily on poetry by blacks, but also includes some poetry by whites about blacks. The works are arranged chronologically by author, from the eighteenth century through 1970. Biographical notes, an author index, and a first line index are included.

SUBJECT(S): American poetry--Afro-American authors. Afro-American race--Poetry.

428. King, Woodie Jr., comp. *The Forerunners: Black Poets in America*. Introduction by Addison Gayle, Jr. Washington, D.C.: Howard University Press, 1975. xxix, 127 p.

This anthology contains poetry by Samuel Allen, Russell Atkins, Arna Bontemps, Gwendolyn Brooks, Sterling A. Brown, Margaret Burroughs, Margaret Danner, Frank Marshall Davis, Owen Dodson, Robert Hayden, Lance Jeffers, Oliver la Grone, Naomi Long Madgett, Dudley Randall, Margaret Walker, and Jay Wright.

SUBJECT(S): American poetry--Afro-American authors. American poetry--20th century.

429. Stetson, Erlene. ed. *Black Sister: Poetry by Black American Women, 1746-1980*. Bloomington, IN: Indiana University Press, 1981. xxiv, 312 p.

An anthology of the works of fifty-eight, representative, black women poets, writing between 1746 and 1980. An introduction attempts to place the poets within a theoretical framework to reveal a coherent and unified literary tradition which has gone virtually unnoticed by literary critics. The collection is divided into two sections: eighteenth and nineteenth centuries (1746-1899) and the twentieth century (1900-1980). Each of these sections is prefaced by introductory essays, which discuss issues unique to each time period, and distinguish the poets from earlier and later periods. It includes a bibliography of poetry anthologies, critical books and articles, and the published works of selected poets.

SUBJECT(S): American Poetry--Afro-American Authors. American Poetry--Women Authors.

430. Wagner, Jean. *Black Poets of the United States: From Paul Laurence Dunbar to Langston Hughes*. Translated by Kenneth Douglas. Urbana: University of Illinois Press, 1973. xxiii, 561 p. SERIES: An Illini Book.

An analysis of the major black poets of the late-nineteenth and twentieth centuries. Important themes and trends, and the lives of the poets are discussed. An introductory section describes black literature in the antebellum South, and the literary styles that later arose from that period. An appendix contains an extensive bibliography.

SUBJECT(S): American literature--Afro-American authors--History and criticism.
Afro-Americans in literature.

Literature for Children and Youths

This section cites bibliographies and reviews of literature appropriate for children and adolescents. Works which appraise this literature are also included.

431. Jackson, Miles M., comp. and ed. *A Bibliography of Negro History and Culture for Young Readers*. With assistance from Mary W. Cleaves and Alma L. Gray. Pittsburgh: Published for Atlanta University by the University of Pittsburgh Press, 1968.

This bibliography cites works for young readers ranging from pre-school through high school. The work is divided into two parts, one covering elementary school and the other covering secondary school literature. Entries are coded for elementary, junior high, and high school readers. All fields of literature are covered including: fiction, the social sciences, pure and applied sciences, arts, drama, poetry, essays, history, and biography. Reference books, magazines and newspapers, audiovisual materials, phonograph records, films and filmstrips, pictures and picture books are also cited. A title-subject and author indexes are included.

SUBJECT(S): Afro-Amercans--Juvenile literature--Bibliography.
Afro-Americans--Bibliography.

432. MacCann, Donnarae and Gloria Woodard, eds. *The Black American in Books for Children: Readings in Racism*. Metuchen, NJ: Scarecrow Press, 1972. 223 p.

This is a collection of critical essays by advocates of a nonracist presentation of characters in children's literature. Criteria for an acceptable presentation of black people are discussed. Some of the articles assess racism in Newberry prize winning, and other noted books for children. A new edition of this work is scheduled for release in the summer of 1985.

SUBJECT(S): Children's literature, American--Addresses, essays, lectures, etc.
Afro-Americans in literature--Addresses, essays, lectures, etc.
Pubishers and publishing--United States--Address, essays, lectures, etc.

433. Mills, Joyce White, ed. *The Black World in Literature for Children: A Bibliography of Print and Non-Print Materials.* Atlanta: Atlanta University, School of Library Service, 1975.

This annotated bibliography lists books, cassettes, records, and posters for children ages 3-13. The items are arranged by subject, and works falling in the categories of folklore, literature, art, biography, history, sociology, fiction and non-fiction are included.

SUBJECT(S): Afro-Americans--Juvenile literature--Bibliography.
Africa--Juvenile literature--Bibliography.

434. Stanford, Barbara Dodds and Karima Amin. *Black Literature for High School Students.* Urbana, IL: National Council of Teachers of English, 1978. xi, 273 p.

This guide to black literature for high school students contains suggestions on teaching black literature and history in high schools, numerous reviews of individual works, and numerous bibliographies. Though its organization may be a bit confusing, and its wide-ranging contents not well integrated, it provides a wealth of material for the high teacher and can be helpful to parents who would like to provide reading materials for their high school aged children. One chapter provides a historical survey of black writers from the pre-Civil War period to 1978, and includes brief biographical information on some of the major black authors along with descriptions of their works, and assessments of suitability for high school students. Another chapter includes reviews of junior novels by black authors which include plot summaries as well as assessments of suitability for high school students; brief summaries of six short stories collections by black authors; and reviews of novels by white authors having black themes. Another chapter lists and discusses biographical and autobiographical works of historical and contemporary figures. The many separate bibliographies scattered throughout the work (some annotated) cover several topics or themes, including blacks on the American Frontier, sports, and sound recordings. Several chapters are devoted to classroom uses of black literature and contain curriculum outlines and suggested activities to aid the teacher in creating and broadening black literature courses. Also included is a directory of publishers. Author and title indexes are included.

SUBJECT(S): American literature--American authors--Study and Teaching (Secondary).
American literature--Afro-American authors--Bio-bibliography.

MASS MEDIA

Mass Media - General Sources

This section contains sources which cover several forms of mass media. Works devoted to Motion Pictures, Television, and Journalism are cited in those sections respectively. See also the Afro-American Librarianship section for additional sources on book publishers and books stores.

435. *Black List: The Concise and Comprehensive Reference Guide to Black Journalism, Radio, and Television, Educational and Cultural Organizations in the USA, Africa, and the Caribbean*. 2d ed. New York: Black List, 1975. 2 vols.

A two-volume directory listing black periodicals, newspapers, publishers, TV and radio stations, and individuals and groups in the visual and performing arts. Grouped according to media category, entries are arranged alphabetically by geographic location. Also included are statistics on blacks employed in the media industry, and a few articles on the subject. Volume I is devoted to the United States. Volume II covers Africa, the Caribbean, and Latin America. Published in 1975, this work tends to be dated, but remains a valuable source of information.

SUBJECT(S): Mass media--Directories.
Afro-Americans--Directories.
Blacks--Directories.
Afro-American universities and colleges--Directories.
Universities and colleges, Black--Directories.

436. Colle, Royal D. *The Negro Image and the Mass Media*. Ph.D. diss., Cornell University, 1967.

This disseration examines the depiction of blacks in mass media from the turn of the century to the mid-1960s, and the efforts of different organizations to effect changes in the images presented. Newspapers, magazines, film, radio, and television are covered. Published materials, news releases, policy statements, codes of performance, personal interviews, letters and other documents were utilized as research sources.

SUBJECT(S): Afro-Americans and mass media.

437. Hill, George H. *Black Media in America: A Resource Guide*. Boston: MA: G.K. Hall, 1984. 352 p. SERIES: (A Publication in Black Studies)

A comprehensive bibliography on black involvement in newspaper, magazine, and book publishing, radio and television broadcasting, and public relations and advertising. Included are citations on marketing, production, editorial publication, and consumer issues concerning each medium. Biographical sources for journalists and performers are also included. Books, dissertations, theses, journal articles, newspaper articles, and magazine articles are cited. Scholarly and popular articles are listed separately, and only the most historic, useful, and informative articles in the periodical section have been annotated. A general index, an index of radio stations, and an index of television statations are included.

SUBJECT(S): Afro-Americans and mass media--Bibliography.

438. Hill, George H. *Black Media, USA*. Chicago: Path Press, 1985. 163 p.

A collection of articles on black involvement in the media. Historical data on books, newspapers, magazines, radio, television, public relations, and advertising is included. Biographical sketches of outstanding communicators such as John H. Johnson, Earl Graves, Ed Lewis, Jack L. Cooper, Al Benson, Max Robinson, Moss H. Kendrix, LeRoy Jeffries, and Barbara Proctor are included. There are also articles on black book publishers, the National Association of Television and Radio Artists (NATRA), Howard University's WHUR Radio, and Atlanta's WERD (the first black-owned radio station). Blacks accredited by the Public Relations Society of America are also listed.

SUBJECT(S): Afro-Americans and mass media--Bibliography.

439. Joyce, Donald Franklin. *Gatekeepers of Black Culture: Black-Owned Book Publishing in the United States, 1917-1981*. Westport, CT: Greenwood Press, 1983. xiv, 249 p. SERIES: Contributions in Afro-American and African Studies, no. 70.

This well documented study provides a detailed examination of black book publishing. It traces the development of black publishing from its origins in the eighteenth and nineteenth centuries through its recent expansion and diversity. The many problems that have plagued black publishers are emphasized, such as lack of funds, administrative inexperience, and limited access to reviews in white journals. Appendices provide historical profiles of publishers, and a statistical analysis of black publishing. Graphs and tables are included. See also Mass Media - General Sources section. A bibliography, an author index, and a name-subject index are also included.

SUBJECT(S): Publishers and publishing--United States.
Book industries and trade--United States.
Afro-American business enterprises--United States.

Motion Pictures

This section cites materials relating primarily to Afro-American involvement in commercial motion pictures. Works dealing primarily with Afro-American involvement in television are cited within the Television section. Works dealing primarily with Afro-American involvement with the theatrical stage, both literary plays and performance, are cited in the Theater Arts - Literature and Performance section. Educational films and multimedia materials are cited under Education - Multimedia.

440. Bogle, Donald. *Toms, Coons, Mulattoes, Mammies, and Bucks: An Interpretive History of Blacks in American Films.* New York: Bantam Books, 1974, xiii, 364 p. SERIES: Bantam Book, B7695.

This history of blacks in films covers the 1910s through the 1960s. The roles played by black stars are analyzed and evaluated for their portrayal of blacks. Included are photo clips, and an index of people, titles, and subjects.

SUBJECT(S): Afro-Americans in motion pictures.
Moving-pictures--United States--History.

441. Cripps, Thomas. *Black Film as Genre.* Bloomington: Indiana University Press, 1978. viii, 184 p.

This work discusses the various genres of black films produced from the early-twentieth century. It contains an account of the growth of black films, an analysis of six major films, and a review of black film criticism. Also included are photo clips, a bibliography, a list of credits, a filmography, and a name-subject-title index.

SUBJECT(S): Afro-Americans in motion pictures.

442. Cripps, Thomas. *Slow Fade to Black: The Negro in American Film, 1900-1942.* New York: Oxford University Press, 1977. xi, 447 p.

A history of Afro-Americans in film, from the silent movies to 1942. Topics discussed include the impact of the *Birth of a Nation*, early black production companies, and the political aspects of cinema production. It includes photographs from films, biographical footnotes, and an author-title-subject index.

SUBJECT(S): Afro-Americans in the motion picture industry.

443. Cyr, Helen W. *A Filmography of the Third World: An Annotated List of 16mm Films.* Metuchen, NJ: Scarecrow Press, 1976. viii, 319 p.

This annotated list of 16mm films cites both fiction and nonfiction films. In the North American section are films by Afro-Americans, Latinos, and Native Americans. Also included are lists of film distributors, directors, cinematographers, scenarists, and composers. A title index is included.

SUBJECT(S): Underdeveloped areas--Film catalogs.
Underdeveloped areas--Social conditions--Film catalogs.

444. Hyatt, Marshall, ed. and comp. *The Afro-American Cinematic Experience: An Annotated Bibliography and Filmography.* Wilmington, DL: Scholarly Resources Inc., 1983. x, 260 p.

This valuable reference and guide covers the portrayal and participation of blacks in films from D.W. Griffith's "Birth of a Nation" to Louis Gossett's performance in "An Officer and a Gentleman." Divided into two parts, the first section is an annotated bibliography of nearly 1,000 popular and scholarly sources, including books, articles, editorials, and film reviews. An index providing access to entries on particular individuals, films, and topics is included for the bibliography. The second section consists of a filmography listing works of interest to students of Afro-American history. Over fifty films of special relevance are cited, with information on casts, plots, and portrayal of the black image. The filmography also includes a list of approximately 1,200 other films listed by categories such as race relations, leading roles, and stereotyped roles.

SUBJECT(S): Afro-Americans in motion pictures--Bibliography.
Afro-American in the motion picture industry--Bibliography.
Afro-American actors and actresses--Bibliography.
Afro-Americans in motion pictures--Catalogs.

445. Klotman, Phyllis Rauch. *Frame by Frame: A Black Filmography.* Bloomington, IN: Indiana University Press, 1979. xvii, 700 p.

This film catalog covers over 3,000 film that have black themes, subject matter, substantial black participation by black writers, actors, producers, directors, musicians, animators, and consultants. Afro-Latins, Afro-Caribbeans, and black Africans are also included. Entries are arranged alphabetically by film title, and include extensive information on the films, including a plot summary. An appendix provides the names, adresses, and phone numbers of motion picture companies mention in the work. There are black performer and director indexes which list their film titles.

SUBJECT(S): Afro-Americans in the motion picture industry--Dictionaries.
Afro-American actors and actresses--Dictionaries.
Moving-pictures--United States--Catalogs.

446. Leab, Daniel J. *From Sambo to Superspade: The Black Experience in Motion Pictures*. Boston: Houghton Mifflin, 1975. viii, 301 p.

A history of Afro-Americans in films, from the earliest silent films through the 1970s. Landmark films, such as *Birth of a Nation*, are discussed in detail. Major actors and actresses and the images they present are also discussed. Several still photographs, notes, a bibliography, and an author-title-subject index are included.

SUBJECT(S): Blacks in moving-pictures.

447. Null, Gary. *Black Hollywood: The Negro in Motion Pictures*. Secaucus, NJ: Citadel Press, 1977. 254 p.

This work is primarily a pictorial collection of stills from black films. It begins with pre-World War I silent films and ends with films of the 1970s. Also included are collections of photos of white performers, appearing as blacks, and an author-title-subject index.

SUBJECT(S): Afro-Americans in motion pictures.

448. Oshana, Maryann. *Women of Color: A Filmography of Minority and Third World Women*. New York, NY: Garland Publishers, Inc., 1985. xii, 338 p. SERIES: Garland Reference Library of Social Science, vol. 173.

An annotated listing of feature films in English which portray a nonwhite female character essential to the plot. Each entry contains: title, studio, release date, running time, producer, director, screenplay, editor, music, photography, cast credits, and a plot synopsis focusing on the woman of color in the film. Director, actress, and film title indexes are included.

SUBJECT(S): Women in moving-pictures--Catalogs.
Minority women in motion pictures--Catalogs.
Developing countries in motion pictures--Catalogs.

449. *Patterson, Lindsay, comp. Black Films and Film-Makers: A Comprehensive Anthology from Stereotype to Superhero*. New York: Dodd, Mead, 1975. xviii, 298 p.

This anthology of twenty-nine essays, written between 1929 and 1973, covers the history of black cinematic activity, major personalities, films released, and economic and political aspects. A selected filmography, a bibliography, and an author-title-subject index are included.

SUBJECT(S): Blacks in moving-pictures--Addresses, essays, lectures.

450. Powers, Anne, ed. and comp. *Blacks in American Movies: A Selected Bibliography*. Metuchen, NJ: The Scarecrow Press, 1974. x, 157 p.

This bibliography emphasizes the social significance of black involvement in films. Serves primarily as a guide to periodical literature, but also cites books, dissertations, biographies, and autobiographies. Access to periodical citations is provided by subject, alphabetically by periodical title, and chronologically by date of article publication. A filmography covering the years 1904 to 1930 lists films chronologically by date, then alphabetically by production company. An author-subject index is included.

SUBJECT(S): Afro-Americans in the moving-picture industry--Bibliography.

451. Sampson, Henry T. *Blacks in Black and White: A Source Book on Black Films*. Metuchen, NJ: Scarecrow Press, 1977. x, 333 p.

A comprehensive historical survey of independently produced all-black films made between 1904 and 1950. It includes chapters on various film companies, synopses of films, and biographies of major stars. Appendices list all-black films produced by independent film makers, 1904-1950; provide a partial list of companies producing black films, 1910-1950; and list film credits for featured players in films, 1910-1950. Illustrations and an author-title-subject index are also included.

SUBJECT(S): Afro-Americans in motion pictures.

452. Sharp, Saundra. *Directory of Black Film/TV Technicians and Artists, West Coast*. Los Angeles: Togetherness Productions, 1980. 310 p.

This directory list around 500 black professional craftspersons working in the film and television industry in Los Angeles, San Francisco, and Seattle. Arranged by several categories, including producers, writers, directors, animators, camera operators, editors, librarians, etc. Brief information is given for individuals, including address, education or training, industry references, and credits and awards. An alphabetical index, a specific categories index, and a general index are included.

SUBJECT(S): Afro-Americans in the motion picture industry--California--Directories.

Television

This section cites materials relating primarily to black participatin in the television industry. The Mass Media - General, and Motion Pictures sections also cite items which included some coverage of television.

453. Berry, Gordon L., and Claudia Mitchell-Kernan, eds. *Television and the Socialization of the Minority Child.* New York: Academic Press, 1982. xvii, 289 p.

This is one of the few sources which deals with television and the minority child. It grew out of an invitational conference convened by the Center for Afro-American Studies at the University of California, Los Angeles. It contains research studies and conceptual papers that systematically examine the unique impact of television on Afro-American, American Indian, Asian American, and Hispanic children. The chapters are written by authorities in communications, education, linguistics, history, psychiatry, psychology, sociology, and the broadcasting industry. References to additional works appear with each chapter. An author index and a subject index are included.

SUBJECT(S): Television and children.
Minorities in television--United States.
Socialization.

454. Hill, George H. and Sylvia S. Hill, eds. *Black on Television: A Selectively Annotated Bibliography.* Metuchen, NJ: Scarecrow Press, 1985. xiv, 223 p.

This first book-length bibliography on black involvement in television cites more than 2,800 entries, and covers the years 1939 to 1984. It is divided into sections citing books, selected biographies, collective biographies, journal articles, and newspaper and magazine articles. Approximately 60 citations to books and dissertations include annotations; the remaining citations are unannotated. The newspaper and magazine articles section, which constitutes the bulk of the bibliography, is subdivided into a number of subject categories (not indicated in the table of contents) including: advertising, awards and honors, broadcasting, children and children's programs, management, music, organizations, actresses, actors, comedians, singers, youth, producers, directors and writers, comedy programs, documentary programs, drama programs, games programs, movie programs, music programs, news/talk programs, "Roots" programs, variety programs, protest/controvery, religious broadcasting, soap operas, sports, and women. Appendices list black-owned television stations, cable companies, and black Emmy Award winners. A program index and a subject-author index are included.

SUBJECT(S): Afro-Americans in the television industry--Bibliography.
Afro-Americans in the performing arts--Bibliography.

455. Hill, George H. *Ebony Images: Black Americans and Television*. Carson, CA: Daystar Publishing Company, 1985. 110 p.

An anthology of articles on black involvement in television. Emmy award winners, black-owned stations and cable facilities, and programs featuring black stars are listed. Black involvement in soap operas, sportscasting, news, cartoons, religious broadcasting, game shows, cable television, the roles of black children, and several historical shows such as "Roots" are covered. Negative images of blacks on television are also dealt with. Also included are biographical sketches of several prominent personalities such as Tony Brown, Bryant Gumbel, Charlene Hunter-Gault, and Ed Bradley.

SUBJECT(S): Afro-Americans in the television industry--History.
Afro-Americans in the performing arts.

456. Jackson, Anthony, ed. *Black Families and the Medium of Television*. Ann Arbor, MI: Bush Program in Child Development and Social Policy, University of Michigan, 1982. 108 p.

This collection of essays by scholars and specialists examines the television image of blacks, with a focus on the black family. Topics covered by the articles include: the importance of television images of black families; blacks and television ratings; contemporary research perspectives on black families; research perspectives on the portrayals of black families on television; the role of advocacy groups; and the role of government. The contributing authors include Anthony Jackson, Deborah Cherniss, James Comer, Lester Strong, Stanley Robertson, Andrew Billingsley, Gordon Berry, Ossie Davis, Pluria Marshall, and Lois Wright. Brief biographies on the authors are included. Bibliographical references are included with some of the articles.

457. Jackson, Harold. *From "Amos 'n' Andy" to " I Spy": A Chronology of Blacks in Prime Time Network Television Programming, 1950-1964*. Ph.D. diss., University of Michigan, 1982. 138 p.

This dissertation identifies and discusses the roles played by black actors and performers who appeared on weekly prime-time network series, 7:00 p.m. to 11:00 p.m., that premiered in the fall of each year, 1950 to 1964. It follows a chronological pattern of the development of characters and personalities on programs that featured blacks on a continuing basis. A number of programs featuring black performers not aired during prime time were also studied to illustrate the performers' television exposure. The research materials utilized included black publications, personal papers on television performers, producers and directors, and information provided by NBC, CBS, ABC, and the Alan DuMont television networks. An alphabetical listing of all black performers and a list of their television credits is included.

SUBJECT(S): Afro-Americans in the television industry--History.

458. MacDonald, J. Fred. *Blacks and White TV: Afro-Americans in Television Since 1948*. Chicago: Nelson-Hall, 1983. xvi, 288 p.

This is the first book-length work on the history of black participation in the television industry. It details the successes and disappointments of blacks working in television, providing names, performers, programs, and specific incidents. The inclusion of illustrations, a bibliography, and an index make this a useful source of reference for those interested in this field.

SUBJECT(S): Afro-Americans in the television industry--History.

459. Withey, Stephen B., and Ronald P Abeles, eds. *Television and Social Behavior: Beyond Violence and Children*. A Report of the Committee on Television and Social Behavior, Social Science Research Council. Hillsdale, NJ: L. Erlbaum Associates, 1980. x, 356 p.

This collection of essays deals with the short and long-term effects of television on children, and is intended to: 1) stimulate others toward a better understanding of television and social behavior, 2) to discuss problems involved in television research, and 3) suggest new directions research in television might take in addition to the traditional focus on violence and children. Of particular interest are three chapters which focus on television's portrayal of blacks: "Television and Afro-Americans: Past Legacy and Present Portrayals," by Gordon L. Berry, pp. 231-248; "Social Trace Contaminants: Subtle Indicators of Racism in T.V.," by Chester M. Pierce, pp. 249-257; and "Psychological Effects of Black Portrayals on Television," by Sherryl Brown Graves, pp. 259-289. The Berry and Graves articles include bibliographical references. An author index and a subject index are included.

SUBJECT(S): Television broadcasting--Social aspects--Addresses, essays, lectures.
Television--Psychological aspects--Addresses, essays, lectures.
Violence in television--Addresses, essays, lectures.

460. Woll, Allen L. and Randall M. Miller. *Ethnic and Racial Images in American Film and Television: A Bibliography*. New York, NY: Garland Publisher, Inc., 1985. 300 p.

This bibliography cites studies on the depiction of racial and ethnic minorities in motion pictures and on television. Afro-Americans and many other ethnic minorities are covered. Historical, sociological, psychological, and humanistic studies from 1940 to the present are included. There is a chapter for each ethnic or racial group, and each chapter contains an introductory essay. A general introduction is also included. Subject, name, film program, and television program indexes are included.

Journalism

See also Mass Media - General Sources section for additional items relating to periodicals and magazines as a form of the mass media.

461. Bullock, Penelope L. *The Afro-American Periodical Press, 1838-1909*. Baton Rouge, LA.: Louisiana State University Press, 1981. 330 p.

This works concentrates on the Afro-American periodical press as opposed to the newspaper press. It presents a narrative history of the beginnings and early development of periodical publishing by black Americans, discusses the individuals and the institutions responsible for the magazines, and attempts to identify the circumstances in American history and culture which helped to shape the black press. It is also intended to serve as a guide to these publications for researchers in black studies. It includes a selected list of periodicals, a chronology of periodicals providing the year and location in which each of the publications was first issued, and a geographical listing of periodicals. Bibliographical notes, a selected bibliography, and an author-title-subject index are also included.

SUBJECT(S): Afro-American periodicals--History.

462. Davis, Lenwood G. *A History of Journalism in the Black Community: A Preliminary Survey*. Monticello, IL: Council of Planning Librarians, 1975. 35 p. SERIES: Council of Planning Librarians. Exchange Bibliography, no. 862.

This bibliography lists material published from the mid-nineteenth century to 1975, dealing primarily with the newspaper press. Reference works, periodicals, books, articles, dissertations, theses, and black newspapers are cited. There are no indexes or annotations.

SUBJECT(S): Afro-American press--Bibliography.

463. Johnson, Ben and Mary Bullard-Johnson. *Who's What and Where: A Directory of America's Black Journalists*. Detroit, MI: Who's What and Where, 1985. xiv, 480 p.

Provides brief biographical information on over 2,500 print and broadcast minority journalists, including education, current and past positions held, current business address and telephone number, and honors. Although focusing primarily on Afro-Americans, some coverage is also given to Native American, Asian American, and Hispanic journalists. Introductory chapters provide self-help information for minority journalists, information for employers seeking to hire minority journalists, and a history of minority journalism. Appendices list black newspapers, radio stations, television stations, cable operations, magazines, and local black journalist organizations.

464. Penn, Irving Garland. *The Afro-American Press and Its Editors*. New York: Arno Press and the New York Times, 1969. 575 p. First published 1891. Reprint from a copy in the collection of Harvard College Library.

This nineteenth century work discusses Afro-American newspapers and magazines, from *Freedom's Journal* (1827) to 1891. A large portion of the work contains biographical sketches of early Afro-American journalists. Illustrations and an index are included.

SUBJECT(S): Afro-American press.
Afro-American newspapers.
Afro-American journalists.

465. Suggs, Henry Louis, ed. *The Black Press in the South, 1865-1979*. Westport, CT: Greenwood Press, 1983. xi, 468 p. SERIES: Contribution in Afro-American and African Studies, no. 74.

The first comprehensive study of the institution of the black press in the postbellum South. Included are: biographies of editors and the history of their newspapers; comparisons and contrasts of the Southern black newspapers, including analyses of the type of news covered, circulation, and the composition of the readership; evaluations of black editorial response to the important social and political issues of the day; and assessments of the press' relationship to other institutions of black life, including churches, civic and social organizations, and schools. A bibliography and an index are included.

SUBJECT(S): Afro-American press.
Afro-American newspapers.
Afro-American journalists.

EDUCATION and MULTIMEDIA

Education

466. Beckham, Berry, ed. *The Black Student's Guide to Colleges*. New York: Dutton, 1982. 336 p.

This guide contains profiles of approximately 110 predominately white as well as historically black colleges. A statistical summary appears at the beginning of each profile, giving data on total student population, number of black graduate and undergraduate students, number of black faculty, and the size of the library collection. The narrative descriptions contain both objective and subjective statements and assessments. This work should be quite helpful in identifying areas of student life which prospective black college students should explore in greater depth, but it is not intended nor recommended as the only basis for selecting one college over another.

SUBJECT(S): Afro-American universities and colleges--United States--Directories.

467. Chambers, Frederick, comp. *Black Higher Education in the United States: A Selected Bibliography on Negro Higher Education and Historically Black Colleges and Universities*. Westport, CT: Greenwood Press, 1978. xxiv, 268 p.

This bibliography on black higher education contains entries arranged in the following categories: doctoral dissertations, institutional histories, periodical literature, masters theses, selected books and autobiographies, biographies, reports, and government publications. Works published from the nineteenth century to 1978 are cited. An Index is included.

SUBJECT(S): Afro-Americans--Education (Higher)--Bibliography.

468. Davis, Lenwood G. *A Working Bibliography on Published Materials on Black Studies Programs in the United States*. Monticello, IL: Council of Planning Librarians, 1977. 31 p. SERIES: Council of Planning Librarians. Exchange Bibliography, no. 1213.

This unannotated bibliography lists materials on black studies in the United States, through 1976. Arranged by format, books, pamphlets, articles, dissertations, and selected reference works are cited. A section on current black studies collections is also included.

SUBJECT(S): Afro-Americans--Study and teaching--United States--Bibliography.

469. *Directory of African & Afro-American Studies in the United States*, Waltham, MA: African Studies Association.

Updated periodically, the sixth edition (1979) lists about 900 universities and colleges offering courses on African and Afro-American studies in the United States, Puerto Rico, and the Virgin Islands. Entries are grouped by state, then alphabetically by institution. The name and address of the department or unit sponsoring the program, department chairperson, a list of faculty, the degrees and courses offered, African languages taught, and a brief description of library facilities are included. Institutions offering only one or two related courses are listed separately in an appendix. When available, details regarding financial aid and related periodical publications of the institutions are also listed. The sixth edition is somewhat dated and incomplete, but remains the most comprehensive and reliable source of information on programs and courses offered in Afro-American studies. The seventh edition (1982), entitled *Directory of Third World Studies in the United States*, omits most of the entries relating to Afro-American Studies, and though more up-to-date, is not as useful as the sixth edition for those interested in Afro-American Studies. Continues: *Directory of African Studies in the United States*.

SUBJECT(S): Blacks--Africa--Study and teaching-- United States--Directories.
Afro-Americans--Study and teaching-- United States--Directories.
Africa--Study and teaching-- United States--Directories.
African studies--United States--Directories.
Afro-American studies--United States-- Directories.

470. *Directory of Special Programs for Minority Group Members*: *Career Information Services*, *Employment Skills Banks*, *Financial Aid Sources*. Garrett Park, MD: Garrett Park Press. 1976-.

Updated periodically, this directory provides information for students, counselors, prospective employers and employees, and program directors. There are three main sections: general employment and educational assistance programs; Federal programs; and college and university awards. Continues: *Directory of Special Programs for Minority Group Members*: *Career Information Services*, *Employment Skills Banks*, *Financial Aid*.

SUBJECT(S): Manpower policy--United States--Directories--Periodicals.
Minorities--Employment--United States--Directories--Periodicals.
Minorities--Scholarships, fellowships, etc.-- United States--Directories--Periodicals.

471. Fleming, Jacqueline. *Blacks in College*: *A comparative Study of Students' Success in Black and in White Institutions*. San Francisco: Jossey-Bass, 1984. SERIES: Josey-Bass Higher Education Series. SERIES: Jossey-Bass Social

and Behavioral Sciences Series.

This interesting study compares the academic success of black students attending predominately black and predominately white colleges in Northern and Southern states. Based on a cross section sample of approximately 3,000 freshman and senior students in eight predominately white and seven black colleges in Georgia, Texas, Mississippi, and Ohio. An index and bibliographical notes are included.

SUBJECT(S): Afro-American college students.

472. *Graduate and Professional School Opportunities for Minority Students*. Princeton, NJ: Educational Testing Service, 1969-.

This directory identifies and describes professional school opportunities in medicine, law, business, and other graduate programs. For each program, the following information is given: contact person, application fee requirements, standardized tests used for admissions, application deadline dates, total number of students, the number of minority students, and the number of minority faculty. It is periodically updated, and continues: *Graduate Study Opportunities for Minority Group Students*.

SUBJECT(S): Professional education--United States--Directories.
Universities and colleges--United States--Graduate work--Directories.
Minorities--Higher education--United States.

473. Gurin, Patricia, and Edgar Epps. *Black Consciousness, Identity, and Achievement: A Study of Students in Historically Black Colleges*. New York: Wiley, 1975. xiv, 545 p.

This important work reports the results of a series of studies conducted in several historically black colleges from 1964 to 1970. A bibliography and an index are included.

SUBJECT(S): Afro-American college students--United States.
Afro-American--Race identity.

474. Harber, Jean R., and Jane N. Beatty, eds. *Reading and the Black English-Speaking Child: An Annotated Bibliography*. Newark, DE: International Reading Association, 1978. 47 p. SERIES: International Reading Association. IRA Annotated Bibliography.

An annotated bibliography arranged according to the following subject catagories: the role of dialect, the influence of other factors on reading performance, teacher attitudes, blacks and standard testing methods, language and reading programs, strategies for change, and recommendations for future work. There is also a table showing the differences between standard English and black English.

SUBJECT(S): Reading--Bibliography.
Afro-Americans--Language--Bibliography.

475. Jones, Leon. *From Brown to Boston: Desegregation in Education, 1954-1974*. Metuchen, NJ: Scarecrow Press, 1979. 2 vols. xiii, 2175 p.

A comprehensive two-volume annotated bibliography of writings and legal cases on school desegregation. Volume one is divided into three sections containing lists of books and articles, arranged chronologically by year of publication. Volume II contains legal cases with annotations, and is also arranged chronologically.

SUBJECT(S): School integration--United States--Bibliography.
School integration--Law and legislation--United States--Bibliography.

476. Newby, James Edward. *Black authors and Education: An Annotated Bibliography of Books*. Washington: University Press of America, c1980. xiv, 103 p.

A bibliography of books in education by blacks, arranged alphabetically by author, and covering the period from the 1800s to 1979. Annotations provide clear and objective descriptions of works cited. Unfortunately, the lack of a subject index does not permit the quick identification of works by subfields in education. An author index and a title index are included.

SUBJECT(S): Afro-Americans--Education--Bibliography.
Afro-American authors--Bibliography.

477. *Plans for Progress. Directory of Predominately Negro Colleges and Universities in the United States of America* (four-year institutions only). Washington, 1969. 85 p.

Fifty-four predominately black schools are listed in this directory. For each, the address, officials, kind and number of degrees granted, enrollment number, a short description, and affiliations are given.

SUBJECT(S): Afro-American universities and colleges--United States-- Directories.

478. St. John, Nancy Hoyt, and Nancy Smith., comps. *Annotated Bibliography on School Racial Mix and the Self Concept, Aspirations, Academic Achievement, and Interracial Attitudes and Behavior of Negro Children*. Cambridge: MA: Cambridge School Integration Research, Graduate School of Education, Harvard University, 1966. 77 p. SERIES: Harvard University. Center for Research and Development on Educational Differences. Monograph, no. 3.

This annotated bibliography lists books, periodical articles, and dissertations. Entries are arranged according to the following subject areas: school racial mix, socio-economic variables, personality and self-concept, aspirations, and interracial attitudes. The materials cited were produced between 1954 and 1966.

SUBJECT(S): Segregation in education--United States--Bibliography.

479. Schlachter, Gail Ann *Directory of Financial Aids for Minorities, 1984-1985.* Santa Barbara, CA: ABC-Clio Information Services, 1984. 305 p.

This work identifies over 850 special resources set aside for blacks, Asians, Hispanics, Native Americans, Hawaiians, Eskimos, and Samoans, as well as minority groups in general. The work is divided into four sections featuring programs designed primarily or exclusively for minorities, a list of state sources of educational benefits, an annotated bibliography of directories listing general financial aids programs, and five indexes. Each entry contains information on: sponsoring organization, purpose of the program, eligibility requirements, remuneration, duration of the aid, special features and limitations, number of awards available, and application deadlines.

SUBJECT(S): Minorities--Scholarships, fellowships, etc.-- United States--Directories--Periodicals.

480. Swanson, Kathryn. *Affirmative Action and Preferential Admissions in Higher Education: An Annotated Bibliography.* Metuchen, NJ: Scarecrow Press, 1981. viii, 336 p.

This bibliography on affirmative action in higher education admissions is divided into three parts: law and the courts; academic and community response; and philosophical debate. Each section is prefaced by an analytical essay which provides an overview and defines the issues. Government publications, court cases, books, periodical and newspaper articles, and selected chapters within collected works are cited. A name index and a title index are included.

SUBJECT(S): Universities and colleges--United States--Admission--Bibliography.
Affirmative action programs--United States--Bibliography.
Discrimination in education--United States--Bibliography.

481. Thomas, Gail E., ed. *Black Students in Higher Education: Conditions and Experiences in the 1970s.* Westport, CT: Greenwood Press, 1981. xx, 405 p. SERIES: Contributions to the Study of Education, no. 1.

A comprehensive volume of twenty-eight essays which review

research findings and provide insights on three issues: Black access to higher education; the academic, social and psychological experiences of blacks in institutions of higher education; and the retention and completion status of black students in higher education. Most chapters include bibliographical references. An index is included.

SUBJECT(S): Afro-Americans--Higher education--Addresses, essays, lectures.

482. Tobin, McLean. *The Black Female Ph.D.: Education and Career Development*. Washington, D.C.: University Press of America, 1980. xii, 123 p.

This published doctoral dissertation contains a unique analysis of black women Ph.D.'s in predominately black colleges and universities. Includes statistical tables, a bibliography, and an index.

SUBJECT(S): Afro-American women--Education (Higher)
Doctor of philosophy degree--United States.
Afro-American women--Social conditions.
Afro-American women executives.
Discrimination in employment--United States.

483. Weinberg, Meyer. *The Education of Poor and Minority Children: A World Bibliography*. Westport, CT: Greenwood Press, 1981. 2 vols.

This unannotated bibliography cites 40,00 items on the education of poor and minority children, particularly as it is affected by social, economic, and political forces. A sizable number of entries are relevant to the education of the black child, and there are sections devoted to Afro-American studies, historically black colleges, the black women. A special effort was made to include publications sponsored by minority groups and written by minority authors. The materials are drawn from a broad range of sources covering the social sciences, law, history. education, and several other disciplines. One-forth of the entries relate to countries and areas outside of the United States. An author index is inlcuded.

SUBJECT(S): Educational equalization--United States--Bibliography.
Minorities--Education--United States--Bibliography.
Educational equalization--Bibliography.
Socially handicapped--Education-- Bibliography.

484. Weinberg, Meyer. *The Education of the Minority Child: A Comprehensive Bibliography of 10,000 Selected Entries*. Chicago: Integrated Education Associates, 1970. xii, 530 p.

This bibliography on the education of minority children focuses primarily on Afro-American children from the colonial period to the present. Books, articles, theses, and dissertations are arranged by subject. Although most of the items cited are on male youths and adults, important chapters on the black woman are also included. Over 500 periodicals and nearly 250 other bibliographies were used as sources for the compilation of this work. Annotations are not included. An author-title-subject index is also included.

SUBJECT(S): Minorities--Education--Bibliography.

485. Weinberg, Meyer. *Minority Students: A Research Appraisal*. Washington: U.S. Dept. of Health, Education, and Welfare, National Institute of Education, 1977. vi, 398 p.

In this important work, research efforts on the minority child are identified and discussed in depth. A comprehensive range of studies are examined in an effort to cover all major approaches and contrasting viewpoints, with special value attached to those studies which included first-hand examination of the ongoing reality of the classroom. Much of the book's content is directly relevant to the black child. An extensive bibliography, an index of persons cited, and a subject index are included.

SUBJECT(S): Minorities--Education--United States.

486. Weinberg, Meyer. *School Integration: A Comprehensive Classified Bibliography of 3,100 References*. Chicago: Integrated Education Associates, 1967. iv, 137 p.

This bibliography on school integration lists books, periodical articles, government hearings and reports on school integration. Areas covered include: the effects of integration on children; legal and governmental aspects; the relationships between integration, school, and work for minority students; and the relationship between integration and the civil rights movement. Also included are a chapter on integration in other countries, and a bibliography of bibliographies. An author index is also included.

SUBJECT(S): Segregation in education--Bibliography.

487. Weinberg, Meyer. *The Search for Quality Integrated Education: Policy and Research on Minority Students in School and College*. Westport, CT: Greenwood Press, 1983. xv, 354 p. SERIES: Contributions to the Study of Education, no. 7.

This work provides a comprehensive, balanced, and detailed analysis of hundreds of studies relating to race and intelligence; desegregation and academic achievement; education in black schools, the education of Mexican and Native Americans; and minority experiences in higher education. It also provides a summary of discriminatory practices within schools. In addition to providing a comprehensive review of the literature, it defines the scope and diversity of minority education studies to date. A bibliography and index are also included.

SUBJECT(S): School integration--United States.
Educational equalization--United States.
Education, Urban--United States.
Minorities--Education--United States.

488. Willie, Charles Vert. *School Desegregation Plans that Work*. Westport, CT: Greenwood Press, 1984. xi, 239 p. SERIES: Contributions to the Study of Education, no. 10.

This work presents a series of court-ordered and community initiated school desegregation plans that have been tested and proven in cities such as Atlanta, Boston, Milwaukee, and Seattle. It includes a review of the recent history of school desegregation planning as mandated or permitted by the courts and discusses local and state responsibilities in planning unitary school systems. The various plans and their implications are assessed, including how cities may prevent violence and foster a sense of community. Finally, there is an analysis of the association between white flight and the kind of plan adopted. Tables, maps, bibliography, and an index are included.

SUBJECT(S): School integration--United States--Case studies--Addresses, essays, lectures.
Discrimination in education--Law and legislation--United States--Address, essays, lectures.

Multimedia Sources

This section cites materials devoted exclusively to educational audiovisual aids or multimedia materials. Some audiovisual materials are also cited in items listed in the Literature for Children and Youth section.

489. Johnson, Harry Alleyn. *Multimedia Materials for Afro-American Studies: A Curriculum Orientation and Annotated Bibliography of Resources*. New York: R.R. Bowker Co., 1971. 353 p.

This annotated bibliography cites films, filmstrips, slides, kits, prints and graphics. For each, the title, creator, cost, length and content are given. In addition, there are essays on the teaching of Afro-American studies, a directory of producers and distributors, and a list of paperbound books. An author-title-subject index is included.

SUBJECT(S): Afro-Americans--Education--United States.
Afro-American studies--Audiovisual aids--Bibliography.

490. National Information Center for Educational Media. *Index to Black History & Studies (Multimedia)*. 2d ed. Los Angeles: National Information Center for Educational Media, University of Southern California, 1973. xi, 189 p.

Arranged by subject, this index provides information on non-print materials in Afro-American studies. It includes 16mm and 35mm films, filmstrips, 8mm film cartridges, overhead transparencies, audiotapes, records, and videotapes. For each item, the title, length, physical description, and intended audience are given. A directory of producers and distributors is also included. Entries are indexed by distributors' code and by title.

SUBJECT(S): Afro-Americans--Study and teaching--Audio-visual aids--Catalogs.

491. Sprecher, Daniel. *Guide to Films (16 mm) about Negroes*. Alexandria, VA: Serina Press, 1970. xxi, 737 p.

A list of films arranged alphabetically by title. All are black and white, unless otherwise noted. Includes running time, year of release, grade level (elementary to adult), and a description of content for each.

SUBJECT(S): Afro-Americans--Film catalogs.

492. Wynar, Lubomyr Roman, and Lois Buttlar. *Ethnic Film and Filmstrip Guide for Libraries and Media Centers: A Selective Filmography*. Littleton, CO: Libraries Unlimited, 1980. 277 p.

This work cites selected audiovisual resources recommended for collection development, curriculum development, reference services, and research. It covers forty-six ethnic groups with blacks represented on pp. 90-143. It also discusses problems of bibliographic control, selection, and evaluation. It includes a directory of producers and distributors, and a title index.

SUBJECT(S): Minorities--United States--Film catalogs.
United States--Ethnic relations--Film catalogs.

FAMILY AND RELATED STUDIES

Family

493. Bass, Barbara Ann, Gail Elizabeth Wyatt, Gloria Johnson Powell. *The Afro-American Family: Assessment, Treatment, and Research Issues*. New York: Grune & Stratton, 1982. xix, 364 p. SERIES: Seminars in Psychiatry.

This book contains selected lectures and research papers by members of a multidisciplinary mental health team. Its aim is to begin to meet the need for the training of mental health professionals involved in the practice of ethnopsychiatry and the delivery of mental health services to Afro-Americans. Bibliographical references and an index are included.

SUBJECT(S): Blacks--psychology.
Cross-Cultural Comparison.
Psychotherapy.
Socioeconomic Factors.

494. Davis, Lenwood G. *The Black Family in the United States: A Selected Bibliography of Annotated Books, Articles, and Dissertations on Black Families in America*. Westport, CT: Greenwood Press, 1978. xii, 132 p.

This bibliography lists books, articles, and dissertations covering the following subjects as related to the black family: the black family and slavery; religion; economics; education; and rural, urban, lower, and middle class blacks. There is an author index and a selective key word index.

SUBJECT(S): Afro-American families--Bibliography.

495. Davis, Lenwood G. *The Black Family in Urban Areas in the United States: A Bibliography of Published Works on the Black Family in Urban Areas in the United States*. 2d ed. Monticello, IL: Council of Planning Librarians, 1975. 84 p. SERIES: Council of Planning Librarians. Exchange Bibliography, nos. 808-809.

This bibliography cites materials on black families, primarily in New York City, Chicago, Philadelphia, Cleveland, Washington D.C., Los Angeles, Newark, and San Francisco. Arranged by form, reference works, books, government documents, and doctoral dissertations, are listed. There is also a chapter providing black population data by state. There are no indexes or annotations.

SUBJECT(S): Afro-American families--Bibliography.
Afro-American women--Bibliography.
Afro-Americans--Economic conditions--Bibliography.

496. Engram, Eleanor. *Science, Myth, Reality: The Black Family in One-Half Century of Research*. Westport, CT: Greenwood Press, 1982. xvii, 216 p. SERIES: Contributions in Afro-American and African Studies, no 64.

This work explores the "scientific" image of the black family as it is known by millions of black Americans. The author demonstrates that social stereotypes, racial myths, and crude folkloric conceptions are evident in even the most careful scientific studies. She finds that common fallacies lead to a failure to consider black people as human with simple human needs, and that there is a widespread failure to understand the complex African-American cultural background. The author proposes a new model for understanding black family life based on fundamental human needs and cultural realities. Each chapter concludes with bibliographical notes. An extensive bibliography and an index are also included.

SUBJECT(S): Afro-American families

497. Gutman, Herbert George. *The Black Family in Slavery and Freedom, 1750-1925*. 1st ed. New York: Pantheon Books, 1976. lxxviii, 664 p.

This important study analyzes and demonstrates the strength of the black family, from 1750 to 1925. It shows that slaves, in quarters away from their owners, lived a stable family life and possessed a culture which was autonomous from that of their owners. Charts and illustrations, tracing the history of particular families, are included. Notes on each chapter, a subject index, and an index of names and titles are also included.

SUBJECT(S): Afro-American families--History.
Afro-Americans--History.
Afro-Americans--Social conditions.

498. King, Lewis M. and Donna T. Davis. *Black Family Development and Mental Health*. Santa Barbara, CA: ABC-Clio, 1985. ca. 300 p.

This bibliography provides access to research findings on black family development and related mental health issues. There are annotations for over 400 important articles, and 500 related references for further exploration. In addition, the existing theoretical perspectives of the black family are critiqued, and an alternative view is presented which focuses on socio-psychological, political, and economic variables. Author and subject indexes are included.

SUBJECT(S): Afro-American families--Bibliography.

499. Klotman, Phyllis Rauch, and Wilmer H. Baatz, comps. *The Black Family and the Black Woman: A Bibliography.* New York: Arno Press, 1978. x, 231 p.

First published in 1972, this bibliography contains the holdings of the Indiana University Library on the black family and the black woman. Entries are organized chronologically by subject with some cross listing of titles. Monographs, children's books, periodicals, audiocassettes, and government documents are cited. An ERIC (Educational Resources Information Center) section is also included. Items are annotated when titles are not self-explanatory, or when only part of the work is relevant to the black family or woman.

SUBJECT(S): Indiana University, Bloomington. Libraries.
Afro-American families--Bibliography--Catalogs.
Afro-American women--Bibliography--Catalogs.

500. McGoldrick, Monica, John K. Pearce, and Joseph Giordano, eds. *Ethnicity and Family Therapy.* New York: Guilford Press, 1982. xxiii, 600 p. SERIES: The Guilford Family Therapy Series.

This work shows how ethnic identity shapes therapeutic relationships. It evaluates the influence of ethnicity on definitions of normality and pathology, and on attitudes toward problem solving, life stage transitions, and appropriate sex and family role behavior. It shows how fundamental differences in background may influence families' and clinicians' perceptions of therapy, and how ethnic variations may be used to formulate intervention strategies tailored to the specific needs of different groups. Afro-Americans and eighteen other ethnic groups are carefully profiled.

SUBJECT(S): Family Therapy.
Ethnic Groups--psychology.

501. Obudho, Constance E., ed. *Black Marriage and Family Therapy.* Westport: CT, Greenwood Press, 1981. xv, 269 p. SERIES: Contributions in Afro-American and African Studies, no. 72.

This collection of essays examines the marital and family lives of black Americans. It is divided into two parts. Part One contains a brief overview and a discussion of several studies and their findings. Topics included the expression of love among blacks, husband-wife relationships, women's feelings about working and being mothers and wives, styles and processes of parenthood, and family planning. Part Two points out the lack of research on black family therapy and stresses the need for developing and testing research techniques. Each chapter is concluded with bibliographical references.

Author and subject indexes are included.

SUBJECT(S): Afro-American families--Addresses, essays, lectures. Family psychotherapy--United States--Addresses, essays, lectures. Marriage--United States--Address, essays, lectures.

Children and Youths

502. Dunmore, Charlotte. *Black Children and Their Families: A Bibliography*. San Francisco: R and E Research Associates, 1976. ix, 103 p.

Books, bibliographies, periodical articles, films, dissertations, and library collections are contained in this bibliography. Most of the materials were produced after 1960. Adoption, family life, ghetto life, mental health, sex, and family planning are covered.

SUBJECT(S): Afro-American children--Bibliography.
Afro-American families--Bibliography.

503. Myers, Hector F., Phyllis G. Rana, and Marcia Harris, comps. *Black Child Development in America, 1927-1977: An Annotated Bibliography*. Westport, CT: Greenwood Press, 1979. xxii, 470 p.

This bibliography of 1,274 annotated entries "represents a comprehensive compilation and catalogue of the social science literature on the Black child in America." Material is arranged in five sections: language, physical, cognitive, personality, and social development. Only literature published in professional journals is listed. Author and subject indexes are included.

SUBJECT(S): Afro-American children--Bibliography.
Child development--United States--Bibliography.

504. Myers, Hector F., comp. *Research in Black Child Development: Doctoral Dissertation Abstracts, 1927-1979*. Westport, CT: Greenwood Press, 1982. xxi, 737 p.

A comprehensive compilation of doctoral dissertations on black child development in the United States completed between 1927 and 1979 in the major social sciences fields. The citations are organized into five areas of emphasis: language, physical, cognitive, personality, and social development. The citations were obtained from *Dissertations Abstracts International*. All abstracts were quoted directly from the original source. Author and subject indexes are included.

SUBJECT(S): Afro-American children--Abstracts. Dissertations, Academic--Abstracts.

Men and Women

This section contains works on the social and psychological aspects of Afro-American females and males and black male/female relationships. Works relating to men or women who are literary authors, musicians, scientists, etc., are cited in the those subject sections.

During the last several years much work has been done to gain greater bibliographical control over works relating to women, and a number of good reference works devoted to women have appeared. On the other hand, there are no reference books which focused on black men. Three reference text sources devoted to men are cited below. Works focusing on women and the family often provide data and views on the black male as well.

505. Cade, Toni, comp. *The Black Woman: An Anthology*. New York: New American Library, 1970. 256 p. SERIES: A Mentor Book.

This anthology includes poems, short stories, essays, and papers primarily devoted to the personal aspect of black women's lives. Biographical information on each author is included.

SUBJECT(S): Afro-American women--Addresses, essays, lectures.

506. Davis, Lenwood G. *The Black Woman in American Society: A Selected Annotated Bibliography*. Boston: G. K. Hall, 1975. xi, 159 p.

This annotated bibliography on black women lists books, articles, general reference works, periodicals, reports, pamphlets, speeches, and government documents. National organizations, newspapers, publishers, editors, elected officials, and libraries with major black history collections, are also listed. Statistics on black women are also provided. Author and subject indexes are included.

SUBJECT(S): Afro-American women--Bibliography.

507. Davis, Lenwood G. *Black Women in the Cities, 1872-1972: A Bibliography of Published Works on the Life and Achievements of Black Women in Cities in the United States*. Monticello, IL: Council of Planning Librarians, 1972. 53 p. SERIES: Council of Planning Librarians. Exchange Bibliography, no. 336.

This brief bibliography on black women in the cities lists books, articles, government documents, reports, pamphlets, speeches, and bibliographies published in the nineteenth and twentieth centuries. Black women's national organizations, and elected black women officials in each state are also listed.

SUBJECT(S): Afro-American women--Bibliography.

508. Harley, Sharon, and Rosalyn Terborg-Penn, eds. *The Afro-American Woman: Struggles and Images*. Port Washington, NY: National University Publications, 1978. xxiii, 137 p. SERIES: Series in American Studies.

This collection of essays examines the public roles of black women from the early-nineteenth to the mid-twentieth century. Black women as workers, educators, artists, and political activists; and the relation between black and white women in feminist activities are addressed. Bibliographical notes accompany each essay, and an author-title-subject index is included.

SUBJECT(S): Afro-American women--Addresses, essays, lectures.

509. Gary, Lawrence E., ed. *Black Men*. Beverly Hills, CA: Sage Publications, 1982. 295 p. SERIES: Sage Focus Editions. vol. 31.

This collection of eighteen, original articles is intended to provide a profile of the black male in the United States. Data is presented to dispel some of the myths and misconceptions about the black male, as well as to focus on his unique needs. There are bibliographical notes at the end of each article. There is no index.

SUBJECT(S): Afro-American men--Addresses, essays, lectures.

510. Hull, Gloria T, Patricia Bell Scott, and Barbara Smith, eds. *All the Women Are White, and All the Blacks Are Men, But Some of Us Are Brave: Black Women's Studies*. Old Westbury, NY: Feminist Press, 1982. xxxiv, 401 p.

This work contains essays on black women's studies written by feminists and scholars. It illuminates recent research and contains practical guidelines for crystallizing black women's studies. It includes a chapter of over one hundred pages devoted to bibliographies and bibliographic essays. It covers the following: Afro-women 1800-1910, poets, novels, playwrights, music composers, non-print materials, and additional references and resources. An index is included.

SUBJECT(S): Afro-American women--Addresses, essays, lectures.
Afro-American women--Study and teaching--Addresses, essays, lectures.

511. Jones, Jacqueline. *Labor of Love, Labor of Sorrow: Black Women, Work, and the Family from Slavery to the Present.* New York: Basic Books, 1985. xiii, 432 p.

SUBJECT(S): Afro-American women--Employment--History.
Afro-American women--History.
Afro-American families--History.

512. Lerner, Gerda. comp. *Black Women in White America: A Documentary History.* New York: Pantheon Books, 1972. xxxvi, 630 p.

This book gathers together a wide variety of documents, many previously unpublished, on the life and history of the black woman in the United States, from the slave era to the early 1970s. Slave narratives, personal testimonies, and excerpts from private and public letters are included. There are also "bibliographic notes," which evaluate information sources on black women; and a list of autobiographies and biographies of black women.

SUBJECT(S): Women, Afro-American--Collections.

513. Loewenberg, Bert James, and Ruth Bogin. *Black Women in Nineteenth-Century American Life: Their Words, Their Thoughts, Their Feelings.* University Park: Pennsylvania State University Press, 1976. xi, 355 p.

Materials taken from diaries, autobiographies, letters, and speeches provide a description of the lives, activities, and thoughts of twenty-four nineteenth century black women. These materials are placed into four groups according to theme: family relationships, religious activities, political and reformist movements, and educational information. A bibliography cites works on each of the twenty-four women and black women in general. An author-title-subject index is also included.

SUBJECT(S): Afro-American women--Biography.

514. Majors, Monroe Alphus. *Noted Negro Women, Their Triumphs and Activities.* 1893. Reprint. Freeport, NY: Books for Libraries Press, 1971. 365 p. SERIES: The Black Heritage Library Collection.

This work includes biographical sketches of noted nineteenth century black women.

SUBJECT(S): Afro-American women--Biography.
Women, Black--Biography.

515. Richardson, Marilyn. *Black Women and Religion: A Bibliography.* Boston, MA: G. K. Hall, 1980. xxiv, 139 p.

This annotated bibliography greatly facilitates access to information on the relationship of the black woman to the black church. Books, articles, musical compositions, works of art, films, and sound recordings are cited. There are sections which cover literature, music, art, and audiovisual media. Also cited are reference sources, theses, and dissertations. The appendix lists autobiographies and biographies. It also contains biographical sketches of a selected list of relatively unknown black women of achievement who were motivated in great part by religious concerns. An author-subject-title index is included.

SUBJECT(S): Afro-Americans--Religion--Bibliography. Afro-American women--Bibliography.

516. Roberts, J.R., comp. *Black Lesbians: An Annotated Bibliography.* Forward by Barbara Smith. Tallahassee, FL: Naiad Press, 1981.

A comprehensive, annotated bibliography of materials by or about black lesbians in the United States, from an ancient legend of black Amazons in what is now California, to present-day activism in the black, third world, and gay rights movements. An effort was made to include every reference available, ranging from substantive works to those which devote only a few pages, paragraphs, or sentences to black lesbianism. The bibliography is organized into seven sections: lives and lifestyles; oppression, resistance, and liberation; literature and criticism; music; periodicals; research, reference, and popular studies; and an addendum. Also included is an appendix of materials relating to the Norton Sound case. A subject-author index, and a directory of selected organizations are included.

SUBJECT(S): Afro-American lesbians--Abstracts.

517. Rodgers-Rose, La Frances, ed. *The Black Woman.* Beverly Hills: Sage Publications, 1980. 316 p. SERIES: Sage Focus Edition, no. 21.

This collection of essays addresses the personal and socio-political facets of the lives of black women. Biographical information on each contributor is provided.

SUBJECT(S): Afro-American women--Addresses, essays, lectures.

518. Sims, Janet L., comp. *The Progress of Afro-American Women: A Selected Bibliography and Resource Guide.* Westport, CT: Greenwood Press, 1980. xvi, 378 p.

A highly comprehensive bibliography of nineteenth and twentieth century sources pertaining to black women. Monographs, periodical and newspaper articles, masters theses, doctoral dissertations, and audiovisual materials are cited. Topics are covered include black women club movements; armed services and defense; the suffrage movement; women's rights and the feminist movement; the church; sports; community organizations; politics; law and law enforcement; and medicine. Many of the subject categories included have not appeared in previously published bibliographies. An index is included.

SUBJECT(S): Afro-American women--Bibliography.

519. Smith, Barbara, ed. *Home Girls: Black Feminist Anthology*. New York: Kitchen Table: Women of Color Press, 1983. 432 p.

This collection of lesbian-oriented poetry, fiction, essays, and interviews attempts to provide a definitive articulation of the black feminist/lesbian experience. The interview and conversation segments are unedited.

SUBJECT(S): Afro-American lesbians.
Afro-American women authors.

520. Staples, Robert. *Black Masculinity: The Black Male's Role in American Society*. San Francisco: Black Scholar Press, 1982. 181 p.

The first singly authored book examining the roles of the black male in the United States. Bibliographical notes providing a comprehensive survey of pertinent literature are included.

SUBJECT(S): Afro-American men.
Masculinity (Psychology).

521. Staples, Robert. *The Black Woman in America: Sex, Marriage, and the Family*. Chicago: Nelson-Hall Publishers, 1974. xv, 269 p. SERIES: Professional-Technical Series.

This work analyzes the personal aspects of black women's lives, including sexual attitudes and experience, prostitution, marriage and family life, and black women and the feminist movement. A bibliography and an author-title-subject index are included.

SUBJECT(S): Afro-American women.

522. Staples, Robert. *The World of Black Singles: Changing Patterns of Male/Female Relations*. Westport, CT: Greenwood Press, 1981. xxi, 259 p. SERIES: Contributions in Afro-American and African studies; no 57.

This study attemps to delineate the characteristics of black singles, their coping mechanisms for dealing with singlehood, and the their life styles. Also included are chapters on interracial dating and alternative life styles such as single parenthood, and gay and lesbians life styles. The study was based on data collected from 100 personal interviews conducted in the San Fancisco Bay area. Included are the questionnaire used and notes on methodology. Bibliographical notes, a bibliography, and an index are also included.

SUBJECT(S): Afro-American single people--California--San Francisco Bay area-- San Francisco Bay area--Case studies.
Afro-American single people.

523. Steady, Filomina Chioma, ed. *The Black Woman Cross-Culturally*. Cambridge, MA: Schenkman Pub. Co., 1981. ix, 645 p.

A pioneer collection of essays which attempts to provide a cross-cultural view of the black woman in Africa, the United States, the Caribbean, and South America. Most articles conclude with bibliographical notes. An extensive bibliography and biographical sketches of the contributors are included.

SUBJECT(S): Women, Black--Africa--Addresses, essays, lectures.
Women, Black--Caribbean Area--Addresses, essays, lectures.
Women, Black--Latin America--Addresses, essays, lectures.
Afro-American women--Addresses, essays, lectures.

524. Young, Glenell S. and Janet Sims-Wood, comps. *The Psychology and Mental Health of Afro-American Women: A Selected Bibliography*. Temple Hills, MD: Afro Resources, 1984. SERIES: Resources on Afro-American Women, no. 1.

525. Wares, Lydia Jean. *Dress of the African Woman in Slavery and Freedom: 1500 to 1935*. Ann Arbor, MI: University Microfilms International, 1983. 251 p.

One of the few works dealing with Afro-American clothing, this Ph.D. dissertation discusses the dress behavior patterns of the African American women, as they existed in slavery and freedom from 1500 to 1935. Emphasis is placed on the West African cultural patterns of dress, which were transmitted as a part of the African American cultural heritage to the United States. An extensive bibliography and a glossary of terms is included. Illustrations are poorly reproduced.

SUBJECT(S): Clothing.
African costume.
Afro-American costume.
Costume.

526. Wilkinson, Doris Y., and Ronald L. Taylor, comps. *The Black Male in America: Perspectives on His Status in Contemporary Society*. Chicago: Nelson-Hall, 1977. viii, 375 p.

An interdisciplinary collection of articles focusing on the social positions and role enactments of black males. The articles are grouped into four sections relating specifically to socialization; stigmatization; the issues of interracial mating; and roles and statuses in post-industrial society. An extensive bibliography cites empirical studies and literature by and about black males, in a variety of disciplines. An author and a subject index are included.

SUBJECT(S): Afro-American men.
Afro-Americans--Psychology.
Afro-American families.

527. Williams, Ora. *American Black Women in the Arts and Social Sciences: A Bibliographic Survey*. rev. and enl. ed. Metuchen, NJ: Scarecrow Press, 1978. xxi, 197 p.

This useful work lists books and periodical articles by or about black women in the arts and social sciences. A chronology of important dates for black women, bibliographies on individual authors, lists of black periodicals and publishers, illustrations, and a name index are included.

SUBJECT(S): Afro-American women--Bibliography.

Interracial Mating

For works dealing with mulattoes and miscegenation, see the section Race and Ethnic Relations - Mulattoes and Miscegenation.

528. Godon, Albert I. *Intermarriage: Interfaith, Interracial, Interethnic*. Boston: Beacon Press, 1964. xiii, 420 p.

A study based on a sample of 5,407 college students in 40 colleges and universities on attitudes toward intermarriage. Tables show the social distance scales with respect to blacks and other racial ethnic groups. One lengthy chapter is devoted to black/white marriages. Bibliographical notes and an index are included.

SUBJECT(S): Interracial marriage.
Miscegenation.
Race relations.

529. Henriques, Fernando. *Children of Conflict: A study of Interracial Sex and Marriage.* New York: Dutton, 1975. xiv, 196 p.

This study covers the United States, Britain, the Caribbean, and Africa, and provides a detailed sociological and historical analysis of the interracial sex and marriage. Photos, bibliographical notes, and an index are included.

SUBJECT(S): Interracial marriage.
Miscegenation.
Race relations.

530. Porterfield, Ernest. *Black and White Mixed Marriages.* Chicago: Nelson-Hall, 1978. xv, 189 p.

A systematic ethnographic description of 40 black/white families, focusing on intrafamilial relations, interactional patterns between families and their kin network, and relations with the larger society. Chapters are devoted to the incidence of black/white marriage, 1874 to 1964; motives of the partners; research methodology; dating, weddings, and marital relations and acceptance/rejection by kin; and relations with the larger community. Statistics on the incidence of black/white marriage are included, though incomplete and fragmentary. Tables, bibliographical notes, an author index, and a subject index are included.

SUBJECT(S): Interracial marriage--United States--Case studies.

531. Stuart, Irving R. and Lawrence Edwin. *Interracial Marriage: Expectations and Realities.* New York: Grossman Publishers, 1973. xiv, 335 p.

A collection of articles grouped into two sections: The first covers the psychodynamics of interracial marriage in the United States, including the emotional, social, and economic aspects. Attention is given to the family, children, couseling, interracial familites through adoption, and interracial dating. A useful review of the literature relating to black/white marriage empirical studies is included. The second group of articles covers comparative and cultural aspects of interracial marriage with a focus on Puerto Rico, Brazil, Trinidad, Cuba, and other geographical locations. Bibliographical references and an index are included.

SUBJECT(S): Interracial marriage.

532. Washington, Joseph R. Jr. *Marriage in Black and White.* Boston: Beacon Press, 1970. 358 p.

This historical study covers the miscegenation laws forbidding marriage and cohabitation and the co-existent non-enforcement of intercourse prohibitions; the perspectives of social scientists on black/white marriages; religious forces impacting on black/white marriages; historic rationalizations and reasoned opposition to black/white marriages; and arguments for interracial marriage. Bibliograhical notes and an index are included.

SUBJECT(S): Interracial marriages.

PSYCHOLOGY AND MENTAL HEALTH

533. Boykin, A. Wade, Anderson J. Franklin, and J. Frank Yates, eds. *Research Directions of Black Psychologists*. New York: Russell Sage Foundation, 1979. xv, 440 p.

This work contains a collection of articles by black psychologists on a variety of scholarly issues in psychology and education, and their implications for the black community. The articles are grouped into six sections: current participation by black psychologists in empirical research; research methodology; self-identity and adjustment; cognitive abilities; motivational issues; and problems for future research. Each article concludes with bibliographical references. An index is included.

SUBJECT(S): Psychological research--United States.
Afro-Americans--Psychology.
Afro-American psychologists.

534. Davis, Lenwood G. *Psychology and the Black Community*. Monticello, IL: Council of Planning Librarians, 1976. 17 p. SERIES: Council of Planning Librarians. Exchange Bibliography, no. 1060.

An unannotated list of articles, books, dissertations, and periodicals on psychology and the black community. Most of the articles cited are contained in the book *Black Psychology*, edited by Reginald L. Jones. Of the periodical titles cited, the *Journal of Black Psychology*, is only one devoted exclusively to black psychology the remaining periodicals include articles in this field.

SUBJECT(S): Afro-Americans--Psychology--Bibliography.

535. Dvorkin, Bettifae E., comp. *Blacks and Mental Health in the United States, 1963-1973: A Selected, Annotated Bibliography of Journal Articles*. Washington, D.C.: Medical-Dental Library, Howard University, 1974. ii, 34 p.

An annotated bibliography covering black mental health problems including mental retardation, schizophrenia, suicide; psychological problems and racial integration; treatment for black patients; interracial analysis and therapy; the mental health workers who deliver services to blacks; and community mental health and mental health planning.

SUBJECT(S): Mental illness--United States--Bibliography.

536. Gary, Lawrence E. ed. *Mental Health: A Challenge to the Black Community*. Philadelphia: Dorrance, 1978. xiii, 365 p.

A collection of articles devoted to a variety of factors and issues affecting the mental health of black people. It focuses on both the pathological and the positive aspects of black mental health. The chapters provide conceptual overviews on mental health, and cover the developmental process of black mental health from childhood through old age. Bibliographical references appear at the end of each chapter. An index is included.

SUBJECT(S): Afro-Americans--Mental health.
Social psychiatry--United States.
Mental health services--United States.

537. Guthrie, Robert V. *Even the Rat was White: A Historical View of Psychology*. New York: Harper & Row, 1976. xii, 224 p.

In this important and well documented work, the author seeks to analyze, document, and illustrate the history of psychology from a black perspective. He exposes the racism which has been inherent in psychological and anthropological research, theories, methodologies, I.Q. testing, and measurements of physical characteristics. In addition, the work contains an overview of the history of psychology and education in black colleges. Biographical sketches and reviews of the works of early black psychologists from 1920 to 1950, and a lengthy essay devoted to Francis Cecil Summer, the "father" of black American psychology, are also included. Each chapter is concluded with bibliographical references. An appendix contains a selected list of psychological studies, 1920 to 1946. A bibliography and an index are included.

SUBJECT(S): Psychology--History.
Afro-American psychologists.
Ethnopsychology--History.
Anthropometry--History.
Blacks--Psychology.

538. *Jones, Enrico E., and Sheldon J. Korchin, eds. Minority Mental Health*. New York: Praeger, 1982. x, 406 p.

A collection of articles, written expressly for this volume, by social scientists and mental health professionals concerned with the mental health problems of minorities and their solution. Some of the chapters present concepts and issues applicable to all minorities. Several chapters focus on issues relating specifically to blacks, i.e., the appropriateness of traditional theoretical models for understanding black behavior; the psychological assessment of blacks; family therapy, and therapeutic interventions with urban blacks. Each chapter contains numerous bibliographical references. An index is included.

SUBJECT(S): Minorities--Mental health--United States.
Minorities--United States--Psychology.

539. Jones, Reginald Lanier, ed. and comp. *Black Psychology*. 2d ed. New York: Harper & Row, 1980. xii, 484 p.

An important collection of core articles in black psychology grouped into the following categories: perspectives, personality, assessment, education, counseling, and psychology and psychologists in the community. Most articles include bibliographical references. An index is included.

SUBJECT(S): Afro-Americans--Psychology--Addresses, essays, lectures.
Afro-Americans--Psychology--Study and teaching.
Afro-Americans--Psychology--Bibliography.

540. Jones, Reginald Lanier, ed. and comp. *Sourcebook on the Teaching of Black Psychology*. Berkeley: Association of Black Psychologists, 1978.

This work contains articles on the teaching of black psychology and education, and outlines of black psychology courses. An extensive instructional resources section includes: descriptions of films of potential interest to instructors of courses on the psychology and education of blacks; comprehensive bibliographies; tests of black cognizance and patterns of communication; and activities, exercises, and excerpts which may be used by instructors of black psychology.

SUBJECT(S): Afro-american--Psychology--Study and Teachings.

541. Samuda, Ronald J. *Psychological Testing of American Minorities: Issues and Consequences*. New York: Harper and Row, 1975. xiv, 215 p.

A comprehensive summary of the various perspectives, findings, issues, instruments, and trends in the use of standardized norm-referenced tests with American minorities. It delineates the important ways in which psychological testing can, and does, impede the parity of American minorities and deny them access to, and participation in, society. It includes an extensive bibliography of references. An appendix contains a "Compendium of Tests for Minority Adolescents and Adults," which lists and describes instruments that are designed for, or advertised as being appropriate for, minorities or the educationally disadvantaged. This "Compendium" includes tests which measure aptitude; personality, interests, attitudes, and opinions; and miscellaneous and sensory-motor skills. Name and subject indexes are included.

SUBJECT(S): Psychological tests--United States.
Minorities--United States.

542. Shuey, Audrey Mary. *The Testing of Negro Intelligence.* 2nd ed. New York: Social Science Press, 1966. xv, 578 p.

Although considered by some to be biased in its conclusions regarding the biological basis of intelligence, this is a major work which work surveys and summarizes a wide range of the studies of black-white differences in mental test performance in the United States through 1960. Tests of pre-school children, elementary, and secondary school and college students, and enlisted men and officers in the armed forces are covered. An extensive bibliography, author index, and subject index are included.

SUBJECT(S): Intelligence levels--Afro-Americans.

543. Smith, William David, Kathleen Hoard Burlew, et. al., eds. *Reflections on Black Psychology.* Washington, D.C.: University Press of America, 1979.

This is a collection of essays grouped together around the following topics: foundations of the discipline of black psychology; African origins of the black personality; the black child; black youth achievement and identity; the delivery of psychological services; and perspectives on the focus, purpose, and direction of black psychological research. Biographical notes on the editors and contributors, and bibliographical notes at the end of each chapter are included. A subject index and a name index are also included.

SUBJECT(S): Afro-American Psychology.

544. Thomas, Alexander, and Samuel Sillen. *Racism and Psychiatry.* New York: Brunner/Mazel, 1972 xiii, 176 p.

This work examines the impact of racist thinking in human behavior disciplines, with a focus on psychiatry. It sharply challenges traditional assumptions and the current more subtle racist ideology. It identifies specific racist practices in psychiatry and makes recommendations for change. A bibliography and an index are included.

SUBJECT(S): Blacks--Psychology.
Psychiatry.
United States--Race relations.

545. Wilcox, Roger, comp. *The Psychological Consequences of Being a Black American: A Source Book of Research by Black Psychologists*. New York: Wiley, 1971. xiii, 492 p.

A representative collection of articles and speeches by blacks that are concerned with black psychological issues. Articles of historical interest are included. The articles are grouped into seven sections covering: cultural disadvantage, minority group and exceptional children; racial integration; intelligence and achievement; higher education; educational psychology; attitude, personality, and emotional consequences; and psychology as a study and as a profession. Most articles conclude with a list of bibliographical references, and each section of articles is concluded with a bibliography. An appendix provides the names and institutional affiliation of some black psychologists. An index is included.

SUBJECT(S): Afro-Americans--Psychology--Addresses, essays, lectures.
Afro-Americans--Education--Addresses, essays, lectures.

MEDICINE AND HEALTH CARE

546. Davis, Lenwood G. *The Black Aged in the United States: An Annotated Bibliography*. Westport, CT: Greenwood Press, 1980. xviii, 200 p.

A comprehensive, annotated bibliography citing books, dissertations and theses, government publications, and periodical articles on black senior citizens. An introduction providing a historical overview on the topic is included. One chapter is devoted to the elderly during the slave era. It also includes a list of black old folks' homes, 1860-1980; and a list of selected periodical titles. An author-subject index is included.

SUBJECT(S): Afro-American aged--Bibliography.
Old age assistance--United States-- Bibliography.

547. Davis, Lenwood G. *A History of Selected Diseases in the Black Community*. Washington D.C.: Council of Planning Librarians, 1976. 28 p. SERIES: Council of Planning Librarians, Exchange Bibliography, no. 1059.

An unannotated list of articles and books on the history of diseases in the black community, written from the mid-1800s through the 1970s. Many of the articles cited deal with sickle cell anemia, cardiovascular diseases, syphillis, and tuberculosis. Most of the books cited include pertinent chapters or passages, but may not be exclusively devoted to diseases.

SUBJECT(S): Afro-Americans--Diseases--Bibliography.
Health and race--United States--Bibliography.

548. Davis, Lenwood G., comp. *Sickle Cell Anemia: A Preliminary Survey*. Monticello, IL: Council of Planning Librarians, 1975 24 p. SERIES: Council of Planning Librarians. Exchange Bibliography, no. 763.

An unannotated bibliography of articles, books, and pamphlets arranged by form. In addition to the citations, the text of the National Sickle Cell Anemia Program; the text of the National Sickle Cell Anemia Control Act; and a list of national, regional, and local organizations that provide services related to sickle cell anemia, are included.

SUBJECT(S): Anemia, Sickle cell--Bibliography

549. Cosminsky, Sheila and Ira E. Harrison. *Traditional Medicine II, 1976-1981: Current Research with Implications for Ethnomedicine, Ethnopharmacology, Maternal and Child Health, Mental Health and Public Health: An Annotated Bibliography of Africa, Latin America, and the Caribbean*. New York: Garland Publishing, Inc., 1984. xvii, 327 p. SERIES: Garland Reference Library of Social Science, vol. 147.

This bibliography surveys traditional medicine and research literature relating to Africa, Latin America, and the Caribbean, published 1976 to 1981. It is a sequal to the authors' *Traditional Medicine, 1950-1975*. Publications relevant to the issues of collaboration between old and new health care methods, the use of healers in national and official health services, the development of primary health care programs, training programs for traditional birth attendants, and the efficacy of medicinal plants and healing rituals and symbols are cited. Author and country indexes are included.

SUBJECT(S): Developing Countries--Abstracts.
Medicine--Africa--abstracts.
Medicine--Latin America--Abstracts.
Medicine, Traditional--Abstracts.
Medicine--Caribbean area--Abstracts.

550. Harrison, Ira E., and Sheila Cosminsky. *Traditional Medicine, 1950-1975: Implications for Ethnomedicine, Ethnopharmacology, Maternal and Child Health, Mental Health, and Public Health: An Annotated Bibliography of Africa, Latin America, and the Caribbean*. New York: Garland Publishing, Inc., 1976. ix, 238 p. SERIES: Garland Reference Library of Social Science, vol. 19.

An annotated bibliography of literature on native medical systems of people of the third world, from 1950 to 1975. The focus is on

Africa, Latin America, and the Caribbean, and is divided into three sections: general, which cites works pertinent to African and Latin American and/or other countries of world; Africa; and Latin America and the Caribbean. Each section is further subdivided into: general; ethnomedical literature on the definitions of illness, beliefs about causation, attitudes and meaning of illness; ethnopharmacology on drugs and medicinal plants; health care delivery; maternal and child health; mental health; and public health. Indexes are included.

SUBJECT(S): Developing Countries--abstracts
Medicine--Africa--abstracts.
Medicine--Latin America--abstracts.
Medicine, Traditional--abstracts.
Medicine, Primitive--Bibliography.
Medical anthropology--Bibliography.
Public health--Africa--Bibliography.
Public health--Latin America--Bibliography.
Underdeveloped areas--Medical care--Bibliography.
Medicine--Caribbean area--Abstracts.

551. Kidd, Foster, ed. *Profile of the Negro in American Dentistry.* Washington: Howard University Press, 1979 viii, 211 p.

This work profiles the contributions and participation of blacks in dentistry. A chapter on black women in dentistry, and information on schools, organizations, and scholarship and loan sources are included. Also included are statistical tables, illustrations, a brief bibliography, and an index.

SUBJECT(S): Afro-Americans in dentistry.
Dentistry--United States--History.
Dentistry--History--United States.
Afro-Americans--History--United States.

552. Kiple, Kenneth F. *Another Dimension to the Black Diaspora: Diet, Disease, and Racism.* Cambridge and New York: Cambridge University Press, 1981 xix, 295 p.

This scholarly and well researched work on black diet, disease and racism is likely to become a classic. It is the first major study which approaches the issues of black health from a interdisciplinary perspective, combining data from the nutritional, biographical, and medical sciences with social history and demography. The author's aim is to show that genetic and biological circumstances, wrought by virtue of West African ancestry, combined with the climatic and cultural circumstances in North America, have produced immunity to certain diseases as well as susceptibility to others. The authors assert that "...blacks do have different nutritional requirements than whites. But because this is not appreciated, diseases that killed blacks on the plantations of the South...are still playing havoc with our Afro-American population..." The book examines the preslavery era in Africa, and the slave societies of the West Indies and the United States, seeking to establish a link between black-related diseases and white racism. A final section traces major black disease susceptibilities from the Civil War to the present and argues that nutritional deficiencies have shaped many of these susceptibilities. Extensive bibliographical notes, a bibliographical essay, and an index are included.

SUBJECT(S): Afro-Americans--Diseases--History.
Slavery--United States--Condition of slaves.
Afro-Americans--Nutrition--History.
Health and race--United States--History.
Blacks--United States.
Diet.
Disease susceptibility--etiology.

553. Morais, Herbert Montfort. *The History of the Afro-American in Medicine*. Cornwells Heights, PA: Publishers Agency, 1978. xiv, 322 p. SERIES: International Library of Afro-American Life and History.

This work discusses Afro-Americans in medical practice from the late-eighteenth century to the 1950s. A bibliography, photographs and drawings, and an author-title-subject index are included. An appendix contains several historical documents.

SUBJECT(S): Afro-Americans in medicine.

554. National Medical Association (U.S.). *Journal of the National Medical Association*. New York: Appleton-Century-Crofts. 1945-.

This technical journal is to serve as the "primary source for enlightening the medical community on specialized clinical research activities related to the health problems of blacks. Published by the National Medical Association (NMA), the black counterpart to the American Medical Association, the articles are on black-related physical and psychological illnesses as well as the activities of the NMA. This journal is not indexed in *Index Medicus* or *Index to Periodical Articles By and About Blacks*.

SUBJECT(S): Medicine--Periodicals.

555. National Sickle Cell Disease Program. Public Education Services. *Listing of National, Regional and Local Groups Providing Services to Persons Who Have Interest in Sickle Cell Anemia*. Bethesda, MD: National Sickle Cell Disease Program, National Heart Lung Institute, National Institutes of Health, 1974. 32 p. SERIES: DHEW publication, nos. 75-714.

A directory of sickle cell anemia prevention and services groups, arranged alphabetically by state. Addresses and contact people are given.

SUBJECT(S): Anemia, Sickle cell--Prevention & control--Directories.
Health services--U.S.--Directories.

556. Savitt, Todd L. *Medicine and Slavery*: *The Diseases and Health Care of Blacks in Antebellum Virginia*. Urbana: University of Illinois Press, 1978. 332 p. SERIES: Blacks in the New World.

This work analyses the diseases which afflicted the black population in the Old South. It describes the medical conditions in antebellum Virginia, and presents a history of the relationship between black health and white society. The author applies the basic principles of public health to antebellum living and working conditions. With the exception of chapter one, in which a general overview of black related-diseases is presented, the focuses is on Virginia from the Revolutionary to the Civil Wars. Health conditions in Virginia during this period are considered typical of those prevailing throughout the antebellum South. The book contains many statistical tables, maps, and photographs. Bibliographical notes appear throughout the text. Notes on sources, a list of major relevant manuscript collections, and an index are included.

SUBJECT(S): History of medicine--Virginia.
Blacks--History--Virginia.
Medicine--Virginia--History--19th century.
Afro-Americans--Diseases--Virginia-- History--19th century.
Slavery--Virginia--Condition of slaves.
Public health--Virginia--History--19th century.

557. Treiman, Beatrice R., Pamela B.Street, and Patricia Shanks, comps. *Blacks and Alcohol*: *A Selective Annotated Bibliography*. Berkeley: Social Research Group, School of Public Health, University of California, 1976. iii, 87 p.

This annotated bibliography cites periodical articles and books that discuss the social aspects of alcohol use by Afro-Americans. Strictly biomedical or physiochemical works are included only if they discuss social implications. Most works listed were written during the 1960s and early 1970s.

SUBJECT(S): Alcoholism--abstracts.
Blacks--abstracts.

558. Watson, Wilbur H., ed. *Black Folk Medicine*: *The Therapeutic Significance of Faith and Trust*. Forward by Doris Y. Wilkerson. Afterword by Nelson McGee, Jr. New Brunswick, NJ: Transaction Books, 1984. xvi, 121 p.

This interesting collection of articles shows that folk medicine is still an important informal and traditional system of social and health care that is widely used in many societies, including the United States. A glossary, bibliography, and an index are included.

SUBJECT(S): Afro-Americans--Folklore--Addresses, essays, lectures.
Folk medicine--United States--Address, essays, lectures.
Blacks--Folklore--Addresses, essays, lectures.
Folk medicine--Addresses, essays, lectures.

559. Watts, Thomas D., and Roosevelt Write, Jr., eds. *Black Alcoholism: Toward a Comprehensive*. Springfield, IL: Charles C. Thomas, 1983. 242 p.

A collection of articles by specialists which brings together much of what is known about black alcohol abuse and alcoholism in the United States. Prevention is the focus. Articles are grouped into sections dealing with etiological factors, treatment, prevention, research, policy, and practice. Although there is no separate bibliography, each article is concluded with numerous bibliographical references, which taken together, may provide the reader with a fairly comprehensive review of the literature. A name index is included.

SUBJECT(S): Afro-Americans--Alcohol use.
Alcoholism--Treatment-United States.
Alcoholism--United States--Prevention.

560. Williams, Richard Allen, ed. *Textbook of Black-related Diseases*. New York: McGraw Hill, 1975. 803 p.

The physical and psychiatric conditions commonly found among Afro-Americans are discussed in this unique medical reference source. Chapters are written by professionals in the various branches of medicine, and the language is often technical. The full spectrum of black-related diseases is covered, and there is even a chapter on voodoo. This work brings together vital and interesting materials which are found scattered throughout the medical literature. A bibliography and an index are included.

SUBJECT(S): Afro-Americans--Health and hygiene.
Afro-Americans--Diseases.

SPORTS AND ATHLETES

561. Chalk, Ocania. *Black College Sport*. New York: Dodd, Mead, 1976. 376 p.

A history of black male participation in college sports, focusing primarily on the mid-nineteenth century through the 1950s. An account of black athletes of predominately black and white colleges is presented. Chapters cover baseball, basketball, football, track and field, and participation in the Olympics. Numerous photographs, and an author-subject index are included.

SUBJECT(S): Afro-American athletes.
College sports--History.
Sports--United States--History.

562. Chalk, Ocania. *Pioneers of Black Sport: The Early Days of the Black Professional Athlete in Baseball, Basketball, Boxing, and Football*. New York: Dodd, Mead, 1975. xiii, 305 p.

A history of blacks in baseball, basketball, boxing, and football. An appendix provides a history of the American Association (a baseball league that had both black and white players in the late-nineteenth century), and newspaper accounts of the 1904 boxing match between Joe Gans and Joe Walcott. Photographs and drawings, and an author-title-subject index are included.

SUBJECT(S): Afro-American athletes--Biography.

563. Davis, Lenwood G., and Belinda S. Daniels, comps. *Black Athletes in the United States: A Bibliography of Books, Articles, Autobiographies, and Biographies on Black Professional Athletes in the United States, 1800-1981*. Westport, CT: Greenwood Press, 1981. xxvi, 265 p.

A comprehensive bibliography of books and articles on blacks in baseball, basketball, boxing, football, and tennis. Appendices list: doctoral dissertations; baseball and basketball most valuable players, and leading scores; boxing champions; football records; hall of fame members and inductees; athletes in motion pictures; documentaries on athletes; and film biographies. A name index is included.

SUBJECT(S): Afro-American athletes--Bibliography.

564. Henderson, Edwin Bancroft. Introduction to, *The Black Athlete: Emergence and Arrival*. by Jackie Robinson. Cornwells Heights, PA: Publishers Agency, 1978. xiii, 306 p. SERIES: International Library of Afro-American Life and History.

A history of Afro-American professional athletes in the twentieth century. Chapters are devoted to boxing, baseball, basketball, football, track, tennis, and golf. Photographs, bibliography, and an index are included.

SUBJECT(S): Afro-American athletes.

565. Young, Andrew Sturgeon Nash. *Negro First in Sports*. Chicago, Johnson Pub. Co. 1963. 301 p.

This work contains biographies of blacks, who were firsts in basketball, baseball, boxing, golf, and other sports. There is also a chapter on the role of black colleges in athletics. An appendix lists sports records, and provides a history of the Harlem Globetrotters. Illustrations and an author-title-subject index are included.

SUBJECT(S): Afro-American athletes.

ARMED FORCES

566. Binkin, Martin and Mark J. Eitelberg, with Alvin J. Schexnider and Marvin M. Smith. *Blacks in the Military*. Washington, D.C.: Brookings Institution, 1982. xiv, 190 p.

This work provides an overiew of black participation in the armed forces from Bunker Hill to Vietnam, with a focus on blacks in post-Vietnam service. It provides statistics on black recruitment, retention, and the racial composition of the armed forces. The controversies surrounding the current twenty percent black United States armed forces are discussed. Numerous statistical tables, an appendix on racialethnic categories in the armed forces, and an index are included.

SUBJECT(S): United States--Armed Forces--Afro-American soldiers.

567. Berlin, Ira, ed. *The Black Military Experience*. Cambridge (Cambridgeshire): New York: Cambridge University Press, 1982. xxxv, 852 p. SERIES: Freedom, A Documentary History of Emancipation, 1861-1867, ser. 2.

This book is composed of documents housed in the U.S. National Archives which cover the wartime and postwar experiences of slaves and ex-slaves. The documents are highly varied in content, and each is accompanied by an annotation explaining its origin, purpose, and other pertinent facts. They were selected to illustrate processes considered central to the transition from slavery to freedom, and are organized into five major parts which parallel the course of emancipation. Each section or group of documents is preceded by a lengthy introductory essay. Each document is reproduced, as far as modern typology allows, exactly as it appeared in the original manuscript. Bibliographical references and an index are included.

SUBJECT(S): United States--History--Civil War, 1861-1865-- Afro-American troops-- Sources.
Afro-American troops--Sources.

568. Dalfume, Richard M. *Desegregation of the U.S. Armed Forces: Fighting on Two Fronts, 1939-1953.* Columbia, MO: University of Missouri Press, 1969. viii, 252 p.

An account of the military service's change in racial policy and black reactions, 1939 to 1953. Includes an extensive classified bibliography and an index.

SUBJECT(S): United States. Armed Forces--Afro-Americans.
Afro-Americans--Segregation.

569. Foner, Jack D. *Blacks and the Military in American History: A New Perspective.* Forward and conclusion by James P. Shenton. New York: Praeger, 1974. x, 278 p. SERIES: New Perspective in American History.

An history of black soldiers and seamen in America, covering the the War for Independance, Civil War, post-Civil War period, Spanish American War, World Wars I and II, desegregation of the armed forces, and the Vietnam War. A bibliographical essay and an index are included.

SUBJECT(S): United States--Armed Forces--Afro-Americans.

570. Fowler, Arlen L. *The Black Infantry in the West, 1869-1891.* Foreward by William H. Leckie. Westport, CT: Greenwood Press, 1971. xviii, 167 p. SERIES: Contributions in Afro-American and African Studies, no. 6.

A well documented history of blacks in the 24th and 25th Infantry Regiments in the Dakotas and Southwest, during the Indians wars period, 1869 to 1891. Illustrations, a extensive bibliography, and an index are included.

SUBJECT(S): United States Army--Afro-American troops.
United States Army. Infantry--History.

571. Johnson, Jesse J., ed. *Black Women in the Armed Forces, 1942-1974: (A Pictorial History).* Hampton, Va.: Johnson, 1974. x. 110 p. SERIES: Missing Pages in U.S. History.

A well illustrated pictorial history of women in the armed forces. Chapters cover race relations; the Army, Air Force, Navy, and Marines; nurses; chaplains; military wives; and military training. It does not include a bibliography or an index.

SUBJECT(S): Afro-American women--Biography.
United States--Armed Forces--Afro-Americans.

572. Johnson, Jesse J., ed. *A Pictorial History of Black Soldiers in the United States (1619-1969) in Peace and War*. Hampton, Va. 1970. 108 p. SERIES: Missing Pages in U.S. History.

A pictorial history of black men and women in the armed forces. Illustrations are arranged by war, beginning with the Revolutionary War and ending with the Vietnam War. Each section is introduced with a brief analysis of the pictures. A brief bibliography is included.

SUBJECT(S): United States. Army--Afro-American troops.
Afro-American soldiers--United States.

573. Lee, Ulysses. *The Employment of Negro Troops*. Washington D.C.: U.S. Government Printing Office, 1966. xix, 740 p. SERIES: Series: United States Army in World War II. SUBSERIES: Special Studies.

A comprehensive, exceptionally well documented, scholarly study of the use of black troops in all branches of the army during WWII. It focuses on combat forces, and places emphasis on the problems of policy development, application, results, and the responses to policy by the military and the general public. Provides general descriptions and outcomes of combat missions. It includes numerous statistical tables, illustrations, maps, bibliographical notes, and an extensive index.

SUBJECT(S): United States. Armed Forces--Afro-Americans.

574. MacGregor, Morris J., and Bernard C. Nalty. *Blacks in the United States Armed Forces: Basic Documents*. Wilmington, DE: Scholarly Resources, 1977. 13 v.

This thirteen volume work contains the basic documents that define and illustrate the status of blacks in the armed forces, from colonial days through the end of the Vietnam War. Letters, decrees, announcements, conference proceedings, and other documents are arranged chronologically. Some are reproduced in entirety, while others are extracts from material that covered subjects not entirely devoted to blacks. There are no indexes.

SUBJECT(S): United States--Armed Forces--Afro-Americans--History--Sources.

575. MacGregor, Morris J., Jr. *Integration of the Armed Forces, 1940-1965*. Washington, D.C.: Center of Military History, U.S. Army. 1981. xx, 647 p. SERIES: Defense Studies Series. Superintendent of Documents #: D114.2In 8/940-65

Describes the successive measures the armed forces and the Office of the Secretary of Defense took, from 1940 to 1965, to eliminate legal and administrative barriers separating the two races, and to bring about integration in all the armed forces. It includes bibliographical references, a bibliography, and an index.

SUBJECT(S): Afro-American soldiers.
United States--Race relations.

576. Mullen, Robert W. *Blacks and Vietnam*. Washington, D.C.: University Press of America, 1981. x, 99 p.

One of the few works relating to blacks and the Vietnam War. The text is polemic and tends to focus on the domestic reactions of blacks to the war. It does not document the presence or experience of black service men in Vietnam, but is useful for its bibliographical notes and bibliography. Includes an index.

SUBJECT(S): Vietnamese Conflict, 1961-1975--Afro-Americans.
Afro-Americans--Civil rights.

577. Nalty, Bernard C., and Morris J. MacGregor, eds. *Blacks in the Military: Essential Documents*. Wilmington, DE.: Scholarly Resources, 1981. xi, 367 p.

This work contains key documents and document excerpts, which chronicle the changing status of blacks in the military service from the colonial period through the early 1970s. Each entry is accompanied with an annotation, which places the document in historical perspective, and a source note which identifies the entry by sender, intended recipient, subject, and date. An index is included.

SUBJECT(S): Afro-American soldiers--History--Sources.

578. Northrop, Herbert R. *Black and Other Minority Participation in the All-Volunteer Navy and Marine Corps*. Philadelphia: Industrial Research Unit, The Wharton School, University of Pennsylvania, 1979. xix, 242 p. SERIES: Studies of Negro Employment, vol. 8 SERIES: Wharton School. Industrial Research Unit. Studies, no. 57.

This is one of the few studies dealing with black participation in and the racial policies of the Navy and the Marine Corps. It is based upon extensive field work at Navy and Marine Corps installations, and a detailed examination of the literature and the statistical record. It seeks to determine the extent to which blacks and other minorities have been integrated into the Navy and Marine corps, and examines the manner in which these branches of the service recruit, train, upgrade, and retain minorities. Chapters include numerous bibliographical notes. Numerous tables, charts, and an index are also included.

SUBJECT(S): United States. Navy--Afro-Americans.
United States. Navy--Minorities.
United States. Marine Corps--Afro-Americans.
United States. Marine Corps--Minorities.

579. Osur, Alan M. *Blacks in the Army Air Forces During World War II: The Problem of Race Relations*. Washington: Office of Air Force History, 1977. 227 p.

A well documented, scholarly account of the racial attitudes of members of the War Department and of the black community during pre-World War II and early-World War II periods. It shows how the Army Air Forces reluctantly opened services to blacks and then hesitatingly utilized them. It also documents the specific problems blacks encountered as they served in the war, and the occurrence and nature of black protest against segregation and discrimination at home and overseas. It reviews the findings of a series of War Department postwar surveys, aimed at the evaluation of the performance of the Air Forces black troops, and the subsequent recommendations for their employment during the postwar period. It includes numerous bibliographical notes and a lengthy bibliography of primary and secondary sources. Also included are photos of top brass pilots training in the Mediterranean Theatre, and illustrations of unit insignia. An index is included.

SUBJECT(S): United States. Army Air Forces--Afro-American troops.
World War, 1939-1945--Afro-Americans.
Afro-Americans--Segregation.

580. Shaw, Henry I., Jr. and Ralph W. Connelly. *Blacks in the Marine Corps*. Washington: History and Museums Division, Headquarters, U.S. Marine Corps: 1975. x, 109 p.

This is one of the few accounts of blacks in the Marines, covering through the early 1970s. It identifies the handful of blacks who served in the Continental Marines during the American Revolution (no blacks were recruited again until June 1942), and covers the formation and activities of the (first), all black, 51st and 52nd Defense Battalions of World War II, through the Vietnam War. It includes many photos and bibliographic notes. Appendices list black Marine units of World War II, and Marine Medal of Honor recipients photos.

SUBJECT(S): United States. Marine Corps--Afro-American troops.
United States. Marine Corps--History.

LATIN AMERICA AND THE CARIBBEAN

The selected works cited below will provide access to a large portion of the literature on blacks living in the Western Hemisphere outside of the United States. The works are arranged in a single alphabet by author. Specific subject and geographical area access is provided through the subject index.

581. Allis, Jeannette B. *West Indian Literature*: *An Index to Criticism*, *1930-1975*. New York: G.K. Hall, 1981. xxxvii, 353 p. SERIES: Reference Publication in Latin American Studies.

This index cites reviews of novels, poetry, and collections of short stories. Reviews of drama are included only when the author is also a poet or novelist, and when the play is treated as a piece of literature rather than a performance. To insure comprehensiveness and objectivity, this index is nonselective with regard to the length, quality, or merit of the items cited.

SUBJECT(S): West Indian literature (English)--History and criticism--Bibliography.

582. Andrews, George Reid. *The Afro-Argentines of Buenos Aires*, *1800-1900*. Madison, WI.: University of Wisconsin Press, 1980. xiv, 286 p.

This work presents a major reconstruction of the history of the black population in Buenos Aires during the post abolitionist period from 1800 to 1900. Tables and illustrations are included. Appendices contain biographical sketches of Afro-Argentine colonies, 1800 to 1900, and identify the origins and names of the African nations of Buenos Aires, 1770-1900. A glossary, bibliographical notes, a bibliography, and an index are included.

SUBJECT(S): Blacks--Argentina--Buenos Aires--History.
Buenos Aires (Argentina)--Race relations . 582

583. Barrett, Leonard E. *The Rastafarians*: *Sounds of Cultural Dissonance*. Boston: Beacon Press, 1977. xxiv, 257 p. SERIES: Beacon Paper Back, 559.

SUBJECT(S): Ras Tafari movement--Jamaica.
Jamaica--Religion.
Jamaica--History.

584. Barrett, Leonard E. *The Sun and the Drum: African Roots in Jamaican Folk Tradition*. Kingston, Jamaica: Sangster's Book Stores, 1976. 128 p.

An introduction to Jamaican folk culture written for non-specialists and others seeking an elementary overview. Included are chapters on folklore, healing and medicine, witchcraft, and psychic phenomena. A glossary, bibliographic notes, bibliography, and index are also included.

SUBJECT(S): Blacks--Jamaica.
Blacks--Jamaica--Folklore.

585. *The Caricom Bibliography*. Georgetown, Guyana: Caribbean Community Secretariat Library, 1977-.

Arranged by the Dewey Decimal classification, this bibliography is a cumulated subject list of current national imprints of the Caribbean community countries. These are: Antigua, Bahamas, Barbados, Belize, Dominica, Grenada, Guyana, Jamaica, Montserrat, St. Kitts, Nevis, Anguilla, St. Vincent, St. Lucia, Trinidad and Tobago. For 1978 and 1979 there are annual cumulations, thereafter cumulations are semi-annual. The bibliography does not include periodicals (except for the first issue of a new title), or internal government publications. In addition to the subject arrangement, there is an alphabetical listing, and a list of publishers and their addresses.

SUBJECT(S): Caribbean area--Bibliography--Catalogs.

586. Carnegie, Jenipher R. *Critics on West Indian Literature: A Selected Bibliography*. Cave Hill: Research & Publications Committee, Univ. of the West Indies, 1979.

This is one of the few bibliographies of criticism of West Indian authors. It contains separate sections on twelve noted authors, including Edward K.Brathwaite, George Lamming, and Derek Walcott. A general section listing bibliographies, indexes, and articles is also included.

SUBJECT(S): West Indian literature (English)--History and criticism--Bibliography.

587. Cassidy, Frederic Gomes. *Dictionary of Jamaican English*. 2d ed. Cambridge, NY: Cambridge University Press, 1980. lxiv, 509 p.

A scholarly, historical, descriptive dictionary of English in Jamaica since 1655. It includes a bibliography, a list of dictionaries and glossaries cited, and an essay on the history of the phonology of Jamaican English.

SUBJECT(S): English language--Jamaica.
English language--Dialects--Jamaica.

588. Cassidy, Frederic Gomes. *Jamaica Talk: Three Hundred Years of the English Language in Jamaica.* New York: St. Martin's Press, 1961. 468 p.

A detailed account of the language, past and present, of Jamaicans of all ranks, written especially for the layman, but also of some interest to the linguist. It covers pronunciation, grammar, and vocabulary. Textual notes give dates, sources, and etymologies. A bibliography of books, periodicals and manuscripts is included. Also included is a word list with page numbers referring the reader to the text where the word is discussed.

SUBJECT(S): English language--Provincialisms--Jamaica.
English language--Dialects--Jamaica.

589. Chambers, Francis. *Haiti.* Oxford, England; Santa Barbara, CA: Clio Press, 1983. xiii, 177 p. SERIES: World Bibliographical Series, no 39.

An annotated list of 550 books and periodical articles on Haiti. Most items cited were published before 1982, and most are in English. The items were selected with the needs of the general reader, the undergraduate, and the librarian involved in collection development in mind. The entries are grouped in several subject categories including the country and its people, flora and fauna, prehistory and archaeology, history, population, emigration, human rights, folklore, religion, voodoo, social conditions, politics and government, economics, statistics, education, language, visual arts, theatre, literature, libraries and archives, newspapers, magazines, and periodicals. A author-title-subject index is included.

SUBJECT(S): Haiti--Bibliography.

590. Clermont, Norman. *Bibliographie Annotee de l'Anthropologie Physique des Antilles.* Montreal Center de Recherches Caraibes, 1972. 51 p.

An annotated bibliography of the scientific literature in the field of physical anthropology of the Antilles. Anthropometric studies, biological studies, and studies relating to interracial crossings are cited. All works cited were originally written in French, Spanish, and English. All annotations are in French, but titles are cited in the original language. Geographic and subject indexes are included.

SUBJECT(S): Anthropometry--West Indies--Bibliography.

591. Cohen Stuart, Bertie A. comp. *Women in the Caribbean: A Bibliography*. Leiden: Dept. of Caribbean Studies, Royal Institute of Linguistics and Anthropology, 1979. 163 p.

This annotated bibliography cites materials on black women in Suriname, French Guiana, Guyana, the Bahamas, Burmuda, and the islands of the Antillean Archipelago. Bibliographies, catalogs, and materials relating to family and household, cultural factors, education, economics, politics, and law are cited. Includes a list of Caribbean womens' organizations. An author index and a subject category index are included.

SUBJECT(S): Women--Caribbean area--Bibliography.

592. Comitas, Lambros. *The Complete Caribbeana, 1900-1975: A Bibliographic Guide to the Scholarly Literature*. Millwood, NY: KTO Press, 1977. 4 vols.

Over 17,000 monographs, texts, proceedings, doctoral dissertations, journal articles, reports, and pamphlets are listed in this comprhensive, bibliographic guide to the scholarly literature on the Caribbean. Volume I is on people, Volume II on institutions, Volume III on resources, and IV contains author and geographical indexes. Areas heavily covered are Suriname, French Guiana, Guyana, Belize, the Bahamas, Bermuda, and the islands of the Antillean Archipelago. Haiti, Cuba, Puerto Rico, and the Dominican Republic are excluded. There are no annotations.

SUBJECT(S): Caribbean area--Bibliography.

593. Conrad, Robert, ed. *Brazilian Slavery: An Annotated Research Bibliography*. Boston: G. K. Hall, 1977. xvi, 163 p.

This outstanding annotated bibliography on Brazilian slavery lists books, articles, government documents and reports, and pamphlets. Areas covered include the slave trade and its suppression, slavery, and abolition. Many of the works cited are in Portuguese, but all annotations are in English. Also included is a section of bibliographies and research aids. An author index is included.

SUBJECT(S): Slavery--Brazil--Bibliography.
Slave-trade--Brazil--Bibliography.
Slavery--Brazil--Anti-slavery movements--Bibliography.

594. Crahan, Margret E., and Franklin W. Knight, eds. *Africa and the Caribbean: The Legacies of a Link*. Baltimore: Johns Hopkins University Press, 1980. xii, 159 p. SERIES: Johns Hopkins Studies in Atlantic History and Culture.

This is a multidisciplinary and interdisciplinary exploration of the cultural continuities that exist between African and Caribbean societies. The first two chapters provide a regional overview and trace the genesis of Caribbean societies. The remaining essays focus on the following: Updican and Creole slave family patterns in Trinidad; Myalism and African religious tradition in Jamaica; Jamaican Jonkonnu and related Caribbean festivals; the African impact on language and literature in the English -speaking Caribbean; and the African presence in the poetry of Nicolas Guillen, the most universally acclaimed of Caribbean poets. Bibliographical notes appear at the end of each essay, and a selected bibliography relating to African cultural survivals in the West Indies is included. Also included are biographical notes on the authors.

SUBJECT(S): Blacks--Caribbean area--Addresses, essays, lectures.
Caribbean area--Civilization--African influences--Addresses, essays, lecture
Caribbean area--Religious life and customs-- Addresses, essays, lectures.

595. Davenport, Charles Benedict, and Morris Steggerda. *Race Crossing in Jamaica*. Westport, CT: Negro Universities Press, 1970. ix, 516 p.

A quantitative study of three groups of agricultural Jamaican adults: blacks, whites, and hybrids; and several hundred children at all developmental stages. The study covers anthropometric, physiological, psychological, developmental, and eugenical factors. The variability of each race and sex, is discussed. Includes many statistical tables and charts, a genealogical table, black and white photos, a bibliography, and an index.

SUBJECT(S): Anthropometry--Jamaica.
Miscegenation--Jamaica.

596. Fernandes, Florestan. *The Negro in Brazilian Society*. Translated by Jacqueline D. Skiles, A. Brunel, and Arthur Rothwell. Edited by Phyllis B. Eveleth. New York: Columbia University Press, 1969. xxv, 489 p.

A classic, socio-historical study of blacks in Brazil, with a focus on the state and city of Sao Paulo. A glossary, a bibliography, and an index are included.

SUBJECT(S): Blacks in Brazil.
Brazil--Race relations.

597. Freyre, Gilberto. *The Masters and the Slaves: A Study in the Development of Brazilian Civilization*. New York: Knopf, 1956. 537 p.

This is a classic study on how the three major ethnic groups of Brazil, the native Indian, African, and Portuguese, mixed and formed the foundations of the unique Brazilian civilization. Some emphasis is placed on the family life of the slaves. One of the book's interesting contributions is its identification of certain African ethnic groups having occupations which were traditional and consistent with their African ethnic heritage. Therefore, during the Brazilian slave era, members of certain African ethnic groups were sought as slaves to perform certain tasks. For instance, the Fulani (Fulah) from Senegambia were preferred and sought as house servants; and the Haussas and Ashanti were preferred for cattle raising. A bibliography and a name-subject index are included.

SUBJECT(S): Brazil--Social Conditions.
Slavery in Brazil.
Blacks in Brazil.
Indians of South America-Brazil.

598. Fontaine, Pierre-Michel. "Research in the Political Economy of Afro-Latin America." *Latin American Research Review*, Vol. 15, no. 2 (1980), pp. 111-141.

This article contains a critical survey of research literature on the political economy of Afro-Latin America, with a focus on Brazil. An extensive bibliography is included which updates and, to some extent, compliments, the bibliographies in the Fernandes and Pierson texts.

SUBJECT(S): Blacks--Brazil--Economic conditions
Blacks--Latin America--Economic conditions.
Brazil--Economic conditions.
Latin America--Economic conditions.

599. Herdeck, Donald E. *Caribbean Writers: A Bio-Bibliographical-Critical Encyclopedia*. Washington: Three Continents Press, 1979. xiv, 943 p.

This work consists of four separate volumes in one cover, encompassing English, French, Dutch, Spanish and Creole literature of the Caribbean. About 2,000 writers and 15,000 works are cited. Brief biographies appear with a list of important works by and about each author. Essays on the literature of each region, and lists of resources on the regions are also included. Volume I covers Anglophone literature of the West Indies. Volume II covers French literature from Haiti and the French Antilles. Volume III covers Dutch literature of the Netherlands, Antilles, and Surinam. The Spanish literature of Cuba, the Dominican Republic, and Puerto Rico are discussed in Volume IV.

SUBJECT(S): Caribbean literature--History and criticism--Bibliography.

600. Herskovits, Melville J., and Frances S. Herskovits. *Suriname Folk-lore*. New York: Columbia University Press, 1936. 766 p.

This work contains folklore (stories, riddles, proverbs, dreams) and folksongs gathered by the authors in Dutch Guiana (Suriname, South America) from the coastal Negroes and the Bush-Negroes of the upper Suriname river). Most of the materials were gathered from the Suriname city of Paramaribo. In addition to the folklore and songs, there is a lengthy chapter on the culture of the Paramaribo Negroes and sections which provide a musicological analysis of the songs. the songs are presented with musical notes and the words transcribed in the native language, with English translations. A bibliography is included.

SUBJECT(S): Folk-lore--Dutch Guiana.
Afro-Americans in Dutch Guiana.
Afro-American--English dialects--texts.
Music--Dutch Guiana.

601. Institute of Jamaica. *The Jamaican National Bibliography, 1964-1974*. Millwood, NY: Kraus International Publications, 1981. 439 p.

The primary purpose of this work is to provide a bibliographic record for material locally published in Jamaica from 1964 to 1974. It is designed to fill a gap in the current Jamaican bibliographic record, and it provides the first complete cumulation of publications on Jamaican life and culture during this period. Entries are organized under broad subject headings. It includes Jamaican authors, published within and outside of Jamaica, as well as works about Jamaica published elsewhere. Books, articles, pamphlets, and microforms are included. For the period covered, the holdings of the West India Reference Library, the Library of the University of the West Indies at Mona, and the Jamaican Library Service are represented. Jamaican periodicals and newspapers, listed alphabetically by title and subject, are also included. Appendices list manuscripts and maps. A general alphabetical index of authors, editors, corporate bodies, and titles is included.

SUBJECT(S): Catalogs, Union--Jamaica.
Jamaica--Imprints--Union lists.
Jamaica--Bibliography--Union lists.

602. Jackson, Richard L. *The Afro-Spanish American Author: An Annotated Bibliography of Criticism*. New York: Garland Pub., 1980. xix, 129 p. SERIES: Garland Reference Library of the Humanities, vol. 194.

This bibliography cites creative works and criticism by twenty-five Afro-Spanish American authors from Colombia, Costa Rica, Cuba, Ecuador, Mexico, Panama, Peru, Puerto Rico, Uruguay, and Venezuela. Books, articles, dissertations, general bibliographies, general studies, and anthologies are cited. It also includes an introductory essay on trends in Afro-Spanish American literary criticism, lists of periodical titles cited, and an index of critics.

SUBJECT(S): Spanish American literature--Black authors-- History and criticism--Bibliography.

603. *Jamaican National Bibliography*. Kingston: Institute of Jamaica, West India Reference Library.

This current bibliography, published quarterly with annual cumulations, "aims to list all material published in Jamaica, works by Jamaicans published outside of the country, as well as works about Jamaica, to describe each work in detail, and to give the subject matter of each work as precisely as possible." Items listed are those received by the National Library of Jamaica. Included in the annual cumulation is a list of articles from selected Jamaican periodicals. Entries appear in two sections: a classified subject section; and an index arranged alphabetically by author, title, and series. Government publications are not included.

SUBJECT(S): Jamaica--Bibliography--Periodicals.
Jamaica--Imprints--Periodicals.

604. Jordan, Alma and Barbara Comission. *The English-speaking Caribbean: A Bibliography of Bibliographies*. Boston: G.K. Hall, 1984. 420 p. SERIES: Reference Publications in Latin America Studies.

An annotated bibliography of bibliographies on the English-speaking areas of the Caribbean, including Jamaica, Antigua, Bahamas, Belize, Bermuda, Guyana, and Trinidad and Tobago. Included are over 4,000 entries for published and unpublished works, arranged by subject, then by country, then alphabetically by author. Each subject section includes works on the West Indies as a whole, followed by works on individual countries. Subject covered include: agriculture, art, biography, biology, commerce and trade, economics, education, folklore, geography, history, language and linguistics, literature, politics and government, transportation, and zoology.

SUBJECT(S): Caribbean area--Bibliography--Bibliography.

605. Laguerre, Michel S. *The Complete Haitiana: A Bibliographic Guide to the Scholarly Literature, 1900-1980*. Millwood, NY: Kraus International Publications, 1982. 2 vols.

This international and comprehensive bibliography on Haiti covers all materials published between 1900 and 1980. It is intended to serve as a companion set to Lambros Comitas' *The Complete*

Caribbeana, 1900-1975: A Bibliographic Guide to the Scholarly Literature, which does not cover the Republic of Haiti. The four main types of publications cited include books, articles, government documents, and essays in books. Contains entries in several languages, including publications written in Haitian creole. The work is divided into eleven general thematic sections: Introduction to Haiti, Ecological Setting, History of Haiti, Population Studies, Haitian Culture, Structure of Haitian Society, Health and Medicine, Educational System, Political and Legal Processes, Socio-Economic System, and Rural and Urban Development. Each section in turn is sub-divided into specific chapters. Library location information is provided. An author index is included. There are no annotations.

SUBJECT(S): Haiti--Bibliography.

606. Levine, Robert M. *Race and Ethnic Relations in Latin America and the Caribbean: An Historical Dictionary and Bibliography*. Metuchen, NJ: Scarecrow Press, 1980. viii, 252 p.

The dictionary consists of selected terms, names, and events related to racial and ethnic questions,. with an emphasis on relations among races and ethnic. Items refer to Spanish American terms, except where indicated. Some French, Dutch, English, Portugese, Aymara, Guarani, and various patois dialect entries are also included. The unannotated bibliography consists of books and articles arranged by region. An index is included.

SUBJECT(S): Latin America--Race relations--Dictionaries.
Latin America--Ethnic relations--Dictionaries.
Latin America--Race relations--Bibliography.
Latin Ameria--Ethnic relations--Bibliography.

607. Luis, William, ed. *Voices from Under: The Black Narrative in Latin America and the Caribbean*. Westport, CT: Greenwood Press, 1984. SERIES: Contributions in Afro-American and African Studies, no. 76.

This collection of essays provides an analysis of slave narratives and insights into the lives of enslaved Caribbean and Latin America blacks. The selected essays are in Spanish, French, English, Spanish, and Portuguese. Bibliographical notes, a bibliographical essay, and an index are included.

SUBJECT(S): Blacks in literature--Addresses, essays, lecture.
Latin American literature--Black authors--History and criticism--Addresses, essays, lecture.
Caribbean literature--Black authors--History and criticism--Addresses, essays, lecture.

608. Massiah, Joycelin, comp. *Women in the Caribbean: An Annotated Bibliography: A Guide to Material Available in Barbados.* With assistance from Audine Wilkinson, and Norma Shorey. Place: Publisher, 1979.

This annotated bibliography cites books, chapters in books, periodical articles, newspaper articles, unpublished theses and dissertations, pamphlets, and government documents, with library location information. The entries are grouped into subject categories then sub-divided by geographical territory. Topics covered included role and status, law and politics, family and fertility, economics and employment, education, literature and the arts, religion, womens organizations, biography and autobiograpahy, and general reference works. Population and census reports are also cited. Most items are in English. A few Spanish, French, and Dutch language publications are also included. An author index is included.

SUBJECT(S): Women--Caribbean area--Bibliography.

609. Mintz, Sidney Wilfred. *An Anthropological Approach to the Afro-American Past: A Caribbean Perspective.* Philadelphia: Institute for the Study of Human Issues, 1976. iii, 64 p. SERIES: Institute for the Study of Human Issues. ISHI Occasional Papers in Social Change, no. 2.

One of the few historical studies of the Afro-Latin American experience from an anthropological perspective. Also useful are the bibliographical notes and the fourteen pages of bibliographical references.

SUBJECT(S): Blacks--Caribbean area.
Slavery--Caribbean area.
Acculturation.

610. Nodal, Roberto, comp. *An Annotated Bibliography of Historical Materials on Barbados, Guyana, and Trinidad-Tobago.* Milwaukee: Dept. of Afro-American Studies, University of Wisconsin, Milwaukee, 1974. 34 p. SERIES: Afro-American Studies Report, no. 7.

An annotated bibliography of books and manuscripts published during the eighteenth, nineteenth, and the early part of the twentieth century.

SUBJECT(S): Barbados--History--Bibliography.
Guyana--History--Bibliography.
Trinidad and Tobago--History--Bibliography.

611. Osei, Gabriel Kingsley. *Caribbean Women: Their History and Habits*. London: African Publication Society. 1979. 191 p.

This text on Caribbean women can serve as helpful introduction and overview to the topic. One chapter contains biographical sketches of selected noted women. A brief bibliography and an index are included.

SUBJECT(S): Women--Caribbean Area.
Women, Black--Caribbean area
Caribbean Area--Social conditions

612. Owens, Joseph. *Dread: The Rastafarians of Jamaica*. Introduction by Rex Nettleford. Kingston, Jamaica: Sangster, 1976. xix, 282 p.

A study on the Rastafarians and the religious contour of their movement.

SUBJECT(S): Ras Tafari movement--Jamaica.
Jamaica--Religion.

613. Pierson, Donald. *Negroes in Brazil: A Study of Race Contact at Bahia*. Carbondale: Southern Illinois University Press, 1967. lxxxiii, 420 p. SERIES: Perspectives in Sociology.

A classic history of blacks in Brazil, with a focus on Bahia. Includes a glossary, bibliographical notes, extensive bibliographies, a name index, and a subject index.

SUBJECT(S): Blacks in Salvador, Brazil.
Salvador, Brazil--Social conditions.
Brazil--Race question.

614. Porter, Dorothy Burnett, comp. *Afro-Braziliana: A Working Bibliography*. Boston: G. K. Hall, 1978. xxii, 294 p.

A monumental annotated bibliography of 52,000 works on blacks in Brazil. Books, pamphlets, periodical articles, and newspaper articles are cited. Many of the works are in Portuguese, but annotations are in English. The bibliography is in two parts. Part I lists bibliographies of bibliographies, general works, and covers subjects such as politics, history and art. Part II is a bibliography of writings by Afro-Brazilian authors. A name-title index is included.

SUBJECT(S): Blacks--Brazil--Bibliography.
Authors, Black--Brazil--Bibliography.
Brazil--Civilization--African influences--Bibliography.

615. Price, Richard *The Guiana Maroons: A Historical and Bibliographical Introduction*. Baltimore: Johns Hopkins University Press, 1976. ix, 184 p. SERIES: Johns Hopkins Studies in Atlantic History and Culture.

A general introduction to the Maroons of Suriname, covering the period from the founding of a permanent colony in 1651 to Suriname independence in 1975. The book is divided into three parts. The first provides a historical framework to the study of the Suriname Maroons. The second consists of an extended bibliographic essay on the literature, which is organized chronologically, for the nineteenth and twentieth centuries, by tribe. The second section also contains four topical sections dealing with linguistics, medical research, the history of missions, and studies on the arts. The third part is a bibliography of over 1,350 items covering the period from 1667 to 1975, and is arranged alphabetically by author, with library location information when known.

SUBJECT(S): Maroons--Suriname--Bibliography.
Maroons--Suriname.
Suriname--History.

616. Price, Richard, comp. *Maroon Societies: Rebel Slave Communities in the Americas*. 2d ed. Baltimore: Johns Hopkins University Press, 1979. ix, 445 p. SERIES: A Johns Hopkins Paperback.

A collection of articles intended primarily for students as an introductory overview of Maroon societies. The articles are grouped by geographical area, and cover the Spanish Americas, the French Caribbean, the United States, Brazil, Jamaica, and the Guianas. Many of the articles conclude with bibliographical references for further reading. Bibliographical notes, an extensive bibliography, and an index are included. The afterword for the 1979 edition reviews the major studies that have appeared since the publication of the first edition in 1973.

SUBJECT(S): Fugitive slaves--America--Addresses, essays, lectures.
Maroons--Addresses, essays, lectures.

617. *Statistical Abstract of Latin America*. Los Angeles: University of California, Latin American Studies Center, 1956-.

Published at varying intervals since 1956, this work contains abstracts of statistical publications covering geographical, social, socioeconomic, economic, international, and political aspects of Latin America. Tables and maps are included. Entries are grouped by country. There is no breakdown by racial groups.

SUBJECT(S): Statistics--Latin America.
Latin America--Statistics.

618. Stinner, William F., Klaus de Albuquerque, and Roy S. Bryce-Laporte, eds. *Return Migration and Remittances: Developing a Caribbean Perspective*. Washington, D.C.: Research Institute on Immigration and Ethnic Studies, Smithsonian Institution, 1982. lxvii, 322 p. SERIES: RIIES Occasional Papers, no. 3.

This collection of papers focuses on two relatively unexplored themes: return migration and remittances to Caribbean nations and societies. The first group of papers deal with three levels of return migration: from urban centers back to rural areas, within particular societies; intraregional, from neighboring islands or other Caribbean societies back to the Caribbean island or nation of origin; international, from the United States or Europe back to the Caribbean. The first group of papers concludes with an extensive bibliography. A second group of papers deal with remittances or homeward transfers of cash and other economic resources, and also concludes with a bibliography.

SUBJECT(S): Return migration--Caribbean area--Addresses, essays, lectures.
Emigrant remittances--Caribbean area--Addresses, essays, lectures.
United States--Emigration and immigration--Addresses, essays, lectures.
Caribbean area--Emigration and immigration--Addresses, essays, lectures.

619. Toplin, Robert Brent, ed. *Slavery and Race Relations in Latin America*. Westport, CT: Greenwood Press, 1974. xiv, 250 p. SERIES: Contributions Afro-American and African studies, no. 17.

An outstanding collection of essays on race relations in Latin America from the period of slavery to modern times. Chile, Colombia, Brazil, Granada, Cuba, Venezuela, and Puerto Rico are coverd. Each chapter includes bibliographical notes. Maps and an index are also included.

SUBJECT(S): Slavery in Latin America-Addresses, essays, lectures, etc.
Latin America--Race questions--Addresses, essays, lectures, etc.

620. West India Reference Library (Jamaica). *The Catalogue of the West India Reference Library*. Millwood, NY: Kraus International Publications, 1980. 2 vols.

"The Institute of Jamaica's West India Reference Library (WIRL) is the world's outstanding collection of printed and manuscript materials relating to the history and culture of the West Indies." This multivolume work is a reproduction of the card catalog of the WIRP and lists all books, pamphlets, and periodical holdings of the library which were cataloged prior to the end of 1975. The earliest of the holdings date from the year 1547. The catalogue is divided, with author-title entries in Part I and subject entries in Part II. As with nearly all reproduced card catalogs, a few of the entries are difficult to read, but this does not reduce the importance or usefulness of this work. Coverage for Jamaica and the English-speaking Caribbean is comprehensive. Coverage for other areas is more selective.

SUBJECT(S): West India Reference Library (Jamaica)--Catalogs.
West India--Bibliography--Catalogs.

621. Wilkinson, Audine. University of the West Indies (Cave Hill, Barbados). Institute of Social and Economic Research (Eastern Caribbean). *A Bibliography of the Caribbean*. Cave Hill, Barbados: Institute of Social and Economic Research (Eastern Caribbean), University of the West Indies, 1974. iii, 167 leaves. SERIES: Occasional Bibliography Series, no. 1.

This is a bibliography of articles, books, documents, papers, and pamphlets, representing the collection of the Institute of Social and Economic Research (Eastern Barbados). Social, historical, financial, and agricultural aspects of Caribbean life are covered. Entries are arranged geographically. Material on the following areas can be found: Bahamas, Barbados, Belize, British Virgin Islands, Cuba, Dominican Republic, French West Indies, Guyana, Haiti, Jamaica, the Leeward and Windward Islands, the Netherlands Antilles, Puerto Rico, Suriname, Trinidad, Tobago, and Venezuela. There are no annotations, or indexes.

SUBJECT(S): University of the West Indies (Cave Hill, Barbados).
Institute of Social and Economic Research (Eastern Caribbean)
Caribbean area--Bibliography--Catalogs.

622. Williams, Joseph John. *Psychic Phenomena of Jamaica*. New York: Dial Press, 1934. Reprint. Westport, CT: Greenwood Press. 309 p.

Though written in 1934, this well documented study on psychic phenomena (witchcraft, magic, etc.) in Jamaica, remains an important contribution to the scientific and scholarly literature. Bibliographical notes, an extensive bibliography, and indexes are included.

SUBJECT(S): Witchcraft--Jamaica.
Magic--Jamaica.
Blacks in Jamaica.
Jamaica--Social life and customs.
Superstitions.
Ashantis.

623. Williams, Joseph John *Voodoos and Obeahs: Phases of West India Witchcraft*. New York: AMS Press, 1932. Reprint. New York: AMS Press, 1970. xix, 257 p.

A well documented study of the practice of Voodoo in Haiti and Obeah in Jamaica. Also included is an account of African Ophiolatry (snake worship) which pre-dates the development of Voodoo and Obeah in the New World. Bibliographical notes, bibliography, and indexes are included.

SUBJECT(S): Witchcraft--West Indies.
Voodooism--West Indies.
Blacks--West Indies.

APPENDIX: LOS ANGELES AND CALIFORNIA

624. Abajian, James de T., comp. *Blacks and Their Contributions to the American West: A Bibliography and Union List of Library Holdings Through 1970*. Boston: G. K. Hall, 1974. xxii, 487 p.

An unique bibliography of 4,320 entries especially useful for identifying information sources on blacks in California. The emphasis is on local imprints, and specific, rather than general works. Entries are arranged by subject and form of material. Library location information is included. An index of subjects, individuals, and organizational names is also included.

SUBJECT(S): Afro-Americans--The West--Bibliography-- Union lists.
Catalogs, Union--The West.
Catalogs, Union--California.
The West--Bibliography--Union lists.

625. Bullock, Paul, ed. *Directory of Community Services Organizations in Greater Los Angeles*. Los Angeles, Institute of Industrial Relations, University of California, Los Angeles, 1979. 252 p.

This directory lists major private and government social services agencies and organizations in Los Angeles County. It is divided into chapters which focus on the following types of agencies and organizations: civil and legal rights; cultural and religious; community and neighborhood; training programs; business assistance; coordinating, research, and referral; political; service, social, and fraternal; labor; communications; and legal services. Each entry includes an annotation giving address, telephone number, contact person, and the purpose and activities of the organization. Continues: *Directory of Organizations in Greater Los Angeles*.

SUBJECT(S): Associations, institutions, etc.-- California--Los Angeles--Directories.
Los Angeles (Calif.)--Societies, etc.

626. California. Dept. of Industrial Relations. Division of Labor Statistics and Research. *Black Californians: Population, Education, Income, Employment*. (Statistical tables and analysis by Division of Labor Statistics and Research). San Francisco: Fair Employment Practice Commission, *1974*. 56 p.

A statistical report on black population, education, labor force and employment, and income in California based on the 1970 Census. Includes metropolitan, county, and statewide tabulations.

SUBJECT(S): Afro-Americans--California--Statistics.
Afro-Americans--California--Economic conditions.
California--Statistics.

627. Collins, Keith E. *Black Los Angeles: The Maturing of the Ghetto, 1940-1950*. Saratoga, CA.: Century Twenty One Pub., 1980. xi, 120 p.

An extension of Lawrence B. de Graaf's "Negro Migration to Los Angeles, 1930 to 1950." It incorporates data from 275 oral interviews of Watts residents and/or others, who were participants, or were close to someone who had first hand knowledge, of events in Watts during this period. Figures, charts, and an extensive bibliography are included.

SUBJECT(S): Afro-Americans--California--Los Angeles-- Social conditions.
Afro-Americans--California--Los Angeles-- History.
Watts (Los Angeles, Calif.)--History.
Watts (Los Angeles, Calif.)--Social conditions.
Los Angeles (Calif.)--History.
Los Angeles (Calif.)--Social conditions.

628. Davis, Lenwood G. *Blacks in the American West: A Working Bibliography*. 2d ed. Monticello, IL.: Council of Planning Librarians, 1976. 1956. 51 p. SERIES: Council of Planning Librarians. Exchange Bibliography, no. 984.

An unannotated bibliography of journals, bibliographies, state libraries, archives, historical societies, books, periodical articles, and unpublished material published in the nineteenth and twentieth centuries.

SUBJECT(S): Afro-Americans--The West--Bibliography.
The West--Race question--Bibliography.
The West--History--Bibliography.

629. Davis, Lenwood G. *Blacks in the Pacific Northwest, 1788-1972: A Bibliography of Published Works and of Unpublished Source Materials on the Life and Contributions of Black People in the Pacific Northwest*. Monticello, IL., Council of Planning Librarians, 1972. 85 p. SERIES: Council of Planning Librarians. Exchange Bibliography, no. 335.

Perhaps the most comprehensive bibliography on this topic. Most citations relate to Oregon and Washington, with a smaller number dealing with Idaho, Montana, and British Columbia. General bibliographical works and primary sources are included.

SUBJECT(S): Afro-Americans--Pacific Northwest--Bibliography.

630. De Graaf, Lawrence Brooks. *Negro Migration to Los Angeles, 1930 to 1950: A Dissertation*. University of California, Los Angeles, 1962. San Francisco: R and E Research Associates, 1974. xiii, 270 p.

This revised doctoral dissertation measures black migration to Los Angeles, 1930-1950, and analyzes the factors which caused it. Numerous bibliographic footnotes and statistical tables are included. An extensive bibliography is also included.

SUBJECT(S): Afro-Americans--Los Angeles.
Rural-urban migration--United States.
Los Angeles--History.

631. *Ethnic Groups in California: A Guide to Organizations and Information Resources*. Edited by the staff of the California Institute of Public Affairs. Claremont: California Institute of Public Affairs, 1981, 58 p. SERIES: California Information Guides Series.

The first, comprehensive guide to organizations and publications concerned specifically with ethnic groups in California. Approximately ninety ethnic groups are covered, from Africans to Zoroastrians. The Afro-American section lists government agencies, university and college programs, museums, associations, bookshops, banks, periodicals, and a selected list of books and articles.

SUBJECT(S): Minorities--California--Societies, etc.--Directories.
Minorities--California--Bibliography.
California--Foreign population--Societies, etc.--Directories.
California--Foreign population--Bibliography.

632. Fikes, Robert. *A Directory of Black People in California Higher Education*. 2nd ed. San Diego, CA: California Black Faculty (and) Staff Association, 1982. 97 p.

This directory lists "every black faculty member, counselor, librarian, and administrator employed on a full-time basis in California's three systems of public higher education and the majority of private institutions offering at least the bachelor's degree." There are approximately 1400 entries. The work is divided into four parts: Part I lists individuals in alphabetical order and (in most cases) gives the year of initial employment, title, institutional affiliation, and academic background. Part II lists entries by discipline or professional assignment. Part III lists people by institutions of employment. Part IV lists California colleges and universities with addresses and telephone numbers.

SUBJECT(S): Afro-American college teachers--California--Directories.
Afro-American college administrators-- California--Directories.

633. Goode, Kenneth G. *California's Black Pioneers: A Brief Historical Survey*. Santa Barbara, CA.: McNally & Loftin, 1974. xiii, 222 p.

This highly informative historical survey covers the presence of blacks in California from the eighteenth century through the early 1970s. Each chapter concludes with bibliographies for further reading. Appendices provide lists of blacks in California politics, including black governors of the nineteenth century, congressmen, state elected officials, and mayors. Appendices also contain statistical tables on characteristics of the black population in California from 1900 to 1970. Photographs, a bibliography, and an index are also included.

SUBJECT(S): Afro-Americans--California.
California--Race relations.

634. Katz, William L. *The Black West*. New York: Doubleday/Anchor Press, 1971. 336 p.

A history of blacks in the West from Oklahoma to California. Included are chapters on explorers, cowboys, fur traders, early settlers, cavalrymen, and homesteaders. An index and bibliography are included.

SUBJECT(S): Afro-Americans--The West (U.S.)--History.
Frontier and pioneer life--The West (U.S.).
West (U.S.)--History--1848-1950.

635. Lapp, Rudolph M. *Afro-Americans in California*. San Francisco: Boyd & Fraser Pub. Co., 1979. 71 p. SERIES: Golden State Series.

A historical overview of blacks in California from the Spanish colonial period through the 1970s. A bibliographical essay of suggested readings and bibliographical notes are included. It does not include an index.

SUBJECT(S): Afro-Americans--California--History.
California--Race relations.

636. Lapp, Rudolph M. *Blacks in Gold Rush California*. New Haven: Yale University Press, 1977. xiv, 321 p. SERIES: Yale Western Americana Series, 29.

A well documented history of blacks in California. focusing on the gold rush generation of black immigrants during the mid-1800s. In addition to discussing the direct role which blacks played in the search and mining for gold, the author also examines the life and conditions of blacks throughout California, with some emphasis on city dwellers. Bibliographical notes, a bibliographic essay on sources used, and an index are included.

SUBJECT(S): Afro-Americans--California--History.
Slavery--California.
Gold mines and mining--California--History.
California--Gold discoveries.

637. Matthews, Miriam. *The Negro in California from 1781-1910: An Annotated Bibliography*. Report Presented to the Graduate School of Library Science, University of Southern California, in Partial Fulfillment of the Requirements for the Research Course Library Science 290ab. Los Angeles, 1944. xxv, 52 l.

The only comprehensive bibliography dealing exclusively with blacks in California through 1944. Books, periodical articles, original documents and manuscripts, unpublished materials, and newspaper articles are included and arranged by form. The annotations to books include brief indexes to the work's content. Some works cited are only partially related to blacks. An author-title-subject index is included.

SUBJECT(S): Afro-Americans--California--Bibliography.

638. *Negro Who's Who in California*. Los Angeles: "Negro Who's Who in California" Publishing Co., 1948. 133 p.

Blacks are listed according to their field of activity: early California pioneers, church leaders, professional people, business and industrial figures, artists and musicians, and civic and social personalities. The dates, education, family, and career of each person is given. Portraits and a name index are included.

SUBJECT(S): Afro-Americans--California.
Afro-Americans--Biography--Dictionaries.

639. Rusco, Elmer R. *"Good Time Coming?": Black Nevadans in the Nineteenth Century*. Westport, CT: Greenwood Press, 1975. xix, 230 p. SERIES: Contributions in Afro-American and African Studies, no. 15.

SUBJECT(S): Afro-Americans--Nevada--History.
Nevada--History.

640. Savage, William Sherman. *Blacks in the West*. Westport, CT: Greenwood Press, 1976. xvi, 230 p. SERIES: Contributions in Afro-American and African Studies, no. 23.

A well documented history of blacks in the western states from 1830 to 1890. It includes an extensive bibliography citing biography and autobiography, manuscripts, state documents, federal documents, books, periodical articles, and newspapers; and numerous bibliographic notes. An index is also included.

SUBJECT(S): Afro-Americans--The West (U.S.)--History.
Frontier and pioneer life--The West (U.S.).
West (U.S.)--History--1848-1950.

641. Thurman, A. Odell *The Negro in California before 1890*. San Francisco: R and E Research Associates, 1973. ii, 71 p.

A brief, but well documented, history of blacks in California before 1890, beginning with the reputed first, Estevanico, in 1535. Bibliographical notes and a bibliography are included.

SUBJECT(S): Afro-Americans--California.

642. Tolbert, Emory J. *The UNIA and Black Los Angeles: Ideology and Community in the American Garvey Movement*. Los Angeles: Center for Afro-American Studies, University of California, 1980. 138 p. SERIES: Afro-American Culture and Society, vol. 3.

A well documented study of the Garvey movement in the black community of Los Angeles. It includes a chapter providing an overview of the Los Angeles black community through 1930, and an essay on sources relating to Afro-American scholarship and the Garvey movement. Each chapter concludes with bibliographical notes. A bibliography of primary and secondary sources, and a name-title-subject index are included. It is a useful reference for sources on Garveyism and on the black community in Los Angeles during the late nineteenth and early twentieth centuries.

SUBJECT(S): Garvey, Marcus, 1887-1940.
Universal Negro Improvement Association.
Afro-Americans--California--Los Angeles--Social conditions.
Afro-Americans--California--Los Angeles--Race identity.
Los Angeles (Calif.)--Race relations.

AUTHOR INDEX

TITLE INDEX

SUBJECT INDEX

ABOUT THE COMPILER

Nathaniel Davis has an M.L.S. from the University of Illinois, Urbana, and has worked as a librarian in several academic institutions. His past positions include: reference librarian for the Brown University Library Reference Department, Head of the Brown University Library Circulation and Interlibrary Loan Department, Research Associate for the University of Illinois Library Research Center, Librarian for the UCLA Center for Afro-American Studies Library and Adjunct Lecturer for the UCLA Graduate School of Library and Information Science.